A Point of Controversy

The Battle of Point Pleasant

Poffenbarger vs. Lewis

By

C. Stephen Badgley

Badgley Publishing Company

ISBN 13 978-1456456467

ISBN 10 1456456466

Copyright © 2010
Badgley Publishing Company
All rights reserved

Contents

Introduction 1

Prelude 3

The Contenders 7

    Olivia Nye Simpson-Poffenbarger 7

    Virgil Anson Lewis 8

Livia Poffenbarger's Book 9

The Battle of Point Pleasant 11

A Battle of the Revolution 11

    Dedication 15

    The Status of the Battle of Point Pleasant 20

Biographical 55

    General Andrew Lewis 55

    Colonel Charles Lewis 56

    Colonel John Field 60

    Colonel William Flemming 60

    Captain Evan Shelby 61

    Isaac Shelby 62

    John Jones 63

    John Draper 63

    Benjamin Logan 64

    William Campbell 64

    Arthur Campbell 65

    John Campbell 65

    Joseph Mayse 65

    General Andrew Moore 65

    George Mathews 66

    Sampson Mathews 67

Colonel Joseph Crockett	67
James Robertson	68
John Smith	69
Benjamin Harrison	69
Hugh and James Allen	69
Judge Samuel McDowell	69
John Sevier	70
Valentine Sevier	71
James Harrod	71
William Russell	71
James Montgomery	71
John Crawford	72
William Christian	72
George Slaughter	72
James Trimble	72
John Dickenson	72
Anthony Bledsoe	73
William Cocke	73
John Sawyer	74
Joseph Hughey	74
Philip Love	74
Ellis Hughes	74
John Steele	75
Azariah Davis	75
John Todd	75
Charles E. Cameron	75
Silas Harlan	76
Jacob Warwick	76

The Van Bibbers	76
Leonard Cooper	77
William Arbuckle	78
John Young	78
John Henderson	79
Lumen Gibbs	79
George Eastham	80
John Stuart	80
Thomas Posey	82
John Lewis	82
William Clendennin	83
Archibald Clendennin	83
Benjamin Logan	84
John Logan	84
George Clendennin	84
Alexander Breckenridge	85
Captain John Lewis	85
Stephen Trigg	85
William Herbert	86
Walter Crockett	86
John Floyd	86
Benjamin Lewis	87
Josiah Ramsey	88
William Bowen	88
Joseph Drake	89
William Edmiston	89
William Ingles	89
Thomas Ingles	89

Henry Pauling	90
Francis Slaughter	90
Lawrence and George Slaughter	90
The McAfee Brothers	90
James Knox	91
John Madison	91
Elijah Kimberling	91
William Ewing	92
William McKee	92
Charles Simms	92
George Moffatt	92
John Murray	93
William Trotter	93
James Bailey	93
Walter Newman	93
William Moore	94
John Lyle	94
William Robertson	94
John Lewis	94
John Frogg	94
William McCorkle	95
Robert Campbell	96
John Carter	96
Matthew Bracken	97
Captain John Lewis	97
Thomas Hacket	97
Captain James Curry	98
Michael See	98

    Col. James Curry 99

    Solomon Brumfield 99

    William Hamilton 99

    Bazaleel Wells 100

    John Murray, Earl of Dunmore. 100

    Logan 101

    Cornstalk 102

    Forts Blair, Randolph and Point Pleasant 104

Participants of the Battle 107

History of the Monument Building 121

Virgil Lewis's Book 171

CHAPTER I 177

    THE VIRGINIA FRONTIER IN 1774 177

    White Settlers West of the Blue Ridge 177

    County Organization West of the Blue Ridge 179

    A SAVAGE EMPIRE 180

CHAPTER II 185

    LORD DUNMORE'S WAR—ITS CAUSES 185

    The House of Burgesses Authorizes Governor Dunmore to Prosecute the War against the Indians 189

CHAPTER III 195

    GATHERING OF THE SOUTHERN DIVISION OR THE LEFT WING AT "CAMP UNION" ON THE BIG LEVELS OF GREENBRIER 195

CHAPTER IV 201

    THE WESTWARD MARCH OF GENERAL ANDREW LEWIS' ARMY FROM CAMP UNION TO 201

    THE OHIO RIVER 201

    THE ARMY LEAVING CAMP UNION 201

    THE ADVANCE THROUGH THE MOUNTAINS 201

TO THE GREAT KANAWHA RIVER THENCE DOWN THAT RIVER TO 201

CAMP POINT PLEASANT ON THE OHIO RIVER 201

Advance of the Augusta Regiment.. 201

Advance of the Botetourt Regiment 203

JOURNAL AND ORDERLY BOOK 203

OF COLONEL FLEMING 203

The March or Lewis' Army 207

From the Mouth of Elk River 207

To the Mouth of the Great Kanawha 207

Departure of the Fincastle Battalion 209

From Camp Union 209

The Detachment Left at Camp Union 210

CHAPTER V 211

The Beginning Of The Battle 213

Isaac Shelby's Account of the Battle 213

COLONEL WILLIAM FLEMING'S 216

ACCOUNT OF THE BATTLE 216

CHAPTER VI 225

THE VIRGINIAN ARMY IN THE OHIO WILDERNESS 225

TREATY OF CAMP CHARLOTTE 225

RETURN OF THE ARMY 225

THE SUPPLEMENTAL TREATY AT PITTSBURG 225

Advance of General Lewis' Army 227

To The Pickaway Plains 227

The Treaty in Progress 230

The Return of the Army 231

The Supplemental Treaty at Pittsburg, 1775 233

CHAPTER VII 237

THE INFLUENCE OF THE	237
BATTLE OF POINT PLEASANT	237
UPON THE SUBSEQUENT HISTORY OF THE UNITED STATES	237
CHAPTER VIII	241
PAY OF THE SOLDIERS IN DUNMORE'S WAR	241
TOTAL EXPENSES OF THATWAR	241
HOW THEY WERE PAID	241
CHAPTER IX	247
HISTORY AND DISCRIPTION OF THE	247
POINT PLEASANT BATTLE MONUMENT	247
The Battlefield Unmarked	247
Steps Leading to the Erection of a Battle Monument	247
Description of the Same	247
Resolutions in the Virginia Assembly	248
Point Pleasant Monument Association Created	249
A Centennial Celebration	249
First Appropriation for a Monument	250
Legislative Action In 1897	251
Legislative Action In 1901	252
The Trustees Appointed—Work Begun	252
Aid from Congress	253
CHAPTER X	255
HISTORY VERSUS TRADITION	255
TRUTH VERSUS ERROR	255
The Alleged Treachery of Lord Dunmore	256
A Resolution by the Officers,	258
Who Served Under Lord Dunmore,	258
Adopted at Fort Gower,	258

Mouth of Hockhocking River, ... 258

November 5, 1774 258

ADDRESS OF THE CITIZENS OF THE CITY OF WILLIAMSBURG, DECEMBER 5, 1774, TO JOHN, EARL OF DUNMORE 258

THE REPLY OF LORD DUNMORE TO THE 259

CITIZENS OF WILLIAMSBURG 259

ADDRESS OF THE PRESIDENT AND PROFESSORS OF WILLIAM AND MARY COLLEGE 260

TO JOHN, EARL OF DUNMORE 260

THE REPLY OF LORD DUNMORE TO THE PRESIDENT AND FACULTY OF 260

WILLIAM AND MARY COLLEGE 260

ADDRESS OF THE MAYOR, RECORDER, ALDERMAN, AND COMMON COUNCIL OF THE BOROUGH OF NORFOLK, TO JOHN, ... 261

EARL OF DUNMORE 261

THE REPLY OF LORD DUNMORE 261

ADDRESS OF THE COUNCIL OF 262

THE STATE OF VIRGINIA, ... 262

TO JOHN, EARL OF DUNMORE 262

THE REPLY OF LORD DUNMORE 263

Resolution adopted by the Virginia Convention which assembled at Richmond, March 20, 1775 263

Address of Freeholders of Fincastle County (Virginia) 264

To Lord Dunmore, April 8, 1775 264

THE REPLY OF LORD DUNMORE 266

What Historians Say 266

Did General Lewis Disobey Orders? 267

CHAPTER XI POETRY OF THE BATTLE OF POINT PLEASANT 269

THE CAMP SONG AT POINT PLEASANT 269

THE SHAWNEE BATTLE ON THE 269

BANKS OF THE OHIO 269

THE BATTLE SONG OF THE GREAT KANAWHA 269

BATTLE OF POINT PLEASANT: 269

A CENTENNIAL ODE 269

CHAPTER XII 277

THE MURDER OF CORNSTALK AT 277

POINT PLEASANT, NOVEMBER 10, 1777. 277

Efforts to Punish the Men Who Killed Cornstalk 281

ADDENDA 283

APPENDIX A 285

THE ONLY ROSTERS PRESERVED OF THE COMPANIES WHICH WERE IN THE BATTLE OF POINT PLEASANT OR ARRIVED WITH COLONEL CHRISTIAN IN THE EVENING AFTER IT HAD BEEN FOUGHT AND WON. 285

APPENDIX B 299

THE AFTER-LIFE OF THE MEN WHO FOUGHT THE BATTLE OF POINT PLEASANT 299

APPENDIX C 301

EXTRACTS FROM THE VIRGINIA GAZETTE, ... 301

RELATING TO LORD DUNMORE'S WAR 301

The First Printed Account of 304

The Battle of Point Pleasant 304

APPENDIX D 307

A PARTIAL LIST OF MEN WOUNDED IN THE BATTLE OF POINT PLEASANT, WHO WERE AFTERWARD GRANTED PENSIONS BY THE COMMONWEALTH OF VIRGINIA 307

APPENDIX E 309

KINSHIP OF THE MEN WHO FOUGHT THE BATTLE OF POINT PLEASANT
.... 309

Some Questions, Facts, Speculations and Assertions 311

By C. Stephen Badgley 311

Excerpt from "The History of Virginia" 1852 319

Preface from the book 319

A Point of Controversy

Introduction

On April 19, 1775, British soldiers under Lt. Col. Francis Smith were marching from Boston towards the town of Concord, Massachusetts to capture and destroy supplies stored there by the Massachusetts Militia. To reach Concord the British had to pass through the town of Lexington where just as the morning sun was coming up over the horizon, they encountered a group of local militia who had gathered there to block their advance to Concord. It was here that a shot rang out and history has it that this Battle of Lexington was the first battle of the American Revolution.

No one knows who fired that shot or where it came from that morning. Could it be that the "Shot heard round the world" was actually an echo from the gently rolling hills that surround the confluence of the Great Kanawha and Ohio Rivers? It was here...six months earlier, that an army of Virginia Militia was attacked by an alliance of Ohio Indians led by the Shawnee Chief Cornstalk.

Was this fight, known as The Battle of Point Pleasant, the last of the Colonial Wars as some noted Historians say or was it the First Battle of the American Revolution as other noted Historians believe?

I want to tell you that I am not a noted Historian nor do I possess any type of degree in History, but I do share one thing in common with those that do. I am a lover of history, especially early American History in general and the 18th & 19th centuries in particular and I have been for most of the 62 years I have been on this planet.

Although I am not considered a noted authority on American History, I can safely say that I have more than a general knowledge of the events that occurred in those centuries.

The controversy surrounding the Battle of Point Pleasant actually began right after the battle with accusations from some of the participants that Dunmore's motives for going to war with the Indians was actually a well-conceived ploy to divert the Virginia Militia to the frontier in face of the impending Revolution which Dunmore undoubtedly knew was going to occur.

The controversy came to a head at the beginning of the 20th century when Livia Nye Simpson-Poffenbarger, newspaper editor and historian at Point Pleasant, began a campaign to preserve the battlefield and erect a monument to those who fought there. At this time the battlefield was actually an eyesore with pig sties, animal pens and gardens under which laid the bones of the gallant men who died there. She was troubled by the conditions of this field of honor where men struggled so valiantly and gave their lives in pursuit of liberty.

Based on her research and that of other noted Historians of the time, she wrote a book and named it *"The Battle of Point Pleasant, A Battle of the Revolution"*. In her book she cites the names of prominent Historians who shared her opinion that this was the first battle of the American Revolution. One of those cited was Virgil Anson Lewis, world-renowned Historian and Archivist for the State of West Virginia who later became her adversary on the subject and wrote a book entitled **"History of the Battle of Point Pleasant"** in which he refutes the claim that it was the first battle of the American Revolution.

This volume contains both of these books and is an attempt to put the views of both sides of the argument out on the table for you to see and help you form an opinion whether or not this fight was indeed the first battle of the American Revolution. I would really like to know your conclusion and am asking that you send me an e-mail or visit the website of Badgley Publishing Company and record your decision.

C. Stephen Badgley

Badgley Publishing Company
WWW.BadgleyPublishingCompany.com
E-mail: BadgleyPubCo@aol.com

A Point of Controversy

Prelude

The British Proclamation of 1763, at the end of the French and Indian war, prohibited colonial expansion and settlement west of the Appalachian Mountains to protect the rights of the Indians occupying the land there. This proclamation did not fare well with the Colonists who claimed that the defeat of the French opened up the territory for settlement by "Right of Conquest" and the most of the Indians living there had sided with the French and therefore had no rights. This proclamation did not stop some from moving into the restricted territory and hostilities on the frontier heightened.

In 1768 the British Government convinced the Iroquois Six Nation Confederation that they (They Iroquois) were the rightful owners of the lands west of the Appalachians by this same "Right of Conquest" (A principal of law recognized at the time, by all the nations of the world, which gave a conquering nation the right to any territories that they had taken by force of arms.) The Iroquois and the British signed the Treaty of Stanwix and the Iroquois sold the lands to the British Government.

This act infuriated the Indians of the Ohio Country who argued that the Iroquois had no rights to sell anything. Some Iroquoian Indians sided with the mostly Algonquin speaking Indians of the Ohio Country. These were mostly from the Cayuga and Seneca tribes who formed the western most arm of the Iroquois Confederacy.

One of these was a Cayuga Indian named Logan. Logan had taken this English name in honor of James Logan, a very close friend of his father Shikellamy. Logan and others received permission from the Delaware Indians to settle on the Ohio River near present day Wheeling, West Virginia. Like his father, Logan was a friend to all men, white or red. He was not a major chief of the Mingo Confederation he helped form but he was noted for his wisdom and ability to communicate and resolve problems between the races. He was well respected by both the whites and Indians and his counsel was sought many times to help settle disputes.

On April 30, 1774, a group of Virginia men led by ruffian Daniel Greathouse travelled downriver from near present day Wheeling to the cabin of Joshua Baker, a rum trader who had settled there across the river from the Mingo Village of Logan. Their intentions were not friendly. Upon arrival Greathouse sent some men across the river to invite Logan and some of his people to come to Baker's cabin for some rum, talk and a little sport. Logan was not at the village. He had gone hunting. Logan's brother, Taylaynee agreed to gather some of his people to cross over the river and join the "party". Among this group were, Taylaynee's son Molnah, Logan's wife Mellana, Logan's sister Koonay and her two year old daughter. Koonay was married to John Gibson, an English trader who at the time was away on business with the Shawnee. She was pregnant with their second child and very near to giving birth.

Greathouse and his gang got the Indians to drink some rum and when they were pretty much intoxicated he proposed a shooting match to see who among them was the best marksman. Of course, he allowed the Indians to take their turn first and as soon as their rifles were emptied, Greathouse and his cutthroats attacked them. They killed, scalped and horribly mutilated their bodies. One of the most brutal acts perpetrated at that awful scene was when Greathouse tied together the wrists of the pregnant Koonay and hoisted her over a tree limb so her feet were just barely touching the ground. He then took his "hawk", which he always kept razor sharp, and with a huge sweep of his arm, slit open her abdomen. He wiped the blood off his hawk and put it back in his belt. Taking his scalping knife, he pulled the baby from her womb and scalped it. When the firing began, two canoes of Mingo warriors were sent to see what was going on. Greathouse and his gang opened fire on them and drove them back across the river.

The only survivor of this massacre was the two year old daughter of Koonay. She was eventually returned to her father by William Crawford.

Logan upon his return to his village was infuriated, and rightfully so. He gathered warriors from his Mingo Confederation as well as from the Shawnee and Delaware nations and began a series of raids on white settlers in western Pennsylvania. Logan and the Mingoes were not the only ones infuriated by this murder. All of the Indians in the Ohio Country clamored for their leaders to strike the war post...take revenge...and drive the English back across the Appalachians. Cornstalk of the Shawnee was one of the few leaders that spoke for reconciliation rather than war but was overruled.

John Murray aka Lord Dunmore was the Royal Governor of the Colony of Virginia...appointed to the post by King George himself. Lord Dunmore was besieged by requests for aid to quell the Indian uprising on Virginia's frontier and he complied by organizing an army of Militia to travel to the Ohio Country, attack the Indians and destroy their villages.

The barbarous, murderous, heinous act perpetrated by the Greathouse gang was the catalyst that started what history has called Dunmore's War and started the chain of events that became a controversy on whether the only major battle of that war was not just a colonial fight but the first battle of the American Revolution.

These events that culminated in the Battle of Point Pleasant and the signing of a treaty at Camp Charlotte have been a matter of debate for many, many years. Even some of the men who served under Dunmore believed he had deceived them and was actually in collusion with the Shawnee. Some historians believe that the whole situation was planned by Dunmore, a staunch British Loyalist, in an effort to help the Loyalist cause by diverting and depleting the Colonist's fighting force in face of the impending Revolution.

The following books portray both sides of the argument.

The Contenders

Olivia Nye Simpson-Poffenbarger

Livia, the name she preferred, was born on March 1, 1862 near the town of Pomeroy, Meigs County, Ohio. When still a young girl, her family moved downriver a few miles and settled in Point Pleasant, West Virginia. In 1888 she purchased the newspaper "State Gazette" and became the managing editor. She ran the paper until she sold it in 1913. She was an Editor, Historian, Writer, Social Activist and a Civic Leader.

In 1901 Livia established a local chapter of The Daughters of the American Revolution in Mason County, West Virginia. She organized the Mason County chapter of the American Red Cross and directed relief efforts during the great flood of 1913. During World War l, Livia personally chaired three very successful Liberty Loan Drives in the state of West Virginia and her techniques were adopted by many other states. In 1919 she received an honorary Doctorate from the West Virginia University.

Her interest in the Battle of Point Pleasant manifested itself in her efforts to have the State of West Virginia purchase the battlefield site and her efforts to have Congress recognize the battle as being a "Battle of the Revolution" and to erect a monument to those who fought and died there. She was successful in her efforts and the park where the monument stands today, named Tu Endie Wei, is a reflection of those efforts.

She died on January 27, 1937 in Charleston, West Virginia.

Virgil Anson Lewis

Virgil was born July 6, 1848 in Mason County, Virginia (West Virginia). He was an Educator, a Lawyer, a Writer and a noted Historian.

In 1890 Virgil was one of the founders of the West Virginia Historical and Antiquarian Society. In 1893 he received an M.A. in History from the West Virginia University.

Virgil became the first Director of the State Department of Archives and History in West Virginia. He was a prolific book writer and renowned speaker.

He became an adversary of Livia Nye Simpson-Poffenbarger and the theory of the Battle of Point Pleasant being the first battle of the Revolution. Virgil was one of the most influential historians in the debate over this theory. He was held in very high esteem by his peers throughout the world.

He died on December 5, 1912 in Mason, West Virginia.

The first book to be presented will be the complete book written by Mrs. Poffenbarger followed by the complete book by Mr. Lewis.

Livia Poffenbarger's Book

The Battle of Point Pleasant
A Battle of the Revolution

October 10, 1774

Biographical Sketches of the

Men Who Participated

By

Mrs. Livia Nye Simpson-Poffenbarger

The State Gazette, Publisher

Point Pleasant, West Virginia

1909

The Battle of Point Pleasant

Dedication

This volume is dedicated to the memory of the brave colonists, who successful at the Battle of Point Pleasant, had fought the opening battle of the Revolution, in preserving the right arm of Virginia for the struggle with the Mother Country; thus making possible the blessings of liberty we now enjoy as a nation.

Mrs. Livia Nye Simpson-Poffenbarger

Andrew Lewis, who commanded the colonial troops in the Battle of Point Pleasant, October 10, 1774, was the son of John Lewis and Margaret Lynn Lewis, his wife.

John Lewis was of Scotch Irish descent, having been born in France, 1673, where his ancestors had taken refuge from the persecution following the assassination of Henry IV. He married Margaret Lynn, the daughter of the "Laird of Loch Lynn," of Scotland, and .emigrated to Ireland, thence to America in 1729, and became the founder of Staunton, Virginia. Here, he planted a colony and reared a family that have given luster to American History.

Governor Gooch, of Williamsburg, then the seat of Government of Virginia, was the personal friend of Mrs. Lewis' father and hence granted her sons, together with one Benjamin Burden a land, warrant for 500,000 acres of, land in the James and Shenandoah Valleys, with the proviso that they were to locate one hundred families within ten years. They induced their friends from Scotland and the north of Ireland, and the Scotch Irish of Pennsylvania, to emigrate to Augusta County, Virginia. In her diary, Mrs. Lewis says: "It sounded like the gathering of the clans to hear the names of these settlers viz: McKees, McCues, McCampbells, McClungs, McKouns, Caruthers, Stuarts, Wallaces, Lyles, Paxtons, Prestons and Grisbys."

We quote the following from the Ohio Archaeological and Historical Quarterly, July, 1903, pp. 288, 289, 290:

"When John Randolph said that Pennsylvania had produced but two great men—Benjamin Franklin, of Massachusetts, and Albert Gallatin, of Switzerland— he possibly did not know that the best blood of his own State was that of the Scotch-Irish people who went down from Pennsylvania and settled in the Valley. He likely did not know that the great and good Dr. Archibald Alexander, the founder of Liberty Hall, now Washington and Lee University (so much loved by Washington,) the very seat of culture and power of the Shenandoah and James, the greatest factor of the State's prowess, was a Pennsylvanian. He possibly did not know that Dr. Graham, the first president of this institution, was from Old Paxtang; that many of the families whose names are in the pantheon of old Dominion achievement, the families that give Virginia her prominence in the sisterhood of States, had their American origin in Pennsylvania—in the Scotch-Irish reservoir of the Cumberland Valley—the McDowells, the Pattersons, the McCormacks, Ewings, McCorcles, Prestons, McCunes, Craigs, McCulloughs, Simpsons, Stewarts, Moffats, Irwins, Hunters, Blairs, Elders, Grahams, Finleys, Trimbles, Rankins and hundreds of others whose achievements mark the pathway of the world's progress. John Randolph possibly did not know that the first Declaration of Independence by the American patriots was issued by the members of Hanover Church out there in Dauphin County, when on June 4th, 1774, they declared "that in the event Great Britain attempting to force unjust laws upon us by the strength of Arms, our cause we leave to heaven and our rifles." This declaration was certainly carried to Mecklenburg to give the sturdy people of that region inspiration for the strong document issued by them a year later, and which gave Jefferson a basis for the Declaration of 1776. There was much moving from Pennsylvania into Virginia and North Carolina before the Revolution, and Hanover Presbytery in the Valley was largely made up of people from Pennsylvania, whose petition of ten thousand names for a free church in a free land, made in 1785, was the force back of Jefferson's bill for religious tolerance, a triumph for freedom that has always been considered a Presbyterian victory by the Scotch-Irish of America.

We know that Dr. Sankey of Hanover Church was a minister in Hanover Presbytery, and that he was followed into Virginia by large numbers of the Hanover congregation, who kept up a constant stream into the Valley. By the way, two settlements were made by this congregation in Ohio. Col. Rogers, Gov. Bushnel's secretary, derives his descent from them. The population of North Carolina at the outbreak of the Revolution was largely made up of Scotch-Irish immigrants from Pennsylvania and the Virginia Valley who had a public school system before the war. These were the people who stood with the Rev. David Caldwell on the banks of the Alamance May 16th, 1771, and received the first volley of shot fired in the contest for Independence. This same blood coursed the veins of the patriot army with Lewis at Point Pleasant, the first battle of the Revolutionary War, fought October 10, 1774, Lord Dunmore having no doubt planned the attack by the Indians to discourage the Americans from further agitation of the then pending demand for fair treatment of the American Colonies at the hands of Great Britain. It was this blood that coursed the veins of those courageous people who, having survived the Kerr's Creek massacre, were carried to a Shawnee village in Ohio, and on being bantered to sing by the Indians in their cruel sport, sang Rouse's version of one of the Psalms. "Un-appalled by the bloody scene," says the Augusta historian, "through which they had already passed, and the fearful tortures awaiting them, within the dark wilderness of forest, when all hope of rescue seemed forbidden; undaunted by the fiendish reveling of their savage captors, they sang aloud with the most pious fervor—

> "On Babel's stream we sat and wept when Zion we thought on,
> In midst thereof we hanged our harps the willow trees among,
> For then a song required they who did us captive bring,
> Our spoilers called for mirth and said, a song of Zion sing."

It was this blood that fought the Battle of King's Mountain, which victory gave the patriots the courage that is always in hope; it was the winning force at Cowpens, at Guilford, where Rev. Samuel Houston discharged his rifle fourteen times, once for each ten minutes of the battle. These brave hearts were in every battle of the Revolution, from Point Pleasant in 1774 to the victory of Wayne at the Maumee Rapids twenty years later, for the War of Independence continued in the Ohio Country after the treaty of peace. And yet, after all this awful struggle to gain and hold for America the very heart of the Republic, one of the gentlemen referred to by Mr. Randolph wrote pamphlets in which he derided as murderers the courageous settlers of our blood on the occasions they felt it necessary to "remove" Indians with their long rifles. After all the struggle, he too would have made an arrangement with England by which the Ohio River would have been the boundary line."

These were the people who in coming to America had not only secured for themselves that personal religious freedom of a church without a Bishop and ultimately a state without a King, but they became recruits in the Army of Andrew Lewis, the hero of the Battle of Point Pleasant, and like many of their countrymen, continued in the army, (those who had not met the fate of battle,) and became the flower of Virginia's Colonial Army.

The Status of the Battle of Point Pleasant

While the Battle of Point Pleasant has always been conceded to have been the most terrific conflict ever waged between the white man and the Indian, its full significance has not been made the text of American history. We quote however, from a few of the American writers, showing their estimate of it.

Roosevelt, in *"The Winning of the West," Vol. II, chap. 2, says: "Lord Dunmore's War, waged by Americans for the good of America, was the opening act in the drama whereof the closing scene was played at Yorktown. It made possible the two fold character of the Revolutionary War, wherein on the one hand the Americans won by conquest and colonization, new lands for their children, and on the other wrought out their national independence of the British King."*

Kercheval's History of the Valley, p. 120, says: *"Be it remembered, then, that this Indian war was but a portico to our revolutionary war, the fuel for which was then preparing, and which burst into a flame, the ensuing year. Neither let us forget that the Earle of Dunmore was at this time governor of Virginia; and that he was acquainted with the views and designs of the British Cabinet, can scarcely be doubted. What then, suppose ye, would be the conduct of a man possessing his means, filling a high, official station, attached to the British government, and master of consummate diplomatic skill."*

Dr. John P. Hale, in writing of the Battle of Point Pleasant, says, in the History of the Great Kanawha Valley, Vol. I, pp. 114, 115, *"Early in the spring of 1774, it was evident that the Indians were combining for aggressive action. It was decided that an army of two divisions should be organized as speedily as practicable—one to be commanded by Gen. Lewis and the other by Lord Dunmore, in person. Gen. Lewis' army rendezvoused at Camp Union (Lewisburg,) about September 1st, and was to March from there to the mouth of Kanawha; while Gov. Dunmore was to go the northwest route, over the Braddock trail, by way of Fort Pitt, and thence down the Ohio River and form a junction with Gen. Lewis at the mouth of Kanawha.*

The aggregate strength of this southern division of the army was about eleven hundred; the strength of the northern division, under Lord Dunmore, was about fifteen hundred. On the 11th of September Gen. Lewis broke camp, and, with Captain Matthew Arbuckle, an intelligent and experienced frontiersman, as pilot, marched through a pathless wilderness. They reached Point Pleasant on the 30th day of September, after a fatiguing march of nineteen days. Gen. Lewis for several days anxiously awaited the arrival of Lord Dunmore, who, by appointment, was to have joined him here on the 2nd of October. Having no intelligence from him, Lewis dispatched messengers up the Ohio River to meet him, or learn what had become of him.

Before his messengers returned, however three messengers (probably McCulloch, Kenton and Girty) arrived at his camp on Sunday, the 9th of October, with orders from Lord Dunmore to cross the river and meet him before the Indian towns in Ohio. This is, substantially, the current version of matters: but authorities differ.

Some say the messenger arrived on the night of the 10th, after the battle was fought; others say they did not arrive until the 11th, the day after the battle, and Col. Andrew Lewis, son of Gen. Andrew Lewis, says his father received no communication whatever from Lord Dunmore after he (Lewis) left camp Union, until after the battle had been fought, and Lewis of his own motion, had gone on into Ohio, expecting to join Dunmore and punish the Indians, when he received an order to stop and return to the Point. This order (by messenger) Lewis disregarded, when Lord Dunmore came in person, and after a conference and assurances from Dunmore that he was about negotiating a peace, Lewis reluctantly retraced his steps. In the very excited state of feeling then existing between the colonies and the mother country, It was but natural that the sympathies of Lord Dunmore, a titled English nobleman, and holding his commission as governor of Virginia at the pleasure of the crown, should be with his own country; but it was not only strongly suspected, but generally charged, that, while he was yet acting as governor of Virginia, and before he had declared himself against the colonies, he was unfairly using his position and influence to the prejudice of his subjects.

According to the account of Col. Stewart, when the interview was over between Gen. Lewis and the messengers of Lord Dunmore, on the 9th, Lewis gave orders to break camp at an early hour next morning, cross the river, and take up their march towards the Indian towns; but the fates had decreed otherwise. At the hour for starting, they found themselves confronted by an army of Indian braves, eight hundred to one thousand strong, in their war paint, and commanded by their able and trusted leaders, Cornstalk, Logan, Red Hawk, Blue Jacket and Ellinipsico, and some authors mention two or three others. Instead of a hard day's marching, Lewis army had a harder day's fighting—the important, desperately contested, finally victorious, and ever-memorable Battle of Point Pleasant. No "official report" of this battle has been preserved, or was ever written, so far as can be learned. There are several good reasons, apparently, for this omission. In the first place, the time, place and circumstances- were not favorable for preparing a formal official report. In the second place, Lord Dunmore, the superior officer, to whom Gen. Lewis should, ordinarily, have reported, was himself in the field, but a few miles distant, and Gen. Lewis was expecting that the two divisions of the army would be united within a few days; and, in the third place, the "strained relations" between the colonies and the mother country were such, and the recent action of Gov. Dunmore so ambiguous, that Gen. Lewis was probably not inclined to report to him at all."

The same author, in the same volume, at pages 122, 128, 129, 130, 131 and 132, says- "Col. Stewart, one of the first to write about the battle, after Arbuckle's short account, was himself present, was well known to Gen. Lewis (and a relative by marriage), says Gen. Lewis received a message from Gov. Dunmore, on the 9th, telling him to cross the Ohio and join him. Burk, and others, say the messengers *came after the battle and mention Simon Kenton and Simon Girty among the messengers. Col. Andrew Lewis says his father received no communication of any sort from Gov. Dunmore, until ordered to return from Ohio."*

It has been stated that there were not only suspicions, but grave charges, that Governor Dunmore acted a double part, and that he was untrue and treacherous to the interests of the colony he governed. As he is inseparably connected with the campaign (often called the Dunmore War), and its accompanying history, and the inauguration of the Revolution, it may be well to briefly allude to this official course just before, during and after the campaign that his true relations to it, and to the colony, may be understood; and, also, to show that the "Revolution" was really in progress; that this campaign was one of the important early moves on the historical chessboard, and that the Battle of Point Pleasant was, as generally claimed, the initiatory battle of the great drama. In the summer of 1773, Governor Dunmore made, ostensibly, a pleasure trip to Fort Pitt; here he established close relations with Dr. Connally, making him Indian agent, land agent, etc. Connally was an able active and efficient man, who thereafter adhered to Dunmore and the English cause. It is charged that Connally at once began fomenting trouble and ill feeling between the colonies of Virginia and Pennsylvania in regard to the western frontier of Pennsylvania, then claimed by both colonies, but held by Virginia, hoping by such course to prevent the friendly co-operation of these colonies against English designs; and, also to incite the Indian tribes to resistance of western white encroachments upon their hunting grounds, and prepare the way forgetting their co-operation with England against the colonies, when the rupture should come. In December, 1773, the famous "coldwater tea" was made in- Boston harbor. In retaliation the English government blockaded the port of Boston, and moved the capital of the colony to Salem. When this news came, in 1774, the Virginia assembly, being in session, passed resolutions of sympathy with Massachusetts, and strong disapproval of the course of England; whereupon Governor Dunmore peremptorily dissolved the assembly. They met privately, opened correspondence with the other colonies, and proposed co-operation and a colonial congress. On the 4th of September, 1774, met, in Philadelphia, the first continental congress—Peyton Randolph, of

Virginia, president; George Washington, R. H. Lee, Richard Bland, Patrick Henry, Benjamin Harrison and Edmund Pendleton members from Virginia. They passed strong resolutions; among others; to resist taxation and other obnoxious measures; to raise minute men to forcibly resist coercion; and, finally resolved to cease all official intercourse with the English government. In the meantime, Dr. Connally had been carrying out the programme of the northwest. He had taken possession of the fort at Fort Pitt, and renamed it Fort Dunmore; was claiming lands under patents from Governor Dunmore, and making settlements on them; had been himself arrested and imprisoned for a time by Pennsylvania; had the Indian tribes highly excited, united in a strong confederacy and threatened war; then came the massacre of Indians above Wheeling, at Capitina and at Yellow Creek, said to have grown out of Connally's orders. While the continental congress was passing the resolutions above mentioned, and which created a breach between the colonies and the mother country past healing, Governor Dunmore and General Lewis were organizing and marching their armies to the west. Instead of uniting the forces into one army, and marching straight to the Indian towns and conquering or dictating a lasting peace, Lord Dunmore took the larger portion of the army by a long detour by Fort Pitt, and thence down the Ohio, picking up on the way Dr. Connally and Simon Girty, whom he made useful. At Fort Pitt, it is said, he had held a conference with some of the Indian chiefs, and came to some understanding with them, the particulars of which are not known. Instead of uniting with Lewis at the mouth of Kanawha, as had been arranged, but which was probably not intended, he struck off from the Ohio River at the mouth of Hockhocking and marched for the Indian towns on the Pickaway plains, without the support of Lewis army, delaying long enough for the Indians to have annihilated Lewis division if events had turned out as Cornstalk had planned. He (Cornstalk) said it was first their intention to attack the "Long Knives" and destroy them, as they crossed the river, and this plan would have been carried out, or attempted, but for the long delay of Lewis' awaiting the arrival of Lord Dunmore. They afterwards, upon consultations, changed their plans, and determined to let Lewis cross the river and then ambush him somewhere near their own homes, and farther from his (Lewis') base; but the Indians had no organized commissary or transportation arrangements, and could only transport such amount of food as each brave could carry for his own sustenance; this was necessarily, a limited amount, and Lewis' delay in crossing had run their rations so short that they were obliged to cross, themselves, and force a fight, or break camp and go to hunting food. They crossed in the night, about three miles above the Point, on rafts previously constructed, and expected to take Lewis' army by surprise; and it will be seen how near they came to accomplishing it. It was prevented by the accident of the early hunters, who were out before daylight, in violation of orders.

Dr. Campbell says there was considerable dissatisfaction in Lewis camp, for some days before the battle growing out of the manner of serving the rations, and especially the beef rations; the men claimed that the good and bad beef were not dealt out impartially. On the 9th, Gen. Lewis ordered that the poorest beeves be killed first, and distributed to all alike. The beef was so poor that the men were unwilling to eat it, and, although it was positively against orders to leave camp without permission, about one hundred men started out before day, next morning (the 10th), in different directions, to hunt and provide their own meat. Many of these did not get back, nor know of the battle until night, when it was all over. This was a serious reduction of the army at such a time.

Col. Andrew Lewis (son of General Andrew,) in his account of the Point Pleasant campaign, says: *"It is known that Blue Jacket, a Shawnee Chief, visited Lord Dunmore's camp, on the 9th, the day before the battle, and went straight from there to the Point, and some of them went to confer with Lord Dunmore immediately after the battle. It is also said that Lord Dunmore, in conversation with Dr. Connally, and others, on the 10th, the day of the battle, remarked that "Lewis is probably having hot work about this time."*

When Lewis had crossed the river, after the battle, and was marching to join Dunmore, a messenger was dispatched to him twice in one day, ordering him to stop and retrace his steps—the messenger in each instance, being the afterward notorious Simon Girty. Gen. Lewis had, very naturally, become much incensed at the conduct of Lord Dunmore, and took the high-handed responsibility— advised and sanctioned by his officers and men—of disobeying the order of his superior in command, and boldly marching on towards his camp.

When within about two and one-half miles of Lord Dunmore's headquarters, which he called Camp Charlotte, after Queen Charlotte, wife of his majesty, George III, he came out to meet Lewis in person, bringing with him Cornstalk, White Eyes (another noted Shawnee chief), and others, and insisted on Lewis's returning as he (Dunmore) was negotiating a treaty of peace with the Indians. He sought an introduction to Lewis' officers, and paid them some flattering compliments, etc.

Evidently it did not comport with Lord Dunmore's plans to have Gen. Lewis present at the treaty, to help the negotiation by suggestions, or to have the moral support of his army to sustain them. So much did Lewis' army feel the disappointment and this indignity, that Col. Andrew, his son, says that it was with difficulty Gen. Lewis could restrain his men (not under very rigid discipline, at best) from killing Lord Dunmore and his Indian escort. But the result of the personal conference was that Gen, Lewis, at last with the utmost reluctance of himself and army, consented to return, and to disband his army upon his arrival at Camp Union, as ordered.

Suppose Lewis had attempted to cross the river, and been destroyed, or had crossed and been ambushed and demolished in the forest thickets of Ohio, or that Cornstalk had succeeded, as he came so near doing, in surprising him in his own camp, on the morning of the 10th, or after that; suppose the Indians had succeeded in turning the so evenly balanced scale in their favor, during the fight, as they came so near doing, and had annihilated Lewis' army, as they might have done, having them penned up in the angle of two rivers, who can doubt in view of all the facts above noted, that Lord Dunmore would have been responsible for the disaster? Who can doubt, as it was, that he was responsible for the unnecessary sacrifice of life at the Point on the 10th? Who can doubt that, with the two divisions of the army united, as per agreement, and Lord Dunmore and Lewis acting in unison and good faith, they could have marched to the Indian towns and utterly destroyed them or dictated a favorable and lasting peace and maintained it as long as they pleased, by holding important hostages? But, clearly, the policy of the governor was dictated by ulterior and sinister motives; his actions were not single-minded. Col. Andrew Lewis says: *"It was evidently the intention of the old Scotch villain to cut off Gen. Lewis' army."* Burk the historian says: *"The division under Lewis was devoted to destruction, for the purpose of breaking the spirit of the Virginians."*

Withers, Doddridge, and others, express the same views. Gen. Lewis and his army were convinced of the fact; Col. Stewart had no doubt of it, and nearly everyone who has written on the subject has taken the same view of it. A few only are willing to give him the benefit of a doubt. If this design to destroy Lewis' army had succeeded, it is almost certain that the English, through Lord Dunmore, would have perfected an alliance, offensive and defensive, with the victorious Indians, against the colonies and every white settlement west of the Alleghenies would probably have been cut off. It would have been difficult or impossible, for a time, to raise another army for the defense of the western border; the Tory element would have been encouraged and strengthened, the revolutionary element correspondingly discouraged, the rebellion crushed, and Lord Dunmore would have been the hero of the age. Upon what slender and uncertain tenures hang the destinies of nations, and the fate of individuals! The closely won success of Lewis was not only an immediate victory over the Indians, but a defeat of the machinations of the double dealing governor and the projected Anglo-Indian alliance.

If this view of it is established the claim of the Battle of Point Pleasant as being the initiatory battle of the revolution; and, although small in itself, when its after results and influences are considered it stands out in bold relief as one of the important and decisive victories of history. A few words more and we shall be done with Lord Dunmore. Upon his return to Williamsburg, the Assembly, upon his own exparte statement of the results of the campaign, passed a vote of thanks for his "valuable services,' etc., which, it is said, they very much regretted when they learned more of the facts. Just after the battle of Lexington (April 19, 1775), he had all the powder that was stored in the colonial magazine at Williamsburg secretly conveyed on board an armed English vessel lying off Yorktown, and threatened to lay Williamsburg in ashes at the first sign of insurrection. Patrick Henry raised a volunteer force to go down and compel him (Dunmore) to restore the powder; but as this was impracticable, he agreed to pay, and did pay for it, and then issued a proclamation declaring *"One Patrick Henry and his followers rebels."*

He had previously threatened Thomas Jefferson with prosecution for treason, and had commenced proceedings. About this time, having previously sent his family on an English naval vessel, he made his own escape, by night, to the English fleet and commenced a system of depredations along the coast, burning houses, destroying crops, etc. He tried to bring his scheme of Indian co-operation to bear, and sent a message to his old friend, Connally, with a commission as Colonel, and instructed him to secure the cooperation of as many of the western militia commanders as possible, by large rewards; to form an alliance with the Indians, collect his forces at Fort Pitt, and march through Virginia and meet him.

Fortunately, Col. Connally was captured and imprisoned, and the scheme exposed and thwarted He (Dunmore) issued a proclamation granting freedom, to all the slaves who would flock to his standard, and protection to the Tories. Among other acts of violence, he burned Norfolk, the then largest and most important town in Virginia. Upon his flight, the Assembly met and declared his office vacant, and proceeded to fill it; and, for the first time, Virginia had entire "home rule."

Upon the petition of citizens of Dunmore County, which had been named in his honor, the name was abolished, and the county called Shenandoah. In 1776, Lord Dunmore and his fleet and hangers-on were at Guynne's Island, in the Chesapeake Bay, where, as an interesting example of poetic or retributive justice, Gen. Lewis in command of the Virginia troops, attacked, defeated, and drove them off, with heavy loss, Gen. Lewis himself, firing the first gun, soon after which the ex-Governor, a sadder and wiser man "left the country for the country's good."

It will thus be seen that Dunmore, the Tory Governor of Virginia, knew that the war of the Revolution was inevitable. John Adams dates the opening of the Revolution in 1760. The people had tired of taxation without representation. In 1764 we find an organized opposition to oppressive taxation in Boston. In 1765, was passed the Stamp Act and in that year was organized the Sons of Liberty. In 1766 the Royal Artillery was in Boston. In 1767, a duty was imposed on tea. In 1768 British troops were sent to Boston. In 1768 in Virginia was passed the non-importation agreement, followed in 1770 by the Boston Massacre.

In the Parliament of England, the discussion of the taxation of the colonies did not tend to allay their determination to thwart all oppression and when George III determined at all odds to impose taxation the matter was settled in the heart of every loyal American, whether the vow was expressed or implied. It is well authenticated that, to occupy the attention of the colonial forces that they might not have so much time in which to brood over the oppression of the mother country, it was necessary to incite the Indians to attack the frontiers and so divert the attention of the colonists from their quarrel with the mother country and at the same time impress upon them a feeling of dependence upon British arms and means for the safety of their lives and homes. One of the quickest to avail himself of this method of resisting the on-flowing tide of this demand for Liberty was Governor Dunmore.

Virginia had been the first in 1764 to pass a Resolution, defying the British authority as is seen by the following, introduced by Patrick Henry, in the House of Burgesses, and carried:

"Resolved, therefore, That the General Assembly of this colony, together with his majesty or substitute, have, in their representative capacity, the only exclusive right and power to lay taxes and impositions upon the inhabitants of this colony; and that every attempt to vest such power in any person or persons whatsoever, other than the General Assembly aforesaid, is illegal, unconstitutional, and unjust, and has a manifest tendency to destroy British, as well as American, Freedom."

In this same year 1764, Patrick Henry originated the great question which led to the final independence of the United States.

When, in January, 1765, the famous stamp act was passed that for a while stunned the whole country, and confounded the people, it was Virginia, led by the matchless Henry, that stood forth to raise the drooping spirits of the colonists, and it is said his election to the House of Burgesses was with express reference to his opposition to the stamp act, and the adoption of a series of resolutions in 1765, chief among which was the one above referred to.

Upon the death of Mr. Henry, in his private papers, was found the original manuscript, embracing the above Resolution with others, bearing the following narrative, written on the back of it by Mr. Henry, himself:

"The within resolutions passed the House of Burgesses in May, 1765. They formed the first opposition to the stamp act, and the scheme of taxing America by the British parliament. All the colonies, either through fear, or want of opportunity to form an opposition, or from influence of some kind or other, had remained silent. I bad been for the first time elected a burgess, a few days before, was young, inexperienced, unacquainted with the forms of the house, and the members that composed it. Finding the men of weight averse to opposition, and the commencement of the tax at hand, and that no person was likely to step forth, I determined to venture, and alone, unadvised, and unassisted, on a blank leaf of an old law book wrote the within. Upon offering them to the house, violent debates ensued. Many threats were uttered, and much abuse cast upon me, by the party for submission. After a long and warm contest, the resolutions passed by a very small majority, perhaps of one or two only. The alarm spread through America with astonishing quickness, and the ministerial party were overwhelmed. The great point of resistance to British taxation was universally established in the colonies. This brought on the war, which finally separated the two countries, and gave independence to ours."

The Virginia House of Burgesses continued to pass resolutions of defiance until the session of 1768-9, when the House was dissolved by the governor. This house had the merit of originating that powerful engine of resistance, corresponding committees between the legislatures of the colonies, a measure so nearly coeval in the two states of Virginia and Massachusetts that it would have been, at that time with their slow methods of communication, impossible to have borrowed the idea one from the other; so that they are equally entitled to that honor, although Mrs. Warren, a Massachusetts historian of that time, admits that the measure originated in Virginia.

It will thus be seen that when the colonists met in Congress in Philadelphia, September 4, 1774, that all over Virginia it was believed, as Patrick Henry had so eloquently asserted, that the war was inevitable, and the people were ready to voice his sentiment, "*Let it come.*"

Considering all these facts, we can well credit Howe, the Virginia historian who says, "*While Virginia was employed in animating her sister states to resistance, her governor was employed in the ignoble occupation of fomenting jealousies and feuds between the provinces, which it should have been his duty to protect from such a calamity, and Pennsylvania, by raising difficult questions of boundary, and exciting the inhabitants of the disputed territory to forswear allegiance to the latter province; hoping thus, by affording a more immediately exciting question, to draw off the attention of these too important provinces from the encroachments of Great Britain."*

This scheme, as contemptible as it was iniquitous, wholly failed, through the good sense and magnanimity of the Virginia council. Lord North, full of his feeble and futile schemes of cheating the colonies out of their rights, took off the obnoxious duties with the exception of three pence per pound on tea; and, with the ridiculous idea that he might fix the principle upon the colonies by a precedent, which should strip it of all that was odious, offered a draw-back equal to the import duty. This induced the importation of tea into Boston Harbor which, being thrown overboard by some of the citizens, called down upon their city all the rigor of the celebrated Boston port bill.

A draft of this bill reached the Virginia legislature while in session; an animated protest, and dissolution of the assembly by the governor, of course followed. On the following day the members convened in the Raleigh tavern and, in an able and manly paper, expressed to their constituents and their government those sentiments and opinions which they had not been allowed to express in a legislative form. This meeting recommended a cessation of trade with the East India Company, a Congress of deputies from all the colonies, declaring their opinion, that an attack upon one of the colonies was an attack upon all British in America, and calling a convention of the people of Virginia. The sentiments of the people accorded with those of their late delegates; they elected members, who et in convention at Williamsburg, on the 1st of August, 1774.

This convention went into a detailed view of their rights and grievances, discussed measures of redress for the latter, and declared their determination never to relinquish the former; they appointed deputies to attend a general Congress, and they instructed them how to proceed. The Congress met in Philadelphia, on the 4th of September, 1774.

While Virginia was engaged in her efforts for the general good, she was not without her peculiar troubles at home. The Indians had been for some time waging a horrid war upon the frontiers, when the indignation of the people at length compelled the reluctant governor to take up arms, and march to suppress the very savages he was thought to have encouraged and excited to hostility by his intrigues.

Lord Dunmore marched the army in two divisions: the one under General Andrew Lewis he sent to the junction of the Great Kanawha with the Ohio, while he himself marched to a higher point on the latter river, with pretended purpose of destroying the Indian towns and joining Lewis at Point Pleasant; but it was believed with the real object of sending the whole Indian force to annihilate Lewis' detachment, and thereby weaken the power and break down the spirit of Virginia. If such was his object he was signally defeated through the gallantry of the detachment, which met and defeated the superior numbers of the enemy at Point Pleasant, after an exceeding hard-fought day, and the loss of nearly all its officers. The day after the victory, an express arrived from Dunmore with orders for the detachment to join him at a distance of 80 miles, through an enemy's country, without any conceivable object but the destruction of the corps. As these orders were given without knowledge of the victory, Col. Lewis was proceeding to the destruction of the Shawnee villages, when he was informed the governor had made peace.

Another evidence of Dunmore's intention to have the army of Andrew Lewis destroyed at Point Pleasant, is found in Kercheval's History of the Valley, p. 118, as follows:

"It was the general belief among the officers of our army, at the time, that the Earl of Dunmore, while at Wheeling, received advice from his government of the probability of the approaching war between England and the colonies, and that afterwards, all his measures, with regard to the Indians, had for their ultimate object an alliance with those ferocious warriors for the aid of the mother country in their contest with us. This supposition accounts for his not forming a junction with the army of Lewis at Point Pleasant. This deviation from the original plan of the campaign jeopardized the army of Lewis and well nigh occasioned its total destruction. The conduct of the Earl at the treaty, shows a good understanding between him and the Indian chiefs. He did not suffer the army of Lewis to form a junction with his own, but sent them back before the treaty was concluded, thus risking the safety of his own forces, for at the time of the treaty, the Indian warriors were about his camp in force sufficient to have intercepted his retreat and destroyed his whole army."

Again, Kercheval says:

"We now proceed to examine the question, how far facts and circumstances justify us in supposing the Earl of Dunmore himself was instrumental in producing the Indian war of 1774.

It has already been remarked that this Indian war was but the precursor to our revolutionary war of 1775—that Dunmore the then governor of Virginia, was one of the most inveterate and determined enemies to the revolution—that he was a man of high talents, especially for intrigue and diplomatic skill—that occupying the station of commander-in-chief of the large and respectable State of Virginia, he possessed means and power to do much to serve the views of Great Britain. And we have seen, from the preceding pages, how effectually he played his part among the inhabitants of the western country. I was present myself when a Pennsylvania magistrate, of the name of Scott, was taken into custody and brought before Dunmore at Prestone old Fort; he was severely threatened and dismissed, perhaps on bail, but I do not recollect how; another Pennsylvania magistrate was sent to Staunton jail. And I have already shown in the preceding pages, that there was a sufficient preparation of materials for this war in the predisposition and hostile attitude of our affairs with the Indians; that it was consequently no difficult matter with a Virginia governor to direct the incipient state of things to any point most conclusive to the grand end he had in view, namely, in weakening our national strength in some of the best and most efficient parts. If, then, a war with the Indians might have a tendency to produce this result, it appears perfectly natural and reasonable to suppose that Dunmore would make use of the power and influence to promote it, and although the war of 1774 was brought to a conclusion before the year was out, yet we know that this fire was scarcely extinguished before it burst into a flame with tenfold fury, and two or three armies of the whites were sacrificed before we could get the Indians subdued; and this unhappy state of our affairs with the Indians happening during the severe conflict of our revolutionary war, had the very effect, I suppose, Dunmore had in view namely, dividing our forces and enfeebling our aggregate strength; and that the seeds of these subsequent wars with the Indians were sown in 1774 and 1775, appears almost certain.

"And the first we shall mention is a circular sent by Maj. Connolly, his proxy, early in the spring of the year 1774, warning the inhabitants to be on their guard—the Indians were very angry, and manifested so much hostility, that he was apprehensive they would strike somewhere as soon as the season would permit, and enjoining the inhabitants to prepare and retire into Forts, &c. It might be useful to collate and compare this letter with one he wrote to Capt, Cresap on the 14th of July following; see hereafter. In this letter he declares there is a war or danger of war, before the war is properly begun; in that to Capt. Cresap, he says, "the Indians deport themselves peaceably when Dunmore and Lewis and Cornstalk we are all out on their march for battle!

"This letter produced its natural result. The people fled into Forts, and put themselves into a posture of defense, and the tocsin of war resounded from Laurel Hill to the banks of the Ohio River. Capt. Cresap who was peaceably at this time employed in building houses and improving lands, on the Ohio River, received this letter, accompanied, it is believed, with a confirmatory message from Col. Croghan and Maj. McGee, Indian agents and interpreters; and he thereupon immediately broke up his camp, and ascended the River to Wheeling fort, the nearest place of safety from whence it is believed he intended speedily to return home; but during his stay at this place, a report was brought to the Fort that two Indians were coming down the River. Capt. Cresap, supposing from every circumstance, and the general aspect of affairs, that war was inevitable, and in fact already begun, went up the river with his party; and two of his men, of the name of Chenoweth and Brothers, killed, these two Indians.

Beyond controversy this is the only circumstance in the history of this Indian war, in which his name can, in the remotest degree, be identified with any measure tending to produce this war; and it is certain that the guilt or innocence of this affair will appear from this date. It is notorious, then, that those Indians were killed not only after Capt. Cresap had received Connolly's letter, and after Butler's men were killed in the canoe, but also alter the affair at Yellow Creek, and after the people had fled into the Forts."

The same author further says, on pages 128-130, inclusive,

"The Governor of Virginia, whatever might have been his views as to the ulterior measures, lost no time in preparing to meet this storm. He sent orders immediately to Col. Andrew Lewis, of Augusta County, to raise an army of about one thousand men, and to march with all expedition to the mouth of the Great Kanawha, on the Ohio River, where, or at some other point, he would join him, after he had got together another army, which tie intended to raise in the northwestern counties, and command in person. Lewis lost no time, collected the number of men required, and marched without delay to the appointed place of rendezvous.

"But the Earl was not quite so rapid in his movements, which circumstance the eagle eye of old Cornstalk, the general of the Indian army, saw, and was determined to avail himself of, foreseeing that it would be much easier to destroy two separate columns of an invading army before than after their junction and consolidation. With this view he marched with all expedition to attack Lewis before he was joined by the Earle's army from the north, calculating, confidently no doubt, that if he could destroy Lewis, he would be able to give a good account of the army of the Earl.

"The plan of Cornstalk appears to have been those of a consummate and skillful general, and the prompt and rapid execution of them displayed the energy of a warrior. He, therefore, without loss of time, attacked Lewis at his post. The attack was sudden, violent, and I believe unexpected. It was nevertheless well fought, very obstinate, and of long continuance; and as both parties fought with rifles, the conflict was dreadful; many were killed on both sides, and the contest was only finished with the approach of night. The Virginians, however, kept the field, but lost many able officers and men, and among the rest, Col. Charles, Lewis, brother to the commander-in-chief.

This battle of Lewis' opened an easy and unmolested passage for Dunmore through the Indian country; but it is proper to remark here, however, that when Dunmore arrived with his wing of the army at the mouth of the Hockhocking River, he sent Capt. White-eyes, a Delaware chief, to invite the Indians to a treaty, and he remained stationary at that place until White-eyes returned, who reported that the Indians would not treat about peace. I presume, in order of time, this must have been just before Lewis' battle; because it will appear in the sequel of this story, that a great revolution took place in the minds of the Indians after the battle.

"Dunmore, immediately upon the report of White-eyes that the Indians were not disposed for peace, sent an express to Col. Lewis to move on and meet him near Chillicothe, on the Scioto River, and both wings of the army were put in motion. But as Dunmore approached the Indian town, he was met by flags from the Indians, demanding peace, to which he acceded, halted his army, and runners were sent to invite the Indian chiefs, who cheerfully obeyed the summons, and came to the treaty—save only Logan, the great orator, who refused to come. It seems, however, that neither Dunmore nor the Indian chiefs considered his presence of much importance, for they went to work and finished the treaty without him—referring, I believe, some unsettled points for future discussion, at a treaty to be held the ensuing summer or fall at Pittsburg.

This treaty, the articles of which I never saw, nor do I know that, they were ever recorded, concluded Dunmore's war, in September or October, 1774. After the treaty was over, old Cornstalk, the Shawnee chief, accompanied Dunmore's army until they reached the mouth of the Hockhocking on the Ohio River; and what was more singular, rather made his home in Capt. Cresap's tent, with whom he continued on terms of the most friendly familiarity. I consider this circumstance as positive proof that the Indians themselves neither considered Capt. Cresap the murderer of Logan's family, nor the cause of the war. It appears, also, that at this place the Earl of Dunmore received dispatches from England. Dodridge says he received these on his march out.

But we ought to have mentioned in its proper place, that after the treaty between Dunmore and the Indians commenced near Chillicothe, Lewis arrived with his army and encamped two or three miles from Dunmore, which greatly alarmed the Indians, as they thought he was so much irritated at losing so many men in the late battle that he would not easily be pacified; nor would they be satisfied until Dunmore and old Cornstalk went into Lewis' camp to converse with him.

Dr. Doddridge represents this affair in different shades of light from this statement. I can only say I had my information from an officer who was present at the time.

But it is time to remind the reader, that, although I have wandered into such a minute detail of the various occurrences, facts and circumstances of Dunmore's war; and all of which as a history may be interesting to the present and especially to the rising generation; yet it is proper to remark that I have two leading objects chiefly in view—first, to convince the world, that whoever might be the cause of the Indian war in 1774, it was not Capt. Cresap. Secondly, that from the aspect of our political affairs, at that period, and from the known hostility of Dunmore to the American Revolution, and withal to the subsequent conduct of Dunmore and the dreadful Indian war that commenced soon after the beginning of our war with Great Britain—I say, from all these circumstances, we have infinitely stronger reasons to suspect Dunmore than Cresap; and I may say that the dispatches above mentioned that were received by Dunmore at Hockhocking, although after the treaty, were yet calculated to create suspicion.

But if, as we suppose, Dunmore was secretly at the bottom of this Indian war, it is evident that he could not with propriety; appear personally in a business of this kind; and we have seen and shall see, how effectually his sub-governor played his part between the Virginians and the Pennsylvanians; and it now remains for us to examine how far the conduct of this man (Connolly) will bear us out in the supposition that there was also some foul play, some dark intriguing work to embroil the western country in an Indian war."

Hon. V. A. Lewis who is the author of the History of the Virginias compiled in Hardesty's Historical and Geographical Encyclopedia of 1883 pays the following tribute to the Battle of Point Pleasant:

"To the student of history no truth is more patent than this, that the Battle of Point Pleasant was the first in the series of the Revolution, the flames of which were being kindled by the oppression of the mother country and the resistance of the same by the feeble but determined colonies. It is a well known fact that the emissaries of Great Britain were then inciting the Indians to hostilities against the frontier for the purpose of distracting attention, and thus preventing the consummation of the Union which was then being formed to resist the tyranny of their armed oppression. It is also well known that Lord Dunmore was an enemy of the colonists, by his rigid adherence to the royal cause and his efforts to induce the Indians to co-operate with the English, and thus assist in reducing Virginia to subjection. It has been asserted that he intentionally delayed the progress of the left wing of the army that the right might be destroyed at Point Pleasant. Then at the mouth of the Great Kanawha River on the 19th (10th) day of October, 1774, there went whizzing through the forest the first volley of a struggle for liberty, which, in the grandeur and importance of its results, stands without parallel in the history of the world. On that day the soil upon which Point Pleasant, now stands drank the first bloodshed in defense of American liberty, and it was there decided that the decaying institutions of the Middle Ages should not prevail in America, but that just laws and priceless liberty should be planted forever in the domains of the New World.

Historians, becoming engrossed with the more stirring scenes of the Revolution, have failed to consider the sanguinary battle in its true import and bearing upon the destiny of our country, forgetting, that the Colonial army returned home only to enlist in the patriot army and on almost every battlefield of the Revolution were representatives of that little band who stood face to face with the savage allies of Great Britain at Point Pleasant."

And, in conclusion, Kercheval says, at page 139:

"I say, from all which it will appear that Dunmore had his views, and those views hostile to the liberties of America, in his proceedings with the Indians in the war of 1774, the circumstances of the times, in connection with his equivocal conduct, leads us almost naturally to infer that he knew pretty well what he was about, and among other things, he knew that a war with the Indians at this time would materially sub-serve the views and interest of Great Britain, and consequently he perhaps might feel it a duty to promote said war, and if not, why betray such extreme solicitude to single out some conspicuous character, and make him the scapegoat, to bear all the blame of this war, that he and his friend Connolly might escape?"

Nothing could more fittingly describe the patriotic sentiment fell in Virginia than the heroic appeal of Mrs. Wm. Lewis. It is related of her that "When the British force under Tarleton drove the legislature from Charlottesville to Staunton, the stillness of the Sabbath eve was broken in the latter town by the beat of the drum, and volunteers were called for to prevent the passage of the British through the mountains at Rockfish Gap." The elder sons of Wm. Lewis, who then resided at the old fort, were absent with the northern army. Three sons, however, were at home; whose ages were 17, 15 and 13 years. Wm. Lewis was confined to his room by sickness, but his wife, with the firmness of a Roman matron, called them to her, and bade them fly to the defense of their native land. *"Go my children."* said she, *"I spare not my youngest, my fair-haired boy, the comfort of my declining years. I devote you all to my country. Keep back the foot of the invader from the soil of Augusta, or see my face no more."*

When this incident was related to Washington, shortly after its occurrence, he enthusiastically exclaimed, "Leave me but a banner to plant upon the mountains of Augusta, and I will rally around me the men who will lift our bleeding country from the dust, and set her free." Howe's Virginia, its History and Antiquities, p. 183.

From Wither's Border Warfare we quote:

"The army under Gen. Lewis bad endured many privations and suffered many hardships. They had encountered a savage enemy in great force, and purchased a victory with the blood of their friends. When arrived near to the goal of their anxious wishes, and with nothing to prevent the accomplishment of the object of the campaign, they received those orders with evident chagrin, and did not obey them without murmuring. Having, at his own request, been introduced severally to the officers of that division, complimenting them for their gallantry and good conduct in the late engagement, and assuring them of his high esteem, Lord Dunmore returned to his Camp; and Gen. Lewis commenced his retreat. "

"This battle (says Col. Stuart, in his historical memoir) was, in fact, the beginning of the revolutionary war, that obtained for our country the liberty and independence enjoyed by the United States— and a good presage of future success; for it is well known that the Indians were influenced by the British to commence the war to terrify and confound the people, before they commenced hostilities themselves the following year at Lexington. It was thought by British politicians, that to excite an "Indian war would prevent a combination of the colonies for opposing parliamentary measures to tax the Americans. The blood, therefore, spilt upon this memorable battlefield, will long be remembered by the good people of Virginia and the United States with gratitude."

Virgil A. Lewis, West Virginia State Historian and Archivist, says, in his History of West Virginia, published in 1889, at page 133:

"To the student of history no truth is more patent than this, that the Battle of Point Pleasant was the first in the series of the Revolution, the flames of which were then being kindled by the oppression of the mother country, and the resistance of the same by the feeble but determined colonies. It is a well known fact that emissaries of Great Britain were then inciting the Indians to hostilities against the frontier for the purpose of distracting attention and thus preventing the consummation of the union which was then being formed to resist the tyranny of their armed oppressors. It is also well known that Lord Dunmore was an enemy to the colonists, by his rigid adherence to the royal cause and his efforts to induce the Indians to co-operate with the English, and thus assist in reducing Virginia to subjection. It has been asserted that he intentionally delayed the progress of the left wing of the army that the right might be destroyed at Point Pleasant. Then, at the mouth of the Great Kanawha River, on the 10th day of October, 1774, there went whizzing through the forest the first volley of a struggle for liberty which, in the grandeur and importance of its results, stands without a parallel in the history of the world. On that day the soil on which Point Pleasant now stands drank the first blood, shed in defense of American liberty, and it was there decided that the decaying institutions of the Middle Ages should not prevail in America, but that just laws and priceless liberty should be planted forever in the domains of the New World. Historians, becoming engrossed with the more stirring scenes of the Revolution, have failed to consider this sanguinary battle in its true import and bearing upon the destiny of our country, forgetting that the colonial army returned home only to enlist in the patriot army, and on almost every battle-field of the Revolution represented that little band who stood face to face with the savage allies of Great Britain at Point Pleasant."

Owing to the importance of the question, we have, at the risk of tiring the reader, given these many details of evidence that the Battle of Point Pleasant, while not a battle between the English and Colonial forces, nevertheless shed the first blood on American soil for national independence. It can be plainly seen that, though at this time these sturdy pioneers were fighting to protect their homes and firesides, the very foundation of national government, Great Britain, through her Tory Governor of Virginia, intended thus to destroy the flower of the Colonial Army of Virginia. It was a stroke which, had it succeeded, would have averted the War of the Revolution many years. The army that Lewis gathered were not the unlettered men of the forest,—they were from among the most highly educated men of the colony and it is said that, to this date, in no army of a similar number, has such a large percentage had a knowledge of the Greek and Latin languages That they were men of education and influence will be seen by following the survivors of that battle, not only through the Revolution, where many of them distinguished themselves, but out into the civil life of the country, during, and subsequent to, the Revolution.

That the battle was the most fruitful, in its results, of any battle ever fought upon American soil, is apparent from the history of the country. The great Northwest Territory, lying north of the Ohio and east of the Mississippi, had long been a bone of contention between France and England and France did not relinquish her claim until driven to recede as the result of the battle upon the Plains of Abraham before Quebec, where the intrepid Montcalm was defeated by the invincible Wolffe.

The treaty that followed at Paris, in 1765, ceded all this territory to England, whose failure to open it to the colonists was a subject of discussion and distrust and rightfully so, as England maintained it to the ex elusion of the colonists, not only that she might, with it, subsidize the savage Indians, but when necessary, secure their services in maintaining control of the colonies.

By the treaty that followed the Battle of Point Pleasant, that of Camp Charlotte, the federation of the five great nations in control of that territory ceded it to Virginia, to hold inviolate, and which treaty lasted without interruption for three years, enabling the colonists not only to enter the Northwest Territory, but to colonize Kentucky and Tennessee. In Dunmore's army was the intrepid George Rodgers Clarke, a Virginian, the Hannibal of the West, who was present at the treaty of Camp Charlotte. The history of the colonization and civilization of this territory is the history of Geo. Rodgers Clarke, too well known here for extended comment. Suffice it to say that, in the struggle led by Clarke to drive the British from the Northwest Territory, it was not the colonies, but Virginia, protecting her own territory, acquired by the Battle of Point Pleasant, that furnished the army for Clark's expedition, Governor, Patrick Henry supplying Clarke from Virginia's funds, the sum of twelve hundred pounds and supplies of boots and ammunition from Pittsburg, then in Virginia. Could any army nave displayed more heroism, an army of one hundred and fifty, starting out to conquer such a wilderness, with no conveyance for their munitions of war, save their own robust and hardy bodies?

The subjugation of this country was not only comparatively broad in its results, but was due alone to Virginia. Of course, such a vast territory opened up, as it thus was, to civilization and habitation, necessarily called for representation in the Congress of the infant nation, and justly so. Virginia would soon, by her great population, control the legislation of the nation. Such, however, was not the purpose of Virginia. That ever generous mother state here had opportunity to be the most magnanimous of them all. She would not, if she could, dominate the policy of the country, and, without a dollar, she donated, actually gave away to the colonies, in fee simple the entire Northwest Territory, to be the territory of the colonists, and to be disposed of as they deemed best.

When we review the acquisition of the other territory of the United States and compare the $15,000,000, expended by our government, for the Louisiana purchase, the cost of the acquisition of upper and lower California, of Alaska, of the Philippines, of the cost of the Mexican acquisition in men and money, and then remember that the settlement of the states of Kentucky and Tennessee were made possible, as well as the colonization of Western Pennsylvania and Western Virginia, together with the acquisition of the Northwest Territory, and the settlement and civilization of the same, and all as a sequel of the Battle of Point Pleasant, considering the history of the ever memorable struggle and the subsequent development of the country, it is very apparent not only that the Battle of Point Pleasant was the initial, the first battle of the Revolution, but also farther reaching in its results than any other battle ever fought upon the American continent.

As we have said before, no official report of the battle was ever made, but a letter from Williamsburg, Va., then the seat of government, under date of November 10, 1774, was published in the Belfast News Letter, yet preserved. Presumably, it was contributed to that paper because many of the Scotch-Irish had emigrated from Belfast, Ulster District, to Pennsylvania and ultimately to Virginia and settled in the sections of Virginia from which the army had been for the most part been made up. This made the event peculiarly interesting to the people of that portion of Ireland. From that publication we quote the history of the battle:

BELFAST

Yesterday arrived a mail from New York, brought to Falmouth by the Harriot packet boat. Capt. Lee. Williamsburg, Va.

November 10th.

"The following letter is just received here from the camp at Point Pleasant, at the mouth of the Great Kenhawa (as then spelled), dated October 17, 1774:

"The following is a true statement of a battle fought at this place on the 10th instant: On Monday morning, about half an hour before sunrise, two of Capt. Russell's company discovered a large party of Indians about a mile from the camp, one of which men was shot down by the Indians; the other made his escape and brought in the intelligence. In two or three minutes after, two of Capt. Shelby's company came in and confirmed the account.

"Col. Andrew Lewis, being informed thereof immediately ordered out Col. Charles Lewis, to take command of one hundred and fifty of the Augusta troops, and with him went Capt. Dickinson, Capt. Harrison, Capt Wilson, Capt. John Lewis of Augusta, and Capt. Lockridge, which made the first division. Col. Fleming was also ordered to take command of one hundred and fifty more of the Botetourt, Bedford and Fincastle troops. Capt. Thomas Buford, from Bedford; Capt Love, of Botetourt; Capt. Shelby and Capt. Russell, of Fincastle, which made the second division.

"Col. Charles Lewis' division marched to the right, some distance from the Ohio, and Col. Fleming, with his division on the bank of the Ohio, to the left.

"Col. Charles Lewis' division had not marched quite half a mile from the camp when, about sunrise, an attack was made on the front of his division, in a most vigorous manner, by the united tribes of Indians—Shawnees, Delawares, Mingoes, Tawas, and of several other nations—in number not less than eight hundred, and by many thought to be one thousand. In this heavy attack, Col. Charles Lewis received a wound which, in a few hours caused his death, and several of his men fell on the spot; in fact, Augusta division was obliged to give way to the heavy fire of the enemy. In about a second of a minute after the attack on Col. Lewis' division, the enemy engaged the front of Col. Fleming's division, on the Ohio, and in a short time the Colonel received two balls through his left arm, and one through his breast, and, after animating the officers and soldiers in a most calm manner to the pursuit of victory, retired to the camp.

"The loss in the field was sensibly felt by the officers in particular; but the Augusta troops, being shortly after reinforced from the camp by Col. Field, with his company, together with Capt. McDowell, Capt. Mathews and Capt. Stewart, from Augusta; Capt. Paulin, Capt. Arbuckle and Capt. McClannahan, from Botetourt, the enemy no longer able to maintain their ground, was forced to give way till they were in a line with the troops, Col. Fleming being left in action on the bank of the Ohio.

"In this precipitate retreat, Col. Field was killed. During this time, which was till after twelve, the action in a small degree abated, but continued, except at short intervals, sharp enough till after 1 o'clock. Their long retreat gave them a most advantageous spot of ground, from whence it appeared to the officers so difficult to dislodge them that it was thought most advisable to stand as the line was then formed, which was about a mile and a quarter in length, and had sustained till then a constant and equal weight of the action, from wing to wing.

"It was till about half an hour till sunset they continued firing on us scattering shots, which we returned to their disadvantage. At length, the night coming on, they found a safe retreat.

"They had not the satisfaction of carrying off any of our men's scalps, save one or two stragglers whom they killed before the engagement. Many of their dead they scalped, rather than we should have them, but our troops scalped upwards of twenty of their men that were first killed.

"It is beyond doubt their loss, in number, far exceeded ours, which is considerable.

"The return of the killed and wounded in the above battle, same as our last, as follows:

—Killed—Colonels Charles Lewis and John Field, Captains John Murray, R. McClannahan, Samuel Wilson, James Ward, Lieut. Hugh Allen, ensigns Cantiff and Bracken, and forty-four privates. Total killed, fifty-three.

"Wounded—Col. William Fleming, Captains John Dickinson, Thomas Buford and I. Skidman Lieutenants Goldman, Robinson, Lard and Vance, and seventy-nine privates. Total wounded eighty-seven; killed and wounded one hundred and forty."

And further from the same publication:

AMERICA

We have it from good authority that his Excellency, the governor, is on his way to this capital, having concluded a peace with the several tribes of Indians that have been at war with us, and taken hostages of them for their faithful complying with terms of it, the principal of which are that they shall totally abandon the lands on this side of the Ohio River, which, river is to be the boundary between them and the white people, and never more take up the hatchet against the English."

"Thus, in a little more than the space of five months, an end is put to a war which portended much trouble and mischief to the inhabitants on the frontier, owing to the zeal and good conduct of the officers and commanders who went out in their country's defense and the bravery and perseverance of all the troops." (*Copied from the Belfast News Letter of February 10, 1775.*)

De Hass, in describing the battle, says:

"The battle scene was now terribly grand. There stood the combatants—terror, rage, disappointment and despair riveted upon the painted faces of one, while calm resolution and the unbending will to do or die were marked upon the other. Neither party would retreat, neither could advance. The noise of the firing was tremendous;—no single gun could be distinguished—was one common roar. The rifle and the tomahawk now did their work with dreadful certainty. The confusion and perturbation of the camp had now arrived at its greatest height. The confused sounds and wild uproar of the battle added greatly to the terror of the scene. The shouting of the whites, the continued roar of firearms, the war-whoops and dismal, yelling of the Indians, were discordant and terrific."

Col. J. L. Peyton, in his valuable history of Augusta County, says:

"It was, throughout, a terrible scene—the ring of rifles and the roar of muskets, the clubbed guns, the flashing knives—the fight, hand to hand—the scream for mercy, smothered in the death-groan—the crushing through the brush—the advance —the retreat—the pursuit, every man for himself, with his enemy in view—the scattering on every side—the sounds of battle, dying away into a pistol shot here and there through the wood, and a shriek the collecting again of the whites, covered with gore and sweat, bearing trophies of the slain, their dripping knives in one hand, and rifle-barrel, bent and smeared with brains and hair, in the other. No language can adequately describe it."

Mr. Stephen T. Mitchell in 1827 in a publication, "The Spirit of the Old Dominion" published at Richmond, Virginia gives the following account of the Battle of Point Pleasant:

"We landed about a mile on the left-hand shore of Kanawha, and climbing a large hill, we were saluted by a hundred Indians, encamped upon the top. Our captors told their adventures, no doubt, with every aggravation; for, after the most frantic expressions of grief and rage, I was bound to a tree, a large pine tree, which stands to this day upon the brow of the hill and the fire was kindled around me. I said my prayers; my time was come; my body felt the scorching heat: but, by a miraculous interposition of Providence, the clouds which had been lowering all day, now burst out in showers, and quenched the flames. The Indians thought the Great Spirit looked over me, and directed the shower for my safety. My bonds were loosened, and I was allowed a little "jirk and hommony" for my refreshment. The next day I could perceive some great expedition on foot; the Indians were running to and fro in every direction; some grinding paint and some cleaning up their arms; and even the squaws and little boys were providing themselves with hatchets and scalping knives, and strewing themselves from the Ohio River all along the cliffs of Kanawha."

"Late in the evening, I saw an uncommon anxiety on the faces of the savages; councils, grand and petty, were held in various places, and so completely were my guards absorbed in the undertaking which was at hand, that they became entirely remiss in their attentions to me. I resolved to seize the propitious moment and make my escape. I sprang: on my feet and ran as fast as my legs would carry me. A loud whoop proclaimed the event, and in a moment, I could perceive myself closely pursued by half a dozen athletic young fellows, with uplifted tomahawks. Fear added to my limbs the agility of the deer. With my head turned back over one shoulder, I bounded through the pine-trees until my speed had carried me unawares to the brink of a precipice. I tried to stop; it was too late; I gave a piercing shriek and bounded over. A rushing sound in my ears, like the roaring of a mill-dam, then the crashing of branches and limbs recalled me to my recollection, and I found myself to my inexpressible delight, breaking my way through the thick branches of a buck-eye tree. I alighted without injury, and looking back upon the cliff above, could see my savage pursuers gaping over the precipice in amazement. I gave not a second look, but darted off towards the point with a heart swelling with praise to the great Creator, who had thus twice rescued me so miraculously from my enemies.

Arriving at the mouth of the Kanawha, I shouted aloud for assistance. But, the whites had too often been decoyed by their own people to the savages, to be easily imposed upon. They answered me they could give no assistance. I could not swim, but my ingenuity, never fertile in expedients, befriended me now for the first time in my life. I rolled down a dry log from the bank into the water, and getting astride of it, I managed by great exertion of hands and feet, to row it across the stream, which at that time, from the great height of the Ohio, was as still as a mill-pond I was received by General Lewis, the commandant of the fort, with great- cordiality and affection; and, being naked and necessitous, I enrolled myself as a regular in the corps; and, being dressed in militaire, with a tremendous rifle in my hand and a thick breast work before me, I felt as brave as Julius Caesar."

"I was in hopes that I might enjoy, within the walls of a fort, some respite from the fears, toils and anxieties which had, for the last two weeks, worn me out both body and mind., But he who undertakes to settle in a new and savage country, must look out for no such respite, until, by hardihood and perseverance, he has leveled the forest, with its inhabitants, to the earth.

On the 10th of October, 1774, about sun-rise, the hunters came in at full speed, and gave the appalling information that a large body of Indians had spread themselves from river to river, and were advancing by slow degrees, towards the fort; at the same instant, we could observe the women and boys skulking up and down the opposite banks of the Ohio and Kanawha.

The position of the fort was peculiarly favourable to a surprise. As I have above mentioned, it was situated at a right angular point formed by the confluence of the Kanawha and Ohio Rivers. The country above the fort was covered with a heavy forest and impervious growth of underwood, through which an invading force might penetrate completely undiscovered, to the very walls of the fort. The garrison was composed of about twelve hundred men entirely Virginians, from the counties of Botetourt and Augusta. The Indians consisted of about the same number, the flower of the Shawnee, Wyandotte and Mingoe tribes, who were commanded by the celebrated Chieftain, Cornstalk.

From the large force which he had collected for this expedition, and from the secrecy of his movements, it was evident that the Indian Chief, in this desperate attempt to recover the country east of the Ohio River, meditated nothing less than an entire extermination of the garrison. General Lewis ordered out about seven hundred of his rangers, under the command of his nephew, Colonel Charles Lewis; with the remaining part of his troops, about five hundred in number, he determined to act as a reserve and defend the fort to extremities."

"I happened to be among those who were ordered out, very much against my will; but it was neck or nothing; we advanced about three hundred yards in front of the fort, toward a deep ravine which intersected the valley at the right angles with the Kanawha. All was still as death; one moment more and a yell mingled with the roar of a thousand rifles, rung from river to river, and at the same moment every bush and tree seemed alive with armed savages.

Col. Lewis was killed at the first fire, but the rangers maintained their ground, and a contest commenced more desperate and more rapidly fatal than any which had ever, been fought with the Aboriginese, excepting that of Talladega. The Indian Chief, with that promptness for seizing an advantage, and that peculiar military tact for which he was so much renowned, extended his line from the Ohio as far as it would stretch across to the Kanawha bank, for the purpose of outflanking the opposing forces. But, in the execution of this manoeuvre, he was completely foiled by the superior address and boldness of the whites who, animated with revenge for the loss of their leader and a consciousness of their desperate situation, fought with a fury that supplied the inequality of numbers, and set at defiance every stratagem of the savages.

Finding that his method of outflanking would not succeed, the Indian Chief concentrated his forces, and furiously attacked the centre of the Virginia line. The savages, animated by their warlike and noble Chieftain, Cornstalk, forgot the craftiness of their nature, and rushing from their coverts, engaged hand to hand with their stout and hardy adversaries, until the contest resembled more a circus of gladiators than a field of battle. I became desperate; hide where I would, the muzzle of some rifle was gaping in my face, and the wild, distorted, countenance of a savage, rendered he more frightful by paint, was rushing towards me with uplifted tomahawk One fellow in particular, seemed to mark me as his victim; I leveled my rifle at him as he came yelling and leaping towards me, and fired. The ball missed my aim. He rose upon his toes with exultation, and whirling his tomahawk round his head, slung it at me with all his powers. I fell upon my face, and it whizzed harmless over my head and stuck into a sapling. I bounded up and forced it from the tree, but the Indian was on me and rescued the hatchet from my hands. I seized him round the waist, enclosing both his arms at the same time and tripping up his heels, we rolled together upon the ground. I at last, grew furious, gouged him with my thumbs in both eyes, and seizing him with my teeth by the nose, I bit the whole of it from his face; he yelled out with pain and rage, and letting loose the hatchet to disengage my teeth, I grasped the handle and buried the sharp point into his brains. He gave one convulsive leap which bounced me from his body, and in a moment after expired. I immediately rose, and gaining a secure position behind a tree, remained there till the close of the fight, and made a thousand resolutions, if I survived this engagement, never to be caught in such a scrape again. I kept my word, for I have never since encountered the savages, and if Heaven forgives me, I never will. There is no fun in it.

But, to return to the history of this ever memorable battle. There was a peninsula extending from a high range of bills, running parallel with the Ohio River, which jutted close to the Kanawha bank, about a half a mile from its mouth. Knowing the importance of securing the narrow pass which ran between its base and the river, the Indian Chief dispatched a picked body of his troops to take possession of it. They entered the dry bed of a small creek which skirted the foot of the hills, and pursued their route unnoticed till they were about to enter the important pass, when a shower of rifle bullets pierced their body and swept down the foremost ranks. A chosen band of rangers at the same moment made their appearance, with whom General Lewis in anticipation had guarded the pass. A yell of surprise and rage burst from the savage line, and they seconded their returning fire by a unanimous and desperate charge with the hunting-knife. The contest now assumed all the wild and terrific cast which a personal struggle, conducted with the deadly feelings of hate and revenge then existing between the whites and Indians, could inspire. The air was filled with the screams of the savages and the deep imprecations of the riflemen; every blow brought death, and the ground was soon heaped with the corpses of the combatants. But the disappointed efforts of savage desperation were ineffectual against the unbroken and impenetrable column which was maintained by the whites; and the Indians were driven, with the loss of half their force, back upon the main body. Here, the fight still raged in the extremity of opposition, every inch of ground was contested, from behind every bush and decayed log the murderous flash arose, and the continued roar of a thousand rifles vibrated through the forest.,

"The savage Chieftain discovered that the chances against him were desperate, yet, by his own personal example of courage and address, was the fight long sustained, even after his line had been driven, step by step, from their original position. His voice could at intervals be heard, rising above the din of the fight like the shrill blast of a bugle; at one moment, his dusky form and glittering ornaments could be seen flitting through the trees upon the Ohio bank, and his war cry in the next would fill the echoes of the hill at the farthest extremity of the line. A sheering ejaculation of triumph would one moment escape him, as an advantage was gained by the devoted gallantry of some Shawnee warrior; an imprecation upon some skulking Mingoe, in a short time afterwards, would be recognized in his voice. "Charge high and aim low" was his command incessantly throughout the day; and, it is one of the circumstances remarked of that fatal fight, that most of the bullet wounds received by the whites proved mortal; but few of the wounded ever recovered. Yet, all the efforts of the old warrior were vain; defeated and discouraged, the savage army almost abandoned the fight in the latter part of the day, and it was reduced to a mere straggling fire between individuals of the contending parties."

"Night closed upon the scene, yet the ground was still occupied by the two armies. Although victorious, the Virginians could neither press their advantage nor retire to rest. An ambuscade or a night attack was expected from the savages, and their behavior warranted the latter supposition. For, behind a long line of watch-fires, they could be discovered as if cautiously examining the points most open to attack. The wild scream of a savage warrior, apparently advancing to the fight, would at intervals break upon the death-like stillness of the night, and cause my heart to leap almost out of my mouth. I confidently calculated that every moment was the time for their attack, and fancied divers times could hear them stealing through the bushes upon us. The gleams of the morning sun, however, at length illumined the scene, but not a vestige of the Indian army remained; the living and the dead had alike disappeared, and it was not until then, it was ascertained or even suspected, that the savages had secure themselves from interruption, under pretense of a night attack, had thrown their dead, with weights attached to them, in the river, and retreated across it under cover of darkness."

Of the men who participated in the Battle of Point Pleasant, we regret that no complete roster has been preserved. However, the men who were in that army were friends and neighbors, and many of them related by ties of blood and marriage, so that a review of a few of them will indicate the character of the men composing the army.

It will be seen by a review of the history of the colonies that prior to the Battle of Point Pleasant, not only the Colonists but England knew, as did Patrick Henry when he made his famous speech that *"The War was inevitable."* The British Government seeing the fomentation in the colonies had made repeated concessions; willing to relinquish, if necessary, all but the principle of the Right of England to levy taxes upon the Colonists without giving them representation in the British Government. The Colonists were astir with intense excitement. The tea had been thrown overboard in Boston Harbor and the Port had been closed by a bill passed by Parliament in March of that year. Meetings had been and were being held protesting against Royal oppression. That powerful engine of resistance, Committees of Correspondence had been formulating their ideas of resistance and the Virginia Assembly convened at Williamsburg in May, had passed an independent resolution setting forth that June 1st, 1774, should upon the making effective of the Port Bill be made "*a day of fasting and prayer to implore the divine interposition for averting the heavy calamity, which threatens the civil right of America;*" whereupon, the Earl of Dunmore, then Governor of Virginia, at once dissolved the Assembly. The Continental Congress had already convened and its every breath was ladened with resistance of British oppression.

Is it to be wondered at and is it not the most natural thing in the world, that Dunmore would try to devise ways and means to prevent Virginia from participating in the federation of the Colonies; and what more powerful instrument could he have set in motion to distract their attention from the clouds gathering in the East, than by setting in motion a band of howling Indians on the frontier, making it an absolute necessity that Virginia protect her homes, her women and children and her property rights, and this danger so eminent, could not be delayed. So calling together the flower of the Colonial Army of Virginia, which he promised should be united and together encounter the Indians in their homes, he should cause one branch to alone be attacked, hoping they would thus be destroyed and if only temporarily defeated, they would be so busy protecting the frontier and their homes they would have no time to go into the Colonial Army, confederated as they would be to resist the British Army, already many of whom were camping upon the plains of Boston. But to the surprise of Dunmore the Division of Lewis' Army was victorious and the tide of American interests was changed.

Without the Army of Lewis, which was the great military training school of the Colony, many of whom went on into the Revolution and became many of them, officers of high rank, it would have been impossible for Virginia to have raised her quota of men and officers to have participated in that struggle for liberty; and without Virginia the Colonists would have thought it impossible, as it would have been, to have undertaken that struggle for independence. Without the entire support that Virginia gave George Rodgers Clark who was in the Dunmore division, but who later conquered the North West Territory, weakening the otherwise impregnable background that constantly threatened the frontier and in whose territory did not close the struggle for American Independence until Wayne's treaty twenty years later.

We think the opinions of the early writers of history we have quoted, the natural circumstances surrounding Dunmore at and previous to the Battle, makes it plain that although the battle was between the Colonists and Indians it is beyond doubt the first Battle of the Revolution, and the Government of the United States, while it has been tardy, is fully justified in making the declaration that the $10,000 appropriated for the erection of a monument is

"An act to aid in the erection of a memorial structure at Point Pleasant, West Virginia, to commemorate the Battle of the Revolution, fought at that point between the Colonial troops and Indians, October 10th, seventeen hundred and seventy four."

While a shaft 82 feet high will stand as a sentinel upon the site where the dead were buried, from whence the battle was directed and subsequently the fort, built, it is a pigmy as compared with the fact that at last, after a lapse of One Hundred and thirty-four years, the Congress of the United States has officially called it as it is, a battle of the Revolution, and if a battle of the Revolution, it must of necessity be the first, as the hallowed Lexington was not fought, until April 19th, 1775, while that of Point Pleasant, was fought October 10th, 1774.

The battle in its acquisition of territory ceded by the Indians and previously ceded by France to Virginia but literally in control of the

Indians until this time, this followed by the ceding of all the vast territory of the Great Northwest by Virginia to the infant republic at the close of the Revolution with the cessation of Indian hostilities following the battle, permitting the Colonists to turn their attention to the expulsion of the English army and the overthrow of the British yoke, the moral effect that it had on Virginia, and thus on the Colonies, made it the farthest reaching in its effect an battle ever fought on the American Continent.

    The name of every man who participated in that struggle whether he protected the frontier nearer home while the band of stalwarts went forth to conquer the Indians and make secure the wilderness, the men of Wm. Christian's Regiment who rendered such valiant service, coming as they did when the battle was over, the army, exhausted wounded and bleeding and in time to gather up and bury the slain, should all be honored and preserved. Christian's men were only delayed by their effort to bring in supplies to the Army of 54000 pounds of flour on 400 pack horses but 108 additional head of cattle. They expected to join Lewis Army and together march on to encounter the Indians upon the Pickaway Planes; so that as a part of the Army they are entitled to be enrolled with the heroes of that battle, which will be followed by the roster so far as the writer has been able to glean from all available sources, after many years of careful research.

Biographical

General Andrew Lewis

General Andrew Lewis, the hero of the Battle, was not only a gentleman of education and refinement but was a past master in the art of military tactics. Having entered upon his career in 1742 as Captain of Militia and ten years later as head of Militia of his county. He was with Washington at Great Meadows and Fort Necessity in 1754, where he was twice wounded. In 1755 he was detailed to build forts hence was not present at Braddock's disaster. In 1756, he led the Big Sandy Expedition against the Shawnees. In 1758, when with Washington and General Forbes at Fort Duquesne, he was wounded.

He surrendered to a French officer, was imprisoned at Montreal, was exchanged and saw active service. In 1762 at his request his company was disbanded. In 1763 he was appointed to Lieutenant of Augusta County.

We next find him a member of the Virginia House of Burgesses and a member of a committee to negotiate treaties. It was while thus engaged at the treaty of Fort Stanwix that the Governor of New York said of him, *"He looks like a genius of the forest, and, the very ground seems to tremble under him as he walks along."*

It is from Colonel Stewart, his biographer; we learn that *"He was upwards of six feet high, of uncommon strength and agility, and his form of the most exact symmetry. He had a stern countenance and was of a reserved and distant deportment, which rendered his presence more awful than engaging."*

While Mr. Alexander Reed, of Rockbridge County, Virginia, who was with him at Point Pleasant, describes him thus; *"He was a man of reserved manners, and great dignity of character—somewhat of the order of General Washington."* General Washington held him in such esteem that he recommended that he be made Commander-in-Chief of the Continental Army.

The Battle of Point Pleasant was not only the pivotal point in the life of the nation, but in the life of General Lewis as well. Heretofore he had fought as a British Subject. In defying the orders of Lord Dunmore, the Tory Governor, he was not only among the first to defy Britain, but the first to take up arms in defiance of British authority and from this time on we find him enlisted in the cause of the colonists as against the English Crown.

It seems the irony of fate that he should not have lived to witness the surrender at Yorktown. While enroute home he died of a fever at the home of his friend, Colonel Buford, and was taken to his own estate "Richfield" where his remains were interred Sept. 20, 1781, near the town of Salem, where they reposed for many years in an unmarked and neglected grave. A few years ago, the Ladies of the Margaret Lynn Lewis Chapter, Daughters of the American Revolution, of Roanoke, Virginia, had his remains (which were found well preserved) removed to the East Hill Salem Cemetery, where, in 1902, they erected a stately shaft to his memory. One of the six figures of Roger's equestrian statute at Richmond, commemorating famous Virginians, is that of General Andrew Lewis, but the greatest of his monuments is builded in the hearts of a grateful American Republic.

Beside his brother Colonel Charles Lewis, and John, son of his brother William, Andrew had three sons in the Battle of Point Pleasant. What greater love can a man have for his country than, like Jacob of old, to lay his sons as a sacrifice on his country's altar?

Colonel Charles Lewis

While Andrew Lewis is known as the "Hero of the Battle of Point Pleasant," his brother, Colonel Charles Lewis, a brave soldier, too, was called "The Idol of the Army." While Andrew had devoted his life to the cause of his adopted country, he having been born in Ireland where his parents were then residing, it was reserved for Colonel Charles to embody the completeness of American association he having been born in America, being the youngest child of John Lewis and Margaret Lynn Lewis. Thus he had the distinction not only of dying on American soil, but also of having been born there; in 1733, in the County of Augusta, State of Virginia, and was thus all his life known of Virginia, loved of Virginia and he sacrificed his life, satisfied that he had given to Virginia her full measure of devotion. He was mortally wounded while leading a division of the army at the outset of the Battle of Point Pleasant and later was led to his tent where in a few hours he expired.

Colonel Andrew Lewis, his nephew who was engaged in the battle, says *"He received his wound early in the action but did not let it be known until he had gotten the line of battle extended from the Ohio to Crooked Creek, after which he asked Captain Murray, his brother in law, to let him lean on his shoulder and walk with him to his tent, where he expired about 12 o'clock."*

Captain Arbuckle states that *"he received a wound which in a few hours caused his death."*

Roosevelt's Winning of the West says *"The attack fell first and with especial fury, on the division of Charles Lewis who himself was mortally wounded at the very outset, he had not taken a tree* (the frontier expression for covering oneself behind a tree trunk) *but was in an open piece of ground, cheering on his men when he was shot. He stayed with them until the line was formed, and then walked back to camp unassisted, giving his gun to a man who was near him."*

Howe says of him. *"Charles Lewis was esteemed the most skillful of all the leaders of the border warfare and was as much beloved for his noble and amiable qualities as he was admired for his military talents."*

On page 182 of Howe's Virginia Its History & Antiquities, we find a sketch from his life;

"Charles Lewis, the youngest son of John, is said never to have spent one month at a time out of active and arduous service. Charles was the hero of many a gallant exploit which is still treasured in the memories of the descendants of the border riflemen, and there are few families among the Alleghenies where the name and deeds of Charles Lewis are not familiar as household words.

On one occasion, Charles was captured by the Indians while on a hunting excursion, and after having traveled some two hundred miles, barefoot, his arms pinioned behind him, goaded on by the knives of his remorseless captors, he effected his escape. While traveling along the bank of a precipice some twenty feet in height, he suddenly, by a strong muscular exertion, burst the cords which bound him, and plunged down the steep into the bed of a mountain torrent. His persecutors hesitated not to follow. In a race of several hundred yards, Lewis had gained some few yards upon his pursuers, when, upon leaping a prostrate tree which lay across his course, his strength suddenly failed, and he fell prostrate among the weeds which had grown up in great luxuriance around the body of the tree, Three of the Indians sprang over the tree within a few feet of where their prey lay concealed; but with a feeling of the most devout thankfulness to a kind and superintending Providence, he saw them, one by one, disappear in the dark recesses of the forest. He now bethought himself of rising from his uneasy bed, when lo, a new enemy appeared, in the shape of an enormous rattlesnake, who had thrown himself into the deadly coil so near his face that his fangs were within a few inches of his nose; and his enormous rattle, as it waved to and fro, once rested upon his ear. A single contraction of the eyelid — a convulsive shudder—the relaxation of a single muscle, and the deadly beast would have sprung upon him. In this situation he lay for several minutes, when the reptile, probably supposing him to be dead, crawled over his body and moved slowly away. "I had eaten nothing," said Lewis to his companions, after his return, "for many days; I had no firearms and I ran the risk of dying with hunger ere I could reach the settlement; but rather would I have died than made a meal of the generous beast."

Kercheval's History of the Valley, describes the attire of Colonel Charles Lewis on that day, at page 114, as follows: "*Colonel Chas. Lewis, who had arrayed himself in a gorgeous scarlet waistcoat, against the advice of his friends, thus rendering himself a conspicuous mark for the Indians, was mortally wounded early in action; yet as able to walk back after receiving the wound, into his own tent, where he expired. He was- met on his way by the Commander-in-Chief, his brother, Col. Andrew Lewis, who remarked to him, "I expected something fatal would befall you." To which the wounded officer calmly replied, "It is the fate of war."* The same author says at page 115, "*Col. Lewis, a distinguished and meritorious officer, was mortally wounded by the first fire of the Indians, but walked into the camp and expired in his own tent.*"

Peyton's History of Augusta County says "*He abandoned himself too much to his passion for glory and forgot the wide difference between an officer and a private. He was not inferior to his brother, the General, in courage, intrepidity and military genius; he surpassed him in other respects. He knew how to oblige with a better grace, how to win the hearts of those about him, with a more engaging behavior. He consequently acquired the esteem and affection of his men in a most remarkable manner. To perpetuate the memory of his public and private virtues, his eminent services in the field and his heroic fate, the General Assembly of Virginia, in 1816, named Lewis County in his honor."*

By his kinsmen be was considered the "Flower of the Flock." Like his brother, he was a man of splendid physique and without disparaging his kindred, he was best loved because of his high degree of morality, spotless integrity and acknowledged bravery. His long and active military career had made him a hero in the eyes of his comrades from the Braddock Campaign to the hour of his death and while had he lived, he doubtless would have added new luster to his name in the continued struggle of the Revolution. After all, he had but one life to offer up to his country and at this crucial moment no doubt it was needed most. His conduct inspired the army. The sacrifice of his life armed anew his companies and stimulated them to greater feats of daring.

Thwaite's "Dunmore's War" says, *"Charles Lewis was popular and beloved by all the western army. His loss was a general affliction."*

Dr. Hale's "Trans-Allegheny "says: *"Colonel Charles Lewis was said to be the idol of the army. He had a large, active and honorable military experience from Braddock's War down to death. And it is believed that he would have achieved greater honors and distinction in the Revolutionary struggle, if his life had been spared, but his brilliant career was ended in glory on this field."*

The charge he made at Point Pleasant was in the face of a fearless band of adversaries. When General Andrew Lewis selected his brother to take command of the left wing of the army in the first attempt to repulse Cornstalk and his fearful braves, he selected his brother to bear that peril, not that he loved him less, but that he knew the army needed his courageous example. Colonel William Preston, in writing of his death to Patrick Henry, said: *"Poor Charles Lewis was shot in clear ground, encouraging his men to advance. If the loss of a good man, a sincere friend, a brave officer deserves a tear he certainly is entitled to it."*

At the close of the conflict, his mortal remains were laid to rest upon the reservation of forty feet square upon the present sight of Tu

Endie Wei Park, where the Kanawha and Ohio meet. Here, he is buried beside the other dead of that battle. No stone as yet has ever marked his resting place, save the four granite corner stones erected in 1905 by the Colonel Charles Lewis Chapter Daughters of the American Revolution at Point Pleasant. While no monument has as yet been reared to mark the last resting place of this great man, a tribute due him from his own loved ones, as well as from a grateful nation; it is equally a matter of congratulation that though tardy the Government has donated a small amount $10,000 which with the $6,000 in the hands of the State Commission has been pledged in the contract let for a monument. But greater than this monument is the recognition of the Government of the status of the battle as regards the Revolution, standing, as it does, on the heels of Indian depredations on the western frontier and on the threshold of the American Revolution for American Independence. This honor so long delayed, will at last have written this page of American history correctly when a stately monument shall bear the inscription:

Battle of Point Pleasant
October 10, 1774
First Battle of the American Revolution

Colonel John Field

Colonel John Field, born in Culpepper County in 1720 of good family, is buried beside Colonel Charles Lewis, his friend and comrade. He received his fatal wound at the Battle of Point Pleasant, while bravely checking the Indians. He rallied his troops who had begun to waver and, for a time, seemed likely to be repulsed. Colonel Field had been with Braddock and had seen frontier service from that date, both as a militia officer and as a surveyor. In 1765 he served in the Virginia Legislature, in 1766 he was made Colonel of Militia. His troops at Point Pleasant were a volunteer company, raised by him in his own county which he united with that of General Lewis.

Colonel William Flemming

Colonel William Flemming was renowned not only as a military genius, but as a learned physician and gentleman of culture. While twice severely wounded at the Battle of Point Pleasant, he recovered and was subsequently acting Governor of the State of Virginia. He was a Scotchman of proud lineage who was born February 18, 1729. Prior to Dunmore's War he was Lieutenant, under Gen. Forbes in 1760-61. In 1762 he was Captain under Colonel Adam Stephens at Vaux's and Stonaker's Forts. In 1763 he married Anne Christian. His home was at "Belmont" in Montgomery Co. The wounds he received at Point Pleasant disabled him for active participation in the war of the Revolution, but he was County Lieutenant in further defense in his country against Indians, State Senator 1780-81 and acting Governor during the Cornwallis invasion 1781. He was twice commissioned to settle local battles with Kentucky and was a member of the Virginia convention ratifying the constitution of 1788. He was benevolent and beloved and as a physician and surgeon his ministration to humanity was most extensive. His death August 24th, 1795 was the result of wounds received at the Battle of Point Pleasant.

Captain Evan Shelby

Captain Shelby, who with his two sons, was in the Battle of Point Pleasant, was the ranking officer after the death of Colonels Lewis and Field and the wounding of Fleming, until the arrival of Colonel Christian's regiment. It was Evan Shelby who, with his and the companies of Mathews and Stewart in the ruse, executed the flank movement up Crooked Creek that led Cornstalk to believe that Lewis had been re-enforced, possibly by Dunmore who had played him false and thus decided the fortunes of the day. Captain Shelby became Colonel Shelby of the Revolution, whose distinguished career is followed in the history of Kentucky and Tennessee.

He was born in Wales in 1720, He early emigrated to Maryland. He commanded a Company under Forbes in 1758. In 1771 he settled on the Holston. In 1776 he was with Christian in the Cherokee Expedition. In 1779 he led a successful expedition upon the Chickamauga towns, having been appointed by Virginia a general of Militia. He continued in the service throughout the Revolution engaged principally upon the sea board. He rose to the rank of Colonel and before the close of the war to that of General. He died at King's Mountain on December, 4th, 1794.

Isaac Shelby

Isaac Shelby served as a Lieutenant under his father, Captain Evan Shelby, at the Battle of Point Pleasant. He was born at North Mountain, Maryland on Dec, 11th, 1750, where his grand-father settled upon his arrival from Wales. He had removed with his father to the present site of Bristol, Tennessee prior to Dunmore's War and was engaged in feeding and herding cattle. He served throughout the Revolution, distinguishing himself at Camden, King's Mountain and Long Island Flats. Governor Patrick Henry promoted him to a Captaincy and commissioned him Commissary General of the Virginia Forces. When Sevier, in 1779, projected the expedition that captured the British stores, at Chickamauga, Shelby equipped and supplied the troops by the pledge of his individual credit. Governor Thomas Jefferson commissioned him a Major of Virginia but a survey proved him to be a resident of North Carolina, when he was appointed a Colonel by Governor Caswell. He distinguished himself at Thicketty Fork, Cedar Springs and Musgrave's Mills. Retreating across the Alleghenies after the disastrous defeat at Camden, he with John Sevier, planned the remarkable campaign which resulted in the Battle of King's Mountain, the high water mark of the Revolution that turned the tide in favor of the Patriot Army. He did valiant service at the Battle of the Cowpens as well as at Charleston. He was largely instrumental in preserving Kentucky to the Colonists as against an alliance with Spain. He was six times chosen a Presidential elector for Kentucky.

In 1812 he became the first Governor of Kentucky, which he accepted with great reluctance and accepted only that he might again aid his country against Great Britain. He organized 4000 volunteers and, at the age of 63 years, led them in person to the re-enforcement of General William Henry Harrison enabling him to profit by the victory of Perry at Lake Erie. Congress voted him a gold Medal, and the Kentucky Legislature a vote of thanks.

In 1783 he married Miss Susannah, daughter of Captain Nathanial Hart. He established himself on the first settlement and pre-emption granted in Kentucky which he made his home, residing thereon 43 years. He died July 18th, 1826, aged 76 years. He was a strict Presbyterian.

John Jones

John Jones was born in Culpepper County, Virginia, in 1755 and enlisted in the army of Andrew Lewis and was in the Battle of Point Pleasant, following which, upon his return to Culpepper, he enlisted in the Patriot Army and served throughout the Revolution. In 1792 he obtained patents for land for 359 acres on the Kanawha River and that same year for 400 acres more. In 1797 he obtained patents for 400 acres in Teays Valley and land on Paint Creek, besides making purchases from the state. He owned from Paint Creek to the Narrows on Kanawha including the present sites of Pratt and Dego. In the Clifton Cemetery above Paint Creek, his remains were interred, a slab bearing inscription:

"In Memory of John Jones
Who departed this life
January 7, 1838, Aged 83 Years."

John Jones married Frances Morris, a sister of William and Leonard Morris. He was hospitable and a good citizen. The Baptist Church founded at Kelley's Creek in 1796, was largely due to his interest and generosity

His will, recorded March, 1838, mentions his wife, Frances and children, Gabriel, who returned to Culpepper County, Va., William, Nancy, who married _____ Huddleston, Thomas, Levi and Frances, who married Sheltons and were the progenitors of the prominent Nicholas County, W. Va., family of that name.

John Draper

Lieutenant John Draper, of the Battle of Point Pleasant, was born in 1730 and was one of the pioneer settlers at Drapers Meadows, where, in 1755, occurred that dreadful massacre in which his wife and sister were captured by the Indians. In 1765, he removed to Drapers Valley on the line between Pulaski and Wythe Counties, Va. He was commissioned a Lieutenant in one of the Fincastle Companies in 1774. He died in 1828 at the age of nearly ninety-four years.

Prominent members of the family are still residents of Drapers Valley. In 1886 John S. Draper, a great grandson of Lieutenant John Draper, was the owner of the beautiful estate. John Draper was twice married. His first wife was Bettie and after her return from captivity, she bore four sons and three daughters, she died in 1774, aged 42 years, and in 1776, he married Mrs. Jane Crockett, who bore him two daughters, Alice and Rhoda. By the first marriage, the sons were George, James, John and Silas. The names of the other two daughters are to us unknown.

Benjamin Logan

Benjamin Logan, born in Augusta County, Va. in 1743, was, in 1764, a sergeant in Bouquet's Army. In 1771, he moved to the Holston Valley. He was a Lieutenant in the Point Pleasant Campaign. In 1775, he moved to Kentucky and built Logan's Station or fort, which was besieged by Indians. Logan went to the Holston settlement for ammunition returning on foot in ten days. In 1779, he was second in command of the Bowman expedition. He was a noted Indian fighter and allied himself with Kentucky against the Spaniards at New Orleans. He removed to Shelby County, Kentucky, where he died in 1802.

William Campbell

William Campbell was born in Augusta County, Virginia, in 1745. He died at Rocky Mills, Hanover County, Va. on August 22, 1781. In 1767 he moved to the Holston Valley. In 1774 he was appointed Captain of Militia and was in Colonel Christian's Regiment at Point Pleasant. In September, 1775 he commanded a company at Williamsburg in Patrick Henry's Regiment and under General Lewis assisted in dislodging Governor Dunmore from Gwynn's Island in July, 1776. In 1777 he was made Lieutenant of Militia in the new County of Washington. In 1779, he aided in driving the Tories from the Holston Valley. In 1780, he was promoted to a Colonel of the regiment and chosen to represent his county in the legislature. At King's Mountain he distinguished himself and was commended by Washington, Gates and Greene. He was with Gen. Greene at Guilford Court House in March, 1781. He was made a Brigadier General of Militia and served under Lafayette in the Battle of Jamestown, soon after which he died. Lafayette said of him *"His services at King's Mountain and Guilford would do his memory everlasting honor and ensure him a high rank among the defenders of liberty in the*

American Cause", while Jefferson declared *"General Campbell's friends might quietly rest their heads on the pillow of his renown."* His wife was a sister of Patrick Henry.

Arthur Campbell

Arthur Campbell, a cousin of General William Campbell, was born in Augusta County, Va. in 1743. At fifteen he was captured by the Indians and carried to Lake Erie. Escaping, he was employed as a guide, receiving therefore one thousand acres of land which he located near the present site of Louisville, Ky. In 1772, he was a Justice of Fincastle County, Va. and later a Major of Militia.

After the Battle of Point Pleasant he represented his county in the Virginia Assembly. In 1776, he was chosen County Lieutenant for Washington County which office he held for thirty years. He joined Sevier in the movement to establish the state of Franklin for which Patrick Henry removed him from office and the legislature re-instated him in his latter life. He joined his sons at Middleburg, Ky. where he died in 1811.

John Campbell

Captain John Campbell, a younger brother of Arthur, a lieutenant at Point Pleasant, was a Captain at the Battle of Long Island Flats (1776) and served as County Clerk of Washington County from 1779 to 1815.

Joseph Mayse

Joseph Mayse, who participated in the Battle of Point Pleasant, was from Bath County, Virginia. In April, 1840 he died, being in his 89th year. He had served as a magistrate in his district for nearly fifty years. He was a man of such remarkable memory he was considered an "official record." He was twice High Sheriff of Bath County. His health was always perfect and he boasted he had never taken a dose of medicine.

General Andrew Moore

Andrew Moore, a lawyer by profession, was born in Conniscello, Augusta, (now Rockbridge) County, Va. In 1774, he was admitted to the Bar. In October of that year he was with Andrew Lewis's Army at Point Pleasant. In 1776, as a Lieutenant in the Patriot Army, he participated at Saratoga, where he was promoted to a Captaincy and served thereafter three years. The Virginia Legislature made him Brigadier General of Militia and in 1808 Major General.

General Moore had the distinction of being the only man west of the Blue Ridge, prior to the Civil War, who had ever represented Virginia in the Senate of the United States; which was during the administration of President Jefferson. He was a member of the Virginia Assembly from 1781 to 1789 and again from 1798 to 1800. In 1788, he was a delegate to the convention which ratified the United States Constitution. He was a member of Congress from Virginia during the entire administration of President Washington. In 1800 he was elected to the United States Senate, where he served three years. In 1810, President Jefferson appointed him United States Marshall for the State of Virginia, which office he was filling at the time of his death. His son, Samuel Moore, represented Virginia in the Legislature and in Congress. He was a member of the Virginia Constitutional Convention 1829. In 1861, Samuel Moore opposed the secession of Virginia but going with his state, be served in the Confederate Army. The family has always been distinguished.

George Mathews

George Mathews was born in Augusta County, Virginia in 1739, and died August 30, 1812. At twenty-two years of age he led a volunteer company against the Indians. He was in command of a company of Augusta troops at Point Pleasant on October 10, 1774 and participated with the Patriot Army throughout the Revolution. He was engaged at Brandywine. At Germantown he received nine bayonet wounds, was captured with his whole regiment and confined in a prison ship at New York until December, 1781. He then joined General Nathaniel Greene's army in command of the Third Virginia Regiment. In 1785, he removed with his family to Georgia and settled in Oglethorpe County. In 1781-1791 he represented Georgia in Congress, was Governor of Georgia 1793-1796. He was Brigadier General of Georgia.

In 1811, he was authorized by the President of the United States to take possession of West Florida and captured Amelia Island. His son, George, became a Supreme Judge of Louisiana. He admitted no superiors but Washington. He was short, stout, erect, features bluff, hair red, complexion florid. He died when on a visit to Washington and is buried in St. Paul's churchyard. His four children were Mrs. Andrew Barry of Staunton, Va., Mrs. General Samuel Blackburn, and Mrs. Isaac Telfair, of Staunton and one son, Judge George Mathews, above mentioned. He was three times married, (1) to Miss Amelia Paul, (2) to Mrs. Margaret Reed, of Staunton, and (3) to Mrs. Flowers, of Mississippi. He was divorced from his second wife.

Sampson Mathews

Sampson Mathews, Commissary of Colonel Charles Lewis's Regiment, was called "Master Drover of the Cattle." In 1756, Deputy Sheriff Sampson Mathews assumed the functions of Chancellor of Augusta County. In 1764, he was appointed a Justice of the Peace for Augusta. In 1776, with Alexander St. Clair, he was appointed by the State of Virginia as trustee *"to erect at public expense and superintend a manufactory at such place as they may think proper for the manufacture of sail duck*, this preparatory for equipment of a Virginia fleet for Revolutionary service. He became Colonel Sampson Mathews of the Revolution. In 1781 he commanded the regiment that repelled Arnold's invasion of Virginia. He was one of a committee to draft instructions for the members of the Virginia Convention at Richmond, February 22, 1775.

Colonel Joseph Crockett

Nothing can be truer than that God provides men for the hour. Among the one hundred men who participated in the Battle of Point Pleasant and went on to become settlers of Kentucky, that state so open to the prey of the Indians that its first three years saw more people slaughtered by Indians than that state had white population at the end of that time had among its other emigrants who were in the Battle of Point Pleasant. Colonel Joseph Crockett, for a sketch of whose life we are indebted to his illustrious grandson, Col. Bennett H. Young, of Louisville, Ky. is as follows:

"My great grandfather, Colonel Joseph Crockett, was born in Albemarle and was one of the men who marched with Andrew Lewis, with Charles Lewis, and with William Russell, and was engaged in the conflict at Point Pleasant. He was then a young man.

He returned shortly after the Battle of Point Pleasant, and remained for several months as First Lieutenant in a company of Colonial Militia that was stationed at Point Pleasant. When the fires of the Revolutionary War were kindled and it was necessary for every man to go to the front to resists British invasions, the Indians were to be left a little while to themselves. Virginia and North Carolina were then sending their pioneers to make the settlements of Kentucky which were, under God's providence and direction, one of the chief agencies in the success of the colonies in their great struggle against the mother country. My ancestor organized a company and marched to the front. He was successively a Captain, Major and Lieutenant-Colonel. He was a Major in Morgan's riflemen and recruited two companies for that celebrated organization. He was a Lieutenant at White Marsh, was a Captain when Burgoyne surrendered and was engaged in all the battles previous to that great event. He was at Princeton and Trenton, and Valley Forge and Red Bank, and in 1779, he raised a regiment known as the Crockett Regiment, which was sent west to assist George Rodgers Clark in his war with the Indians and was with that distinguished soldier, second in command, in all the skirmishes and battles with the northwestern Indians on the Ohio and Miami Rivers, and helped to destroy Chillicothe and the Indian towns on the Wabash, and throughout the northwest, and in these battles stayed the uplifted hand of the cruel and avenging Indian, who would otherwise have wreaked his cruelties upon the frontier settlements of both Pennsylvania and Virginia and thus coming in the rear of these enemies, avenged many, of the wrongs heaped upon the Virginia, Pennsylvania and Kentucky settlements."

James Robertson

James Robertson, (by some authors written Robinson), with Valentine Sevier, discovered the Indians before the Battle of Point Pleasant. He was born in Brunswick County, Va. in 1742 and died in Chickasaw County, Tenn. on Sept. 1, 1814.

He was a personal friend of Daniel Boone. He did more to consummate a peace between the Indians and whites than any man in Tennessee. He became the founder of Nashville, where he withstood, with a handful of men, a siege of one thousand Indians. Flattering offers were made him by the Spanish government to cut the territory of Tennessee loose from the government and, with Watauga and Kentucky, establish an independent country which he indignantly declined. In 1790, he was appointed a Brigadier General by Washington. He shared with Sevier the honors and affections of Tennessee.

John Smith

Ensign John Smith, of the Battle of Point Pleasant, left sons, Abraham, of Rockingham County, Joseph and Silas H. of Augusta County and daughter Nancy, who married William Crawford, His family has been distinguished.

Benjamin Harrison

Benjamin Harrison commanded a company at Point Pleasant. In July, 1775, he was appointed Captain of a Company of Minute Men. In 1778, he was appointed Lieutenant Colonel of Militia for Rockingham County. He was a native of Loudon County, Virginia. He was the founder of Harrisonburg, Va. He died in 1819.

Hugh and James Allen

Hugh Allen was a Lieutenant in Col. Charles Lewis's Regiment at Point Pleasant where he lost his life and was buried beside Colonel Lewis. His three sons, John, William and Hugh, all settled in Kentucky. His brother, James Allen, who lived eight miles from Staunton, was Captain of Militia in 1756 and was in the Battle of Point Pleasant and witnessed the death of his brother. He died in 1810, aged ninety-four years and was an elder in the Augusta Stone Church for sixty-four years.

Judge Samuel McDowell

Judge Samuel McDowell, who as Captain McDowell, commanded a company of Augusta troops at the Battle of Point Pleasant. He was a native of Rockbridge County, Va. He married Mary McClung and, with his seven sons and two daughters, in 1784, emigrated to Danville, Ky. He was one of the first Kentucky Court and was a member of the convention that framed for Kentucky the first Constitution. He presided over nine political conventions which convened in Danville from 1784 to 1790.

In 1776 he was a member of the Virginia House of Burgesses, representing Rockbridge County. As Colonel McDowell, he commanded a Rockbridge Company during the Revolution. On April 20, 1781 he wrote the Governor of Virginia, when a draft had been ordered from his county for April 26th, that if the men were drawn, the county would be ruined as two thirds of the men had been engaged in the services all the time and there were no new ones to put in the crops and that he had marched with 200 men to join General Greene before the battle of Guilford Court House.

John Sevier

John Sevier was born in Rockingham County, Va. on September 22, 1745 and died near Fort Decatur, Ga. on September 24, 1815. He was educated at Fredericksburg, Va., married at 17 years of age and became the founder of New Market on the Shenandoah. In 1772, he was appointed Captain of the Virginia Line and moved to Watauga. In the Dunmore War, he resumed his rank in the Virginia Line and participated in the Battle of Point Pleasant.

When what is now Tennessee was organized into Washington District, North Carolina, John Sevier was chosen a delegate to the legislature. In 1777, he again represented Watauga and procured for his State, courts and rights of extension. He was appointed Clerk of the Court and District Judge and, with his friend, James Robertson, was in control of the judicial and administrative functions of the settlement.

He was elected Colonel and enlisted, without exception, every able bodied man between the ages of 16 and 50. With Colonel Isaac Shelby he planned the Battle of King's Mountain. He continued to command the forces against the Indians. When the new state, Franklin, afterwards Tennessee, was organized, he took the oath of Governor on March 1, 1785. When the new state became a part of the Union, he was the first representative to Congress from the Valley of the Mississippi, 1789-1790, and in 1796, when Tennessee became a State," he was elected its first Governor which office he filled for three years. He three times represented Tennessee as a State in Congress. He was in the active service of his country from the age of 17 years to 70. As long as he lived, he was the real seat of power in Tennessee. A monument in Nashville attests to his memory and Sevier County in Tennessee commemorates his fame.

Valentine Sevier

Valentine Sevier was a Sergeant in Evan Shelby's Company and a younger brother of General John Sevier. In 1779 he was a Captain in the Chickamauga Campaign and led a company against the British in North Carolina in 1780, which culminated in the Battle of King's Mountain. He rose to the rank of Militia Colonel and died at Clarksville, Tenn. in 1800.

James Harrod

James Harrod, who had been in Kentucky in the spring and summer of 1774, was with Colonel Charles Lewis. He built the first cabin in Kentucky. He became Colonel Harrod of the Revolution. H e was a member of the first Kentucky Legislature. He was an able assistant of George. Rodgers Clark in securing ammunition. He declined to accept the appointment of Major of the first Regimental Militia of Kentucky. Harrodsburg, Kentucky is named for him. A man named Bridges, with whom he had had litigation, murdered him. That date is thought to be in July, 1793.

William Russell

William Russell was but fifteen years of age when participating in the Battle of Point Pleasant. During the Revolution he rose to the rank of Colonel. He was a Lieutenant at the Battle of King's Mountain and Guilford Court House. After the Revolution he settled in Fayette County, Kentucky. He was appointed to command a regiment in the regular army. In 1792, he represented Fayette County in the Kentucky legislature which was repeated a dozen times until 1825, when he contracted a cold at a public meeting where he was called to preside, which resulted in his death.

James Montgomery

Captain James Montgomery, who was in the Battle of Point Pleasant, settled in Kentucky, as did James Knox, who was in Isaac Hite's Company. Others of Isaac Hite's Company who settled in Kentucky were James McCulloch, John Shelp, William Field, Thomas

Glenn, David Williams, James Brown, John Cowan, John Wilson, Abraham Chapline and John Clark.

John Crawford

John Crawford represented Montgomery County, Kentucky, in the Legislature in 1812.

William Christian

While Colonel William Christian was not an actual participant in the Battle of Point Pleasant, he, with his three hundred volunteer troops, not arriving until 11 p. m., the night of the battle, yet they did noble services to the bleeding army and the valiant dead. He was a native of Augusta County and educated at Staunton. He participated in the Braddock Campaign. He married a sister of Patrick Henry and settled in Botetourt County. In 1775, he settled in Kentucky and Christian County is named in his honor. In April, 1776 he was killed by a party of Indians who had stolen his horses and in whom, with a party of friends, he was in pursuit.

George Slaughter

Colonel George Slaughter, a son-in-law of Colonel Field, after the Battle, settled in Kentucky and was one of eight delegates to Congress out of the City of Louisville.

James Trimble

James Trimble, a participant in the Battle of Point Pleasant, aged then but eighteen years, had in 1770 been a prisoner of the Indians. In 1780 or 1781, he emigrated to Woodford, Kentucky, being one of the earliest settlers. In 1804, he died in Kentucky, having made preparations to move to Hillsborough, Ohio, where his family removed after his death. The Trimbles became eminent. Allen Trimble became Governor of Ohio. William A. Trimble was a Major in the War of 1812 and in 1819 a Lieutenant Colonel in the Regular Army and a United States Senator from Ohio.

John Dickenson

Captain John Dickenson, who commanded one of Colonel Charles Lewis' Companies of Augusta County Troops and who was wounded during the Battle of Point Pleasant, was left with Colonel Fleming at the fort when Andrew Lewis, with his troops, advanced into Ohio. In 1785, he surveyed 502 acres of land at the mouth of Campbell's Creek on the Kanawha River. In 1777, he commanded, as a Colonel with Major Samuel McDowell, the Botetourt Troops, as well as troops, from Augusta County, and marched to the defense of the fort at Point Pleasant, accompanied by Capt. Hall's company of Rockbridge Volunteers, numbering in all about 700 men, and he witnessed the murder of Cornstalk, which with the officers in command he tried to prevent. In 1791, when Bath County was organized, he was appointed one of the first gentlemen justices of that county which honor he declined. He died in 1799, owning large tracts of land in Bath, Greenbrier and Kanawha Counties, besides large holdings in Kentucky. He left sons, Adam and John and daughters. Nancy, married Joseph Kincaid, Mary married Samuel Shrewsbury and Jane, who was the wife of Charles Lewis son of Colonel Charles Lewis, some of the descendants of the latter still being residents of this county.

Anthony Bledsoe

Anthony Bledsoe was born in Culpepper County in 1733. In 1774 he moved to the neighborhood of the Shelby's. He was a Magistrate of Botetourt, Fincastle and Washington Counties and a member of the Virginia Assembly from Washington County in 1777-1778. He moved to Bledsoe's Lick, North Carolina and represented his district in the assembly of his State from 1785 to 1788 when he was killed by Indians. He was in charge of the Commissary under Colonel Christian at Point Pleasant with the rank of Major. He commanded the forces at Long Island until July, 1777 and in 1779 went out against the Chickamaugas and did not participate in the Battle of King's Mountain because he felt it was his duty to remain at home and protect the frontier.

William Cocke

Captain William Cocke, of the Battle of Point Pleasant, served in the legislature of four states and in the federal senate, as well as was prominent in his military career. He was born 1748, in Amelia County, Virginia. He studied law and removed to the Holston Valley. He was a brilliant orator and popular. After Dunmore's War he settled for a while in Boonesborough, Kentucky but returned to the Watauga and participated in the Cherokee Campaign. In 1777 he was a member of the Virginia Assembly. In 1780 he led a company at King's Mountain. He was made a Brigadier General of Tennessee and, in 1796, one of the federal senators. He was reelected in 1799. In 1809 he was elected a circuit judge of Tennessee. In 1812 he removed to Columbus, Mississippi and enlisted as a private in the war of that year and soon rose to distinction. He died in 1828 at Columbus, Mississippi.

John Sawyer

Col. John Sawyer was born in Virginia in 1745. He died in Knox County, Tennessee in 1831, and was with the Shelby's at Point Pleasant. In 1776, he served in the Cherokee Campaign and in 1779 in the Chickamauga Expedition and commanded under General Shelby, a company at King's Mountain. He was first a Major, next a Colonel and was a representative to the state assembly, of Tennessee.

Joseph Hughey

Joseph Hughey, of Shelby's Company, was killed when attempting to bring the news of the Indians' presence to camp before the battle. James Mooney, who accompanied him, succeeded in reaching the camp, but was killed during the battle.

Philip Love

Captain Philip Love later served as a Colonel in Christian's Cherokee Campaign in 1776.

Ellis Hughes

Ellis Hughes, who is thought to have been the last survivor of the patriots of the Battle of Point Pleasant, went, after Wayne's treaty, to Ohio and died March, 1845, at Utica, N. Y. where he was highly respected. He was buried with military honors.

Reared in his native state of Virginia, nurtured amid the scenes of forest savagery wherein by Indian depredations he lost his father and sweetheart. It is not surprising that he pursued the dusky foe until he had disappeared from Virginia and from his adopted home, Ohio.

John Steele

John Steele, who was wounded during the engagement at Point Pleasant, was born in Augusta County, Virginia, about 1755. He was an officer in the Battle of Point Pleasant and served throughout the Revolution. He was again wounded at the Battle of Germantown. He was for many years a member of the Executive Council of Virginia and in the administration of President John Adams, was a commissioner to treat with the Cherokee Indians. From 1798 to 1801 he was Secretary of the Mississippi Territory.

Azariah Davis

Azariah Davis, of the Battle of Point Pleasant, was a member of Harrod's Company. He was one of the members of the First Kentucky Legislature and is mentioned (1775) among the first settlers of Harrodsburg, Kentucky.

John Todd

John Todd became one of the founders of Louisville, Ky. He was with Colonel George Slaughter.

Charles E. Cameron

Charles. E. Cameron and his brothers, Hugh and George Cameron, were with the Virginia Troops at Point Pleasant in which engagement George Cameron was killed. They were brothers-in-law of Colonel Charles Lewis who was killed in that battle, whose wife Sarah Murray was their half sister. George Cameron resembled in person and being his distinguished father, Dr. John Cameron, of Staunton, who had emigrated from Scotland. Charles Cameron served throughout the Revolution, as a Lieutenant and was with the Virginia Troops at the surrender of Yorktown. In 1790 he was one of the gentlemen justices of Augusta County. On December 14, 1790, he received a land grant in Bath County, Va., where he located, about four miles from Warm Springs. He accumulated large land interests. His residence of stone was magnificent for its time and overlooked the Jackson River. Major Cameron became the first Clerk of Bath County, serving both courts for a number of years. After the Revolution, he became Colonel of Militia. As a personal friend of General Lafayette, he was presented by him with a beautiful cane which he used and prized until his death, which occurred June 14, 1829. He was survived by his widow, Mrs. Rachel Primrose Warwick and one son, Andrew Warwick Cameron.

Silas Harlan

Silas Harlan, of Berkeley County, Virginia, was in Captain Harrod's Company and after the Battle of Point Pleasant he emigrated to Kentucky. In 1779, he commanded a company of spies under General George Rodgers Clark in the Illinois campaign. General Clark pronounced him one of the bravest and most accomplished soldiers who ever fought by his side. He was a Major at the Battle of Blue Licks, where he fell. He was but thirty years of age and unmarried.

Jacob Warwick

Jacob Warwick, of Bath County, Virginia, on the morning of the Battle of Point Pleasant, had gone out early to kill beeves and prepare rations for the army. He and the men who accompanied him hearing the first shots of battle, thought Dunmore had arrived and that the guns were a salute. Later they thought it a practice exercise, but determining to see for themselves, they joined the army in time to help materially in turning the tide of victory.

Jacob Warwick is buried beside his wife at Clover Lick Cemetery in Bath County, Va. where he died in January of 1826 in his 83rd year. He died at the home of his daughter, Mrs. Major Charles Cameron, on Jackson River.

The Van Bibbers

The brothers, John, Isaac and Peter Van Bibber and Jesse, son of Peter, were participants in the Battle of Point Pleasant. Mrs. Miriam Donley, a Van Bibber descendant, writing for the July, 1903, West Virginia Historical Magazine, says *"Isaac had come from the Carolinas on a visit to his brother in Botetourt County, when the call to arms resounded through the land. Although a Baptist minister, he could and would not resist, as hearts were that day attuned to martial music, and he responded to its call.*

He fell mortally wounded besides Colonel Charles Lewis. Peter fought with such bravery he was promoted and complimented on the battlefield.

John Van Bibber was written of by all historians as Captain and family notes say he was made Captain after the Battle of Point Pleasant and Commissary of Fort Randolph. The Van Bibbers continued to defend the border although Isaac, the son of Isaac, fell at Point Pleasant while Jacob and Mathias Van Bibber died twenty years later. As late as 1843, Captain Jesse Van Bibber was still residing on Thirteen Mile Creek in Mason County, now West Virginia. He with his brother, John Van Bibber were among the earliest settlers of that County.

Howe, the Historian, who in writing the History of Virginia in 1836, said *"There is living upon Thirteen Mile Creek, Mr. Jesse Van Bibber, and aged pioneer in this county. His life, like his own mountain stream therein, was rough and turbulent at its commencement; but as it nears its close, calm and peaceful, beautifully reflecting the Christian virtues."*

Leonard Cooper

Captain Leonard Cooper, another Revolutionary soldier who is buried in Mason County, West Virginia, participated in the Battle of Point Pleasant. Prior to the Revolution, he held a commission in the Colonial Army of Maryland. Learning of Dunmore's War, he hastened to Staunton, Virginia and entered the Army of General Lewis. He remained in the service until the close of the Revolutionary struggle. In 1789 Major Cooper removed with his family from Maryland to Fort Randolph, later erecting a Block House, known as Cooper's Block House, (where Mr. George W. Pullin now resides) in Cooper District, nine miles from the mouth of the Kanawha, on the upper side. He there removed with his family.

In 1804, when the new County of Mason was organized, Major Cooper was appointed a Justice of the Peace in which capacity he served until his death which occurred in 1808. His remains were buried near his home. His son, Leonard, born in 1791, was the first white child born at Point Pleasant. Another of Leonard Cooper's children, Mary, became the wife of William Trotter, son of Richard Trotter, killed in the Battle of Point Pleasant and Anne (Trotter) Bailey, who, going from Cooper's Block House, by canoe to Gallipolis, wherein 1800, their marriage ceremony was performed. This is said to have been the first Virginia marriage performed in the French Settlement.

William Arbuckle

Captain William Arbuckle, of Rockingham County, Virginia, deserves to rank with Daniel Boone and Simon Kenton in the valor displayed in wresting from savagery the vast domain in which his expedition laid. He was not only with General Andrew Lewis at the Battle of Point Pleasant, where as a pilot (having first visited the mouth of the Kanawha in 1764) he safely conducted that wing of the army, but when George Rodgers Clark was organizing his expedition against the French Forts in Illinois from which the Indians were known to receive supplies, he (Captain Arbuckle) tendered his services which were accepted and he acquitted himself with credit in that ever memorable campaign. He defended the fort at Point Pleasant. He married Catherine Madison, widow of Capt. Robert McClannahan, who fell in the Battle of Point Pleasant. He remained in command of Fort Randolph until 1795 when Wayne made his treaty with the Indians, when he bought land and located on the Kanawha four miles below the present town of Buffalo, where he and his wife passed a peaceful and honored old age. Among their descendants yet on the Kanawha are the families of Arbuckle, Craig, Alexander, Miller and others. William Arbuckle had two children born within the fort at Point Pleasant. He and his wife both are buried in the church yard at the Arbuckle Church in Mason County West Virginia, Simple stones are thus engraved:

Wm Arbuckle, born March, 1752,	Kitty Arbuckle
Died March 21, 1836,	Died July 18, 1818
Aged 84 years	Aged 64 years

John Young

John Young became a settler in the present Kanawha County and, in the military organization of the County, was a Lieutenant of Militia. He left a son, Joseph. Young, from whom descend many residents of the valley.

John Henderson

John Henderson, about 1740, with his brothers James and Samuel, came to Augusta County, Virginia, from Scotland.

Descending from James, John his second son, was born 1740, and died March 24, 1787. In 1765 he married Ann Givens, sister to the wife of Gen. Andrew Lewis, and buying 300 acres of land, he settled in Greenbrier. In 1786, he was granted by Governor Randolph 350 acres now in Greenbrier County, and 1400 acres on the South Side of the Kanawha in what is now Clendennin and Arbuckle Districts, Mason County, West Virginia.

In Greenbrier County he became a Lieutenant of Militia and ranked as such in Captain Herbert's Company at Point Pleasant. Later he was Captain of the Greenbrier Militia and later was a Corporal in Capt. Gregory's Company in Daniel Morgan's Virginia Regiment, serving until April, 1779. In 1780 he was elected a Justice of the Peace of Greenbrier County, which office he held in 1787, the time of his death. He was survived by his widow who died May 28, 1819 and children, Samuel, John, Margaret, James, Jean and William. John and Samuel inherited the lands on Kanawha where they made permanent homes. Samuel, building his cabin home at the mouth of Kanawha and in 1810 burned the cabin and erected a commodious brick house, the second one in the county, now occupied by his granddaughter, Mrs. Ella M. Henderson Hutchinson and family.

John Henderson second, son of Captain John Henderson, was a man prominent in the public affairs of Mason County and he occupied and inherited that part of the tract of land adjoining his brother Samuel but running further up the Kanawha.

Lumen Gibbs

Lumen Gibbs was but 16 years of age when, with the army of General Andrew Lewis, he participated at the Battle of Point Pleasant. He was left as a part of the Garrison at the Fort. He became a noted scout and for twenty years he served in that capacity, wandering over the hills of the present County of Mason. His weekly route proceeded from Fort Randolph up the Kanawha to the Mouth of Eighteen Mile Creek, thence across to Letart Falls, thence down the Ohio to Point Pleasant, and his "All's Well" for twenty years dispelled the fears of the early settlers in and about the fort. The early settlers knew the route as "Gibb's Track." He married and located permanently in Mason County, where he has many descendants.

He had emigrated to Augusta County, Virginia in 1755, coming from New Hampshire where he was born. He engaged at once in the Colonial Army in that year with Andrew Lewis in the Braddock Campaign and again enlisted in his command for the Point Pleasant Campaign. He was as noted for his sunny disposition as for his bravery. He lived to a great old age and died 1837 and is buried in the Gibbs Family burying ground eight miles from Point Pleasant. In the same graveyard are buried Revolutionary soldiers James Ball and Isaac Robinson who too participated in the Battle of Point Pleasant and became residents of Mason County.

George Eastham

George Eastham, of Fauquier County, Va., who was in one of the companies with Colonel Field at the Battle of Point Pleasant, was born in 1758, and hence was but a youth when engaged in that battle. He participated in many struggles throughout the Revolution. He married (1) Susan Woodside, who bore him nine children, among whom was Colonel Lawson Eastham; his second wife, Mrs. Mary Brown, widow of James Brown, bore him three children, viz., Lucinda, Albert G. and Saunders. In 1817, he moved to Arbuckle district, Mason County, Virginia, known as Five Mile Creek, and in the following year died. His son, Albert G. Eastham, born in 1805, father of a large family in Mason County, died Feb. 23, 1890, at his home in Arbuckle District being the last real son of "The Revolution" in the County of Mason. He left many descendants in that County who do honor to his name.

John Stuart

Colonel John Stuart was the son of Colonel David Stuart, County Lieutenant of Augusta County when that county extended from the Blue Ridge to the Mississippi, 1755.

John Stuart, son of Daniel and Margaret Stuart, was born in 1749, in Augusta County and emigrated to Greenbrier in 1769 and built a house of hewn logs two and a half stories high which he used as a residence and fort, known as Fort Union.

When his cousin Andrew Lewis rested his army at Fort Union and was ready to continue the march to Point Pleasant, his forces were augmented by Colonel Stuart's and one company commanded by Captain Robert McClannahan.

At Point Pleasant Captain Stuart's Company was one of the three sent up Crooked Creek in the flank movement that successfully put Cornstalk to rout.

Colonel Stuart did not go on with the further battles of the Revolution, but continued the defense of Fort Union and organized a force that went to the successful relief of Fort Donnally when that fort was so vigorously attacked by the Indians.

November 25, 1780, Col. John Stuart became clerk of Greenbrier. At the close of the first deed book he makes valuable historical notes including an account of the Battle of Point Pleasant.

Col. Stuart married Agatha, the widow of John Frogg, killed in the Battle of Point Pleasant, she the daughter of Thomas Lewis, hence already his kinswoman. They had four children, Margaret, who married General Andrew Lewis, son of Col. Charles Lewis; Jane married Robert Crockett; Charles A. married Elizabeth Robinson and Lewis, who married, Sarah, the second daughter of Col. Charles Lewis.

Col. Stuart became one of the best business men and largest landowners of Greenbrier County. In the splendid stone mansion he had built, he lavishly entertained. Here were wont to meet the most intelligent, polished and distinguished men, not only of Virginia, but of other states and nations and his generosity was only bounded by the demands of his neighborhood.

In 1788, he was a member of the Virginia Constitutional Convention. In 1793, he was appointed Lieutenant Colonel of the 79th Regiment of Militia. In 1776, he and his wife each contributed 500 pounds sterling to build the old stone church at Lewisburg, yet beautifully preserved. He was a member of seven literary societies including the American Philosophical Society. His library was extensive and valuable. He built in his own yard the first clerk's office of the county which is still standing. He presented the county the lot upon which the first court house at Lewisburg was built. He died August 23, 1823, and is interred in the old family burying ground.

Thomas Posey

Thomas Posey was born on the Potomac River in Virginia on July 9, 1750. He early participated with the Virginia Militia and with the rank of Captain, was Quartermaster to the Army of General Lewis.

In 1775, he was appointed a member of the Committee of Safety and that year raised a company which he commanded and assisted General Andrew Lewis in driving Governor Dunmore from Gwinn's Island, July 8, 1776. In 1777, he joined the Continental Army at Middle Brook, N. J. Here he became one of the distinguished picket men of Morgan's Riflemen, distinguishing himself at Piscataway, Bennington Heights and Stillwater. In 1778, he was promoted to the rank of Major, in command of the Morgan Riflemen. In 1778, he commanded the 11th Virginia Regiment. At the close of that year he entered the artillery service and was in charge of a battery under Wayne in the attack upon Stony Point, one of the most thrilling incidents of the Revolution, being the first field officer to enter the enemy's works. He witnessed the surrender at Yorktown. He retired with the rank of Brigadier General, settling at Spotsylvania Court House, Virginia. In 1793 he removed to Kentucky where he was elected Lieutenant Governor and, as such, President of the Senate. Moving to Louisiana in October, 1812, he was chosen to fill a vacancy in the United States Senate. President Harrison appointed him Governor of Indiana Territory which honor he declined. He was agent of Indian affairs from 1813 to 1816. He died at Shawnee Town, Illinois on March 19, 1818. His first wife was the daughter of Colonel Sampson Mathews, of Virginia; his second wife, widow of Major George Thornton, and daughter of John Alexander.

Posey County, Indiana, commemorates his name which name adds lustre to the roll of the army of General Lewis.

John Lewis

Major John Lewis, a nephew of General Andrew Lewis with whom he was engaged at Point Pleasant, died in 1823, at his home at Sweet Springs. He was the son of William Lewis, brother of General Andrew Lewis. He was noted for his courage, integrity and high sense of honor and continued in the service of the Colonies throughout the Revolution. As a Lieutenant he was engaged at Monmouth, Saratoga, and Trenton. He spent the winter of 1777 at Valley Forge. He rose to the rank of Major, which rank he held at Monmouth. In 1783 he returned to his Virginia home but was much engaged on the frontier until the close of Wayne's Campaign. He was five feet, ten inches high, compactly built, muscular, strong and courageous. At the time of his death, he was an Elder in the Presbyterian Church.

William Clendennin

William Clendennin was a private in the Battle of Point Pleasant. Later he was commissioned Major in the Kanawha Militia. He represented Kanawha County in the Virginia Assembly in 1706-1801-1803. He was a Collector of Levies 1792-1793-1794. He was a Justice of the Peace and member of the first Court in the County, held at his house in 1789. In 1790, he settled in what is now Mason County, W. Va. In 1804, be carried the petition to the Virginia Assembly asking for the organization of Mason County Virginia and in 1805, was the first representative of that county.

Major Clendennin had settled about 1797 at Eight Mile, Mason County. In 1802 he purchased a part of the Hugh Mercer tract and built the first log cabin in Clendennin District, Mason County, and many of his descendants are living in Mason and adjoining counties in West Virginia and Ohio. By his son Charles, whose son William married Sophia Neale of Gallipolis, their son, James B. Clendennin, is survived by a daughter, Mrs. George Wallis, of Apple Grove.

Sophia, daughter of William Clendennin, married John Miller, and her sister Ann, married Henry Miller, both of Gallipolis. Another sister, Elizabeth, married John Bing of Gallia County, Ohio, from whom descended a large family. Their second child, Martha Young Bing, born in Gallia County, Ohio, Oct. 24, 1805, died Oct. 30, 1900, was the ancestor of the Filson and Cable families of Mason County, West Virginia.

Archibald Clendennin

Archibald Clendennin, brother of William and George, married Nancy Ewing and lived on a farm a mile from Lewisburg. The family was attacked by Indians, and Archibald Clendennin was killed. His wife was captured by the Indians, but made her escape.

Benjamin Logan

Benjamin Logan was born in Augusta County, Virginia, in 1752. He immigrated to Pennsylvania from Ireland when a child and when but fourteen, emigrated with his parents from Pennsylvania to Virginia, where his father died. By the law of entail then prevailing in Virginia, he became the heir of his father's estate but he divided it with his mother, brothers and sisters. He married and settled on the Holston River and was with Colonel Henry Bouquet in his expedition against the Indians. He was in the Battle of Point Pleasant. In 1775 he emigrated to Kentucky with Daniel Boone and established Logan's Fort where he moved with his family the following year. He was one of the most daring of Kentucky pioneers and his defense and relief of his fort is one of the most thrilling pages in Kentucky history. His expedition against the Indians at Chillicothe in which the Indians were put to rout and their supplies captured, including 150 horses, was admirably planned and executed. In 1788 he led a regiment of 600 men against the Indians of the Northwest. He passed his declining years in Shelby County, Kentucky on his extensive farm, dying, Dec, 11, 1802. He was six feet three tall, powerfully built with nerves and courage like a lion. His son William was the first white child born in Kentucky and became an eminent lawyer, being twice appointed Appellate Judge of Kentucky and in 1820 was a United States Senator from Kentucky.

John Logan

John Logan, brother of Benjamin, was engaged in the Battle of Point Pleasant. He emigrated from Virginia to Kentucky where he was a military leader and several times was a representative.

George Clendennin

George Clendennin, who participated in the Battle of Point Pleasant, represented Greenbrier County in the Convention at Richmond in 1788 that ratified the Federal Constitution of Virginia. In that year he purchased 1030 acres of land, the site of the present city of Charleston, and in that year built Fort Lee, afterward called Fort Clendennin. In 1794, the town of Charleston was laid off, which was not named, but finally called Charlestown in honor of Charles Clendennin, father of George. The first court was held in Kanawha

County on Oct. 5, 1789, at the residence of George Clendennin, a County Lieutenant. He was one of the first representatives of Kanawha County, 1790-1791-1792-1794-1795. In 1794 he was made a trustee for the newly laid off town of Point Pleasant.

His wife was Jemima, claimed by some to be the sister of Thomas Ewing, of Ohio, but which has been found to be an error. He died after 1795, when his name last appears as signing a deed and in 1797 his wife appeared in court as his widow, when she gave bond as administratrix.

Parthena, daughter of George and Jemima Clendennin married John Meigs of Marietta, Ohio. John Meigs dying, his widow married Major Andrew Bryan, their daughter Mary married John McCulloch, from whom descended Mrs. M. M. Moore, Mrs. P. S, Lewis, Mrs. J. J. Bright, John A. and Charles E. McCulloch, who were reared on a farm below Kanawha in Arbuckle District, Mason Co., West Virginia.

Mary, the third daughter of George Clendennin, married Major John Cantrell whose only daughter became the wife of the late C. C. Miller, of Mason County who has left many descendants.

Alexander Breckenridge

Alexander Breckenridge named for his maternal grandfather Alexander Breckenridge was in the Battle of Point Pleasant and later served as Colonel in the 7th, Virginia in the Revolution, resigning in 1778. He was for many years Clerk of Augusta County. He and Patrick Henry married sisters.

Captain John Lewis

Captain John Lewis eldest son of Thomas Lewis was a nephew of General Andrew Lewis. He was born in 1749. He was wounded at the Battle of Point Pleasant. He engaged in the struggles of the Revolution and was at Valley Forge and Jersey. He witnessed the surrender of Cornwallis.

Stephen Trigg

Captain Stephen Trigg of the Battle of Point Pleasant was a member of the Virginia Assembly from Fincastle in 1774, when Governor Dunmore dissolved that body. He signed the Articles of Association of the Colonies in 1775 and was active in protecting the frontier during the Revolution. In 1779 he emigrated to Kentucky and represented that county in the Virginia Assembly in 1780. While leading a charge at the Battle of Blue Licks, 1782, he was killed.

William Herbert

Captain William Herbert was a Captain of Fincastle Militia, who participated in the Battle of Point Pleasant. He died 1776.

Walter Crockett

Captain Walter Crockett was born on the South Fork of the Holston River. He was a County Magistrate. He continued in the Patriot Army after the Battle of Point Pleasant and distinguished himself at King's Mountain in 1780.

John Floyd

John Floyd, who was a school teacher, made his home with Colonel William Preston of Fincastle County. He was a native of Virginia, born 1750. In 1774, he was appointed a deputy sheriff. In the spring of 1774, he led a surveying party to Kentucky and, returning, joined William Christian in the Point Pleasant Expedition Arriving too late to actively engage in the battle, he was active in the good offices of his company in ministering to the needs of the army. He married Jane Buckhannon, niece of Col. Preston, and in 1779 located in Kentucky where, in 1783, he was killed by Indians. His son, John Floyd, who was born in Jefferson County, Virginia, 1770, represented Virginia in Congress 1817-1829, Governor of Virginia 1829-1834. South Carolina cast her electoral vote for him for president in 1832. His son, John B. Floyd, grandson of the John Floyd of Point Pleasant campaign, was a member of the Virginia Legislature 1847 and was Governor of Virginia 1850-1853 and was Secretary of War under President James Buchannan. He was indicted by the government, charged with the misuse of government supplies and funds. He demanded a trial and was exonerated. He resigned his position and became General John Floyd of the Confederate Army. He married Sallie Buchannan, granddaughter of William Campbell, of the Battle of Point Pleasant, and a niece of Patrick Henry. They had no children.

Benjamin Lewis

Quoting from the biography of his descendant, State Historian and Archivist Virgil Anson Lewis in "Men of West Virginia" (1903) page 31, *"His paternal ancestors were among the first settlers of the Shenandoah Valley, where they were founders of the city of Staunton. They were active frontiersmen and participants in the Revolutionary and Indian Wars. His great grandfather, Benjamin Lewis, was wounded in the Battle of Point Pleasant and after the wars were over in 1792 settled in what is now Mason County, West Virginia, and is buried in Waggoner District, near the spot where he thus found a home."*

The following from the War Department Adjutant General's Office, Washington, D. C, under date March 28, 1908, is authoritative that after the Battle of Point Pleasant, he continued to serve in the patriot army: *"It is shown by the records that one Benjamin Lewis who served as a Sergeant in Capt. John Spotswood's Co. 10th Virginia Regiment Commanded successively by Col. Edmond Stevens and Major Samuel Harnes and Col. John Green, Revolutionary War. He enlisted November 29, 1776, to serve three years and was discharged July 5, 1778.*

Signed, F. C, Ainsworth

The Adjutant General

That Benjamin Lewis above referred to was not a descendant of John Lewis, the founder of Staunton, we quote from a memorandum of Mrs. Sarah Lewis Rodgers, who was raised at the old Lewis home on Muddy Creek, in Greenbrier County and who moved in pioneer days to Illinois. Writing to her nephew, Rev. Jacob H. Lewis, a Presbyterian minister, of Greenbrier County, the latter dying at 92 years of age, the manuscript is yet preserved and says:

"Our Lewis family in Greenbrier County originated from three brothers, John, George and Benjamin Lewis who came to the county in an early day from the Valley of Virginia. About the close of the Revolution, Benjamin went to the Ohio. George Lewis never married. John married Miss McCrary and their sister, a Mrs. Van Orzel, is buried in the old Caraway graveyard."

None of the sons of John Lewis, founder of Staunton, Virginia, left descendants such as those above described, but it has been claimed that the above Benjamin was the son of Thomas, he the son of John.

Mrs. M. L. Price, West Virginia historian of the John Lewis family from whom she descends, says Thomas Lewis' son, William Benjamin, was born 1778 (four years after the Battle of Point Pleasant, in which the family traditions and papers have always shown Benjamin Lewis to have been born) while L. L. Lewis, of Richmond, recognized as an authority on the John Lewis, Staunton, branch, says: "*Thomas Lewis had a son Benjamin, but he lived and died in Rockingham County, Virginia.*"

As early as 1812 we find in Mason County that Benjamin Lewis conveyed land which was acquired before Mason County was formed, as the land books show no transfer to him in that county prior to 1812 and he continued to buy and convey lands as the records show and that in 1831 there was much conveying of titles of his lands by his children which would indicate that he died on or before that year. Land conveyances show the given name of the wife of Benjamin Lewis to have been Nancy and their children to have been Sarah, who married Samuel Edwards, John who married _____ Edwards, Benjamin, Jr., who emigrated to Iowa, Catherine who married Michael Newhouse, George who married Margaret Winkleblack, William who married Lucinda Clendennin, Andrew, Isaac and probably others.

Josiah Ramsey

After being engaged in the Battle of Point Pleasant, Josiah Ramsey returned to Augusta County. He served as a scout in the Cherokee Campaign of 1776. In 1778, he removed to Kentucky. In 1779, he moved to Cumberland Settlement where he was appointed Major of Militia and was frequently engaged against the Indians. He lived to an advanced age spending the close of his life with a son in Missouri.

William Bowen

William Bowen often related a hand to hand encounter with an Indian antagonist at Point Pleasant whom he finally overpowered. He was a native of Maryland, born 1744. In 1759 he engaged in the border warfare with William Christian. In early life, he had moved to Augusta County, Virginia. In 1784 he removed to Summers County, Tennessee, where he passed the remainder of his life.

Joseph Drake

Joseph Drake who was with William Christian's Regiment at Point Pleasant, had served as a private in Bouquet's expedition in 1764. He was one of the Long Hunters 1770-71. In 1773 he married Margaret, daughter of Col. John Buchanan. In 1775, he visited Kentucky and in June of that year led an exploring party on Green River. He resided at Abington, Virginia until 1778, when he moved to near Boonesborough, Ky., and in August of that year was killed by the Indians. He was a typical frontiersman.

William Edmiston

Lieutenant William Edmiston (Edmondston) a native of Maryland, born 1734, moved at an early date to Augusta County, Virginia. He was a private in the French and Indian War and the Cherokee Campaign 1760. In 1763 he was appointed Lieutenant of Militia for Augusta County. He was in Captain William Campbell's Company at Point Pleasant and was his second in command at King's Mountain, in which eight members of his family were engaged, three of whom were killed. One of those who survived of that family was James Edmiston who has descendants living in many counties in West Virginia, including the County of Mason.

William Ingles

Major William Ingles who, at the Battle of Point Pleasant, was in charge of a commissary with the rank of Major, was a native of Ireland, born 1729, immigrating with his father when a child to Pennsylvania, settling with John Draper at Draper's Meadows in 1748. In 1750 he married Mary Draper, whose capture by and escape from the Indians, is one of the thrilling pages of pioneer history. During the Indian Wars, William Ingles was active in defense of the frontiers. In 1756 he was a Lieutenant in the Sandy Creek Expedition. In 1758-1760, he defended the fort at Ingle's Ferry. In 1777 he was made Colonel of Militia in the organization of Montgomery County. In 1782, he died at his home at Ingles Ferry.

Thomas Ingles

Thomas Ingles was with his mother, Mary Ingles, when captured by the Indians, remaining with them until 1768, practically becoming a young Indian in his habits. Returning to his home for a few years, he tried to adopt the habits of civilization and education but he never forgot his Indian friends. He was in the Battle of Point Pleasant, remaining the following winter in the Fort during which time he visited the Indians at Scioto. In 1782 his wife was captured by the Indians and his home burned. He removed afterward to Tennessee, thence to Mississippi, where he died.

Henry Pauling

Captain Henry Pauling who commanded a company of Botetourt Troops at Point Pleasant, continued in frontier service and in 1777 went with Colonel Bowman to the relief of the Kentucky frontier soon after which he settled in that state and represented Lincoln County, Kentucky in the convention of that state that ratified the Constitution of the United States, but he voted against the ratification of that instrument.

Francis Slaughter

Colonel Francis Slaughter who was at the Battle of Point Pleasant was a member of one of the best Virginia Families. He married a daughter of Robert Coleman of Dunmore and in 1785 moved to Kentucky, settling in Hardin County.

Lawrence and George Slaughter

Lawrence and George Slaughter each married a daughter of Colonel John Field and both were in his regiment at the Battle of Point Pleasant. Colonel George Slaughter in 1776, raising a company, participated in the 8th Va. Reg. at Brandywine and Germantown. In 1779 he joined Shelby in the Chickamauga Campaign and in that winter started to reinforce George Rodgers Clark, but was obliged to winter at Louisville, Ky., joining him the following June, after which be returned to Virginia and in 1784 represented his county in the House of Delegates. Later he moved to Jefferson County, Kentucky, thence to Charleston, Ind., where he died June 17, 1819.

The McAfee Brothers

McAfee Station on Salt River, in Mercer County, Kentucky, commemorates the name of five McAfee brothers, James, Robert,

George, William and Samuel, who lived on Sinking Creek, Botetourt County, Virginia, from which place they finally all emigrated to Kentucky, in 1779. The first three named with James McConn Jr. and Samuel Adams, were Kentucky explorers in 1773 with Col. Bullit and Hancock Taylor. They all participated in the Battle of Point Pleasant.

William McAfee was in the George Rodgers Clarke expedition and was killed in 1780. George died in 1803 at his home on Salt River. Samuel died in 1801, James in 1814, and Robert who was one of the early dealers, who, by flat boat, took large cargoes of produce to New Orleans, in 1795, when on such a mission, was killed by a Spaniard in that city, who was attempting to rob him. They left descendants, many of whom are yet residents of Kentucky.

James Knox

Major James Knox served under Col. Chester in the capacity of scout in 1774. During the Revolution he commanded a company of Morgan's Riflemen engaged at Saratoga and Stillwater, returning with the rank of Major. Settling in Kentucky, he married Mrs. Logan, the widow of Benjamin Logan, who was in the Battle of Point Pleasant. James Knox died in 1822. He had accumulated a good fortune and was respected by all who knew him.

John Madison

John Madison was of the distinguished Virginia family that gave to America the president of that name, being a first cousin of President Madison. His son, James Madison, was the first American Episcopal Bishop. Other of his sons who distinguished themselves were Thomas, Rowland and George, who emigrated to Kentucky. John Madison was the first Clerk of Augusta County and represented that county in the Virginia Assembly in 1751-1752. He married a Miss Strother, sister to the wives of Thomas Lewis and Gabriel Jones of Augusta County.

Elijah Kimberling

Elijah Kimberling of Bath County, Va., who was-engaged in the Battle of Point Pleasant, returned to Bath County, Va. where he resided until the time of his death. So pleased, however, were his sons with his description of the Kanawha Valley, that his four sons, Joseph,

James, Jacob and Nathaniel emigrated to Mason County, West Virginia and located on farms in Union District, near Arbuckle Post office. They became the progenitors of a large and influential family in the Kanawha Valley. Among whom were Elijah Kimberling, for many years a public official of Mason County, who married Margaret Catherine Jones, a native of Culpepper County, Virginia, daughter of Joseph Jones, and Ann Winn, his wife.

William Ewing

William Ewing, a member of Arbuckle's company at Point Pleasant, settled on Swago Creek, tributary to the Greenbrier, near Buckeye, Va. He was a member of the garrison at Point Pleasant and witnessed the murder of Cornstalk.

William McKee

William McKee, born in Ireland in 1732, emigrated when a youth to the Valley of Virginia and was in the Braddock Campaign. At Point Pleasant he was a Lieutenant in Captain *Murray's* Company. He later represented Rockbridge County in the Virginia Legislature and voted in favor of the adoption of the Constitution. He emigrated to Lincoln County, Kentucky, where he died in 1816.

Charles Simms

Charles Simms was in the division commanded by Colonel Lewis who expired in his arms. In the continental army he was first Major of the 12th Virginia, later Lieut. Col. of the 6th Va. and later of the 2nd Virginia Regiment. On Dec. 7, 1777, he resigned from the army and practiced law at Alexandria, Virginia, where he continued to reside until the time of his death.

George Moffatt

Captain George Moffatt was born in 1735. His father was killed by Indians in 1749, enroute to South Carolina. In 1763, George was Captain of a company of Rangers in pursuit of Indians that had killed his stepfather, John Trimble and captured his sister and half brother. He rescued his loved ones. Colonel William Christian was his uncle and Samuel McDowell his brother-in-law and in the battle at Point Pleasant, with him were many of his kindred. In the war of the Revolution he was active and commanded a regiment at Guilford

Court House. From 1781to 1783 he was County Lieutenant of Augusta. He died at his home, eight miles northwest of Staunton in 1811.

John Murray

Captain John Murray, killed in the Battle of Point Pleasant, was a brother-in -law of Colonel Charles Lewis, and a half-brother of Charles Cameron and George Cameron, the last named, was killed in the battle.

William Trotter

William Trotter, who was engaged in the Battle of Point Pleasant, was an Englishman by birth, coming to America as an indentured servant. Coming at the same time with Ann Hennis, who, like him, was "sold out" to defray the expense of their passage. They were bought in Augusta County, Va., and when his term of service had expired he enlisted with Colonel Charles Lewis and was killed in the Battle of Point Pleasant. This so incensed his widow that she donned semi-male attire and with rifle and tomahawk she was seen at musters like a man. Later she married James Bailey.

James Bailey

James Bailey, who was with Colonel Charles Lewis and who afterward married Ann Hennis, the widow of Richard Trotter, is more noted for being the husband of Ann Bailey, the heroine of the Kanawha Valley than for his own achievements. He was assigned to garrison duty at Fort Clendennin where the present city of Charleston is now located. Ann Bailey was the mother of one son, William Trotter, who located in Harrison Township, Gallia, Ohio, where his descendants yet reside.

Walter Newman

Walter Newman, a native of Pennsylvania, was in the Battle of Point Pleasant and was one of the first to locate here when the new town was laid off. He purchased the grounds upon which the Mansion House in Tue Endie Wei Park now stands and built the first hewn log house in the county, which, for its beauty and size, was called the Mansion House. The house was built in 1796. In August, 1804, he was licensed to establish a ferry across both the rivers, Ohio and Kanawha and granted a license to sell spirituous liquors and keep an ordinary at his house in the town of Point Pleasant. This was the first place in which liquor was ever legally sold in the county. Mr. Newman was also the first man in the county to support a missionary, sending his nephew, Rev. James Newman, as a missionary to South America.

William Moore

William Moore, of Rockbridge County, after the Battle of Point Pleasant, became Captain William Moore of the Revolution. He was a merchant of Lexington, Virginia, and purchased the first bag of coffee ever purchased in Virginia, which he found slow sale for. Later, he built an iron furnace at South River in Rockbridge County. He was a Justice of the Peace for many years and served as High Sheriff of Rockbridge for two terms. He died in 1841 aged 93 years. His wife was Miss Nancy McClung by whom he had children, Samuel, David, John, Eliab, Joseph, Isabella, Elizabeth and Nancy.

John Lyle

John Lyle, of Captain McDowell's Company, became Rev. John Lyle, of Hampshire County, now West Virginia, a pioneer minister who proved to be a power for good in that region.

William Robertson

William Robertson of Augusta County was commissioned a Lieutenant July, 1775. He distinguished himself at Great Bridge, Brandywine and Germantown. He died Nov. 12, 1831.

John Lewis

Captain John Lewis, son of Thomas Lewis, of Augusta County was with his uncle, Andrew Lewis, at Point Pleasant, where he was wounded. He was born in 1749, died 1788, leaving four children. He served under Washington at Valley Forge and in the Jerseys and witnessed the surrender of Cornwallis.

John Frogg

The Sutler of the Army, was killed at Point Pleasant, Oct. 10 1774, by the Indians and was there buried.

He came to Staunton from the Rappahannock and married, Miss Agatha Lewis, a daughter of Thomas Lewis, a brother of General A n d r e w and Colonel Charles Lewis, and when the Army started for the Ohio River, Mr. Frogg was appointed the Sutler and went with them.

He was a handsome young man, gallant, generous and fond of display and spoken of as a very worthy gentleman and popular with the men, and by one writer, when giving a list of the dead, spoke of him, as "*poor John Frogg.*"

When he went into the battle, he had on a brilliant red jacket, which made him a prominent mark for Indians and when he fell, there were no less than five Indians that had made an attempt to secure his scalp, and all five of them were found dead on the ground where poor John lay. It is tradition that the little daughter was awakened from her sleep at age three several times by the dream of her father being killed by the Indians, which she related to her mother several days before it was known that there had been a battle. Mr. Frogg was related to the Strother family, one of whom was the wife of John Madison, Clerk of Augusta Co., one was the wife of Gabriel Jones, the Crown's Attorney for said County and the other was the wife of Thomas Lewis, the Surveyor of said County.

His widow became the wife of Captain John Stuart of Greenbrier who was also in said battle; and his daughter married a Mr. Estill.

It may not have been the duty of Mr. Frogg to go into the battle at all, but it is certain he was not required to attire himself in a brilliant red jacket and make of himself a mark for sharpshooters and loose his life, but, it required five Indians to pay for his life.

Agatha Lewis, his wife, was born May 18, 1753 and she married Capt. John Stuart Nov. 18, 1776.

William McCorkle

William McCorkle, who engaged in the Battle of Point Pleasant, was the son of Alexander McCorcle (McCorkle) who had his American origin in Pennsylvania, in the Scotch-Irish reservoir of the Cumberland Valley, among the other Scotch Irish, who, emigrating to the Valleys of the Shenandoah and James, became the very seat of culture and the greatest factors in Virginia's power, and gave that state her prominence in the sisterhood of states.

In the spring of 1774 William McCorkle was making preparations to emigrate with a great body of Virginians to Kentucky and, on June

3rd of that year, a survey of 1,000 acres of land was set aside for him near the present city of Louisville.

Indian hostilities necessitating the protection of the frontier, and although not a young man, William McCorkle enlisted as a volunteer in Captain John Murray's Company from Botetourt and engaged in the Point Pleasant Campaign. He returned to Rockbridge County to the lands be held near Lexington, and which had continued in the possession of his descendants until 1894, when it passed into the hands of strangers.

Soon after the Battle of Point Pleasant, William McCorkle died but he had offered upon his country's altar his son, John McCorkle, who, when but twenty-three years of age, was killed at the Battle of Cowpens, while serving under Gen. Morgan.

John McCorkle married Rebecca Nutt, and was survived by his two sons, Alexander and Samuel, the younger Samuel being the progenitor of five sons, the youngest of whom was William McCorkle, whose oldest son is Ex-Governor William A. McCorkle, who served as Governor of West Virginia, from March 4, 1893, to March 4, 1897, and is now located at Charleston, West Virginia, where, as a historical memorial, he has erected the most beautiful home in the state, "SUNRISE", on the summit of the mountain; embellished with historic stones and furnished and decorated with historic mementoes, demonstrating that his heredity has made him revere the past as it has made him bountifully prepare for the future.

Robert Campbell

Robert Campbell, who was engaged in the Battle of Point Pleasant, was born in the Valley of Virginia in 1755. He was engaged throughout the Revolution. He displayed great bravery in his conflicts with the Cherokees. He was in command of a Regiment at King's Mountain, Oct. 7, 1780. For forty years he was a Magistrate of Washington County, Virginia. In 1825, he emigrated to Tennessee with his children and there died.

John Carter

John Carter became a pioneer of Tennessee. During the Revolution he was elected with John Sevier and Charles Robertson to the Convention that assembled at Hartford, N. C. in 1785, and framed a

Constitution for the State of Franklin, which was reunited with North Carolina in 1788.

Matthew Bracken

Matthew Bracken had been a surveyor with Thomas Hanson from Virginia in the exploration and surveying expedition to Kentucky, which left Fincastle on April 7th, 1774. "Bracken Creek" in Mason County, Kentucky, commemorates his name. He returned to Kentucky in time to enlist as an ensign in the company of Capt. Robert McClennahan's Company of volunteers from Botetourt. He was killed in the Battle of Point Pleasant and his remains were buried within the forty foot reservation, now a part of Tu-Endie Wei Park, at the mouth of the Kanawha.

Captain John Lewis

Capt John Lewis eldest son of General Andrew Lewis married Miss Patsy Love of Alexandria, Virginia who had four children. His eldest son Andrew married Jane McClennahan of Botetourt County Virginia and they were the parents of six children who lived to maturity. Jonn, William and Samuel locating in Kanawha County near the mouth of Scary.

John Lewis known as "Coal River John" was a man of great wealth and prominence and from him through his daughter Marjorie, who married 1st Edward Kenna and 2nd Richard Ashbey, has descended through this first marriage Hon. John E. Kenna who represented the old third district of West Virginia three times in Congress and was twice elected to the United States Senate, each time being the youngest member in either branch of Congress. There are many descendants of Captain John Lewis living on the Kanawha including Mr. Kenna's family, the family of Mr. Kenna's sister Mrs. Gentry, the family of Hon. Joseph Gaines, M. C., Mr. Walter Ashby and many others.

Thomas Hacket

Thomas Hacket (Haket) of Rich Creek Virginia was a member of Captain Michael Woods Company at Point Pleasant, soon after which he settled at Petersburg, Virginia where he continued to reside until after Wayne's Treaty. Lured by the beauty and fertility of the Ohio

Valley he settled at Kyger, Ohio in Gallia County, where he died and is buried, having lived to the advanced age of 104 years.

Among other children, he left a daughter Mary Ann Hacket who married Nimrod Kirk whose daughter, Elizabeth (Betsey) Kirk, married George Knight. From George Knight descended the distinguished Dr. A. L. Knight of Mason County, prominent farmer James Knight of Pleasant Flats, the late Samuel Knight of Marietta, Ohio, Mr. George Knight of Clifton, and Mrs. Louise Meeks of Dallas, Mrs. Rebecca Brown of Hartford, and Mrs. Susan Hogg of Point Pleasant and their descendants.

Captain James Curry

Captain James Curry served under General Andrew Lewis and was severely wounded in the right arm at the Battle of Point Pleasant. His home at that time was near Staunton, Virginia. When at the age of 22 years he enlisted as a private.

Michael See

While at work outside the fort at Point Pleasant in a field near where James Capehart now resides, in August 1791 Michael See and Robert St. Clair were killed by Indians. Thomas Northrop and a colored boy belonging to See were captured and carried away prisoners.

Michael See who had been engaged in the Battle of Point Pleasant was living with his family within the fort where the night of his death his wife gave birth to a son, William See from whom descend the Sees of Mason County West Virginia

We are indebted to Rev. Price, of Marlinton and Rev. C. W McDonald, of Huttonsville, Randolph County, descendants of Michael See who send the following, gleaned from the history of Randolph County:

"Michael See, of German ancestry, and using the language in his family is believed to have been born in Pennsylvania. He came from that state to South Branch, what is now Hardy County, W. Va. about 1765. His father's name was Frederick Michael See, of him but little is known except he had a son named Adam, but Adam never lived in Randolph County. Michael See, son of Frederick See was among the early settlers of Tygart's Valley, Randolph County and his children

intermarried with the following prominent families more than a century since.

Anthony See married Julia Leonard; Adam See married Margaret Warwick, daughter of Jacob Warwick, the pioneer of whose name appears in this Pocahontas sketches; Polly See, of Michael married George See. Her daughter Georgiana became Mrs. Capt. J. W. Marshall, a noted confederate officer and promoter of public improvement. Barbara See married William McCleary; John See married Miss Stewart, and Noah married Margaret Long.

Col. James Curry

March, 1900, Mr. W. S. Curry of Columbus, Ohio, Registrar of the Sons of the Revolution, sent us an account of his grandfather Colonel James Curry, above referred to. It follows:

"James Curry was closely engaged throughout the greater part of the day fighting from behind first one tree and then another but later in the day was shot through the right elbow. It is said he asked the surgeon who dressed his wound *"If it would hurt him to take a drink of wine?"* to which the surgeon replied *"No, if you take it with the Surgeon."* He remained in the garrison until recovered from his wounds.

He served in the army throughout the Revolution as Captain in the Fourth Va. Infantry, participating in the Battle of Brandywine and Yorktown. He was wounded at the siege of Charleston, S. C. and taken prisoner May 12, 1871 by General Lincoln's Army.

After the Revolution he settled at Staunton and served a term as Clerk of the Court for Augusta County. In 1797 he moved to Highland County, Ohio where he entered a Virginia Military tract of land.

Solomon Brumfield

Solomon Brumfield, who enlisted under General Andrew Lewis at Staunton, resided where the city of Washington is now built.

William Hamilton

William Hamilton was an orderly at Point Pleasant in the army of General Lewis and when the battle began was sent as a messenger to hasten the regiments in command of Capt. Wm. Christian whom he met at the mouth of 13 Mile Creek, the present site of the village of

Leon. Here a few were left in charge of supplies while the remainder of the companies marched on to Point Pleasant arriving at about 11 o'clock.

Bazaleel Wells

Bazaleel Wells, afterward General Wells of the Revolution, became the founder of Steubenville, Ohio and helped to form the first Constitution of Ohio. He was then a member of the Ohio Senate and was probably the wealthiest man in Eastern Ohio.

At the beginning of the century, it was he who financed the building of the Zanesville road, the great highway of Ohio that proved to be the great artery of commerce of that successful, progressive new state.

John Murray, Earl of Dunmore.
(LORD DUNMORE.)

In reviewing, (by many historians,) the life and character of Lord Dunmore, there are none who have more truly recorded his character than H. Maxwell, in his "History of Hampshire County", who says on page 51:

"Before proceeding to a narrative of the events of the Dunmore War, it is not out of place to inquire concerning Governor Dunmore, and whether from his past acts and general character he would likely conspire with the British and the Indians to destroy the western settlements in Virginia. Whether the British were capable of an act so savage and unjust as inciting savages to harass the western frontier of their own colonies is not a matter for controversy. It is a fact that they did do it during the Revolutionary War."

As to a confirmation of the character of Dunmore and his methods we quote again from the same author, relating to events subsequent to the Battle of Point Pleasant:

"Dunmore had trouble elsewhere. His domineering conduct and his support of some of Great Britain's oppressive measures caused him to be hated by the Virginians and led to armed resistance. Thereupon he threatened to make Virginia a solitude using these words:

"I do enjoin the true and loyal subjects to repair to my assistance, or I shall consider the whole country in Rebellion and myself at liberty to annoy it by every possible means, and I shall not hesitate to reduce houses to ashes, and spreading devastation wherever I can reach. With a small body of troops and arms, I could raise such a force from among Indians, negroes and other persons as would soon reduce refractory people of them."

The patriots finally rose in arms and drove Dunmore from the country. Some of these events occurred after the Dunmore War, but they serve to show what kind of a man the Governor was."

He was born in England in May, 1709, descending from the house of Stuart. He succeeded to the peerage in 1756, appointed Governor of New York 1770; of Virginia, July, 1771. With a band of Tory followers, he plundered the inhabitants, residing on the James and York Rivers. He and his followers suffered defeat at the battle of Great Bridge, shortly after which he burned Norfolk, then the most prosperous city in Virginia In 1779, he returned to England, and, in 1786, was appointed Governor of the Bermudas.

Logan

Tah-gah-jute, son of Shikellamy, chief of the Cayuga Indians, was born in about 1725. He was named Logan by the whites for James Logan, (the Secretary of William Penn,) who had been such a friend of the Indians, that they accepted the name as a badge of honor.

Logan was reared near the Moravian settlements and his relation to the whites had been most friendly. Throughout Virginia and Pennsylvania he was known for his commanding presence and engaging qualities. Residing with his family near Readsville, Penn., he supported them by hunting and trapping and dressing hides which, he disposed of to the whites. At this time, the Mingo tribe of Indians chose him as their chief. About 1770, he moved to the banks of the Ohio where, in the spring of 1774, his family was massacred, whereupon he sent a declaration of war to Michael Cresap, whom he believed had ordered the massacre. Thus began the fearful depredations that burst upon the frontier and Logan is said to have taken thirty scalps himself before the termination of hostilities at Point Pleasant, where he was engaged that fearful October day. Subsequent to the battle when the other Indian chiefs sued for peace,

Logan disdained to participate in the treaty. Governor Dunmore sent John Gibson to personally invite him to the council and he then gave out that classic in English literature that has made so famous the name of Logan. It is as follows:

"I appeal to any white man to say if he ever entered Logan's cabin hungry, and he gave him not meat; if he ever came cold and naked and he clothed him not. During the course of the last long and bloody war, Logan remained idle in his cabin, an advocate of peace. Such was my love for the whites that my Countrymen pointed as they passed and said Logan is the friend of the white men. I had even thought to have lived with you but for the injuries of one man. Cresap, the last spring, in cold blood and unprovoked, murdered all of the relations of Logan, not even sparing my women and children. There runs not a drop of my blood in the veins of any living creature. This called for my revenge. I have sought it; I have fully glutted my vengeance. For my country I rejoice at the beams of peace. But do not harbor the thought that mine is the joy of fear; Logan never felt fear He will not turn on his heel to save his life. . Who is there to mourn for Logan? Not one."

The speech was written down, when Gibson repeated it to an officer, and published in the Virginia Gazette. Thomas Jefferson, a great admirer of Logan, took pains to establish its authenticity and published it in his Notes on Virginia.

Logan was killed by his nephew at Lake Erie in the summer of 1780.

Cornstalk

Cornstalk, the celebrated Shawnee warrior, is first mentioned in Colonial History in 1763, when about sixty Indians, led by Cornstalk attacked the settlement on Muddy Creek, in Greenbrier County, Virginia, when they pretended to be on a friendly mission, at which time they arose and murdered all except a few women and children, whom they took prisoners. From there the Indians went on to the Levels in the same county, to the home of Alexander Clendennin, where many were gathered enjoying the fruits of a successful chase and the Indians, too were treated with the utmost hospitality, but they again murdered most of the inmates of that place. Mrs. Clendennin was carried away a prisoner and with others taken to Muddy Creek.

For a year the Indian depredations were continued until there was not a white settler left in Greenbrier County, which was not again inhabited by whites until 1769, when Col. John Stuart and a few others became permanent settlers.

It is said that Cornstalk was born in the Kanawha Valley about 1727.

In the Battle of Point Pleasant, he commanded the army consisting of the flower of the Shawnee, Delaware, Wyandotte, Mingo and Cayuga braves, he being the King of the federation, in their herculean efforts to stay the oncoming tide of Saxon civilization. These Indians were fighting to maintain their homes and their hunting grounds and if the whites were ever to be repelled, it must be now. This was not the first time in battle array that the Shawnees had shown their skill as warriors. In the Braddock defeat and other campaigns they had proven themselves valiant. They despised treaties and had chafed under that with Bouquet so that at the Battle of Point Pleasant, they had determined to be victorious. It was not that they favored Great Britain. All whites were alike to them except as they availed to help them save their hunting grounds and here were gathered their ablest leaders: Cornstalk, Red Eagle, Scoppathus, Blue Jacket, Logan, Chief of the Cayugas, Ellinipsico, Red Hawk ,the noted Delaware Chief and others commanding the most formidable army every arrayed as an Indian phalanx. The story of their bravery has already been related in the accounts of the Battle of Point Pleasant, here in published.

It would have been well for the white settlers, if the history of Cornstalk could have ended with the Battle at Point Pleasant. The treaty with the whites following the battle was maintained in the highest sense of honor by Cornstalk.

In the spring of 1777, when the great Indian uprising was again taking place, Cornstalk came to Fort Randolph at Point Pleasant to warn the whites of their danger and was retained as a hostage, during the whole of the summer. In November, his son, Ellinipsico, came in search of his father, hallooing to be brought across the river. The next day two hunters crossed the Kanawha and returning, one was killed by Indians. Some of the whites made a rush for the Indians detained at the fort. Captain Arbuckle in command tried to stay them, but incited by one of the Gilmores whose kindred had been massacred at Muddy Creek, Cornstalk and his son, Ellinipsico and Red Hawk were murdered in cold blood, by Captain James Hall and Hugh Galbraith leading the men. The bravery of Cornstalk called forth the admiration of even his brutal murderers, as he thus addressed Ellinipsico.

"*My Son, the Great Spirit has seen fit that we should die together, and has sent you here to that end. It is His will and let us submit; it is all for the best!*" and then turning his face to his murderers at the door, he fell without a groan, pierced with seven bullets.

Cornstalk said the day before he was killed while attending a conference with the whites. "*When I was a young man and went to war, I often thought each might be my last adventure and I should return no more. I still lived. Now l am in the midst of you and if you choose you may kill me. I can die but once. It is alike to me whether now or hereafter.*"

From the records of Rockbridge County we quote the following.

"*At a court held in Rockbridge County, April 18, 1778, for the examination of Capt. James Hall and Hugh Galbraith, charged with the murder of Cornstalk, no witnesses appearing, they were acquitted for the murder of Cornstalk and two other Indians in November, 1777, they denying their guilt.*"

The remains of Cornstalk were interred at Point Pleasant outside the fort, where Viand intersects with First Street, but in August 4, 1840, when Viand Street was opened, his remains were removed to the Court House yard. Dr. Samuel G. Shaw made a memorandum at the time of his burial. His grave is thirty yards in the rear of the Court House where the grave is neglected.

On October 13, 1899, a monument to Cornstalk with the simple inscription "CORNSTALK" was erected in the Court House yard near Sixth Street. The monument is of grey limestone the stone for which was donated by Mr. S. H. Reynolds, then Superintendent of Construction at Kanawha Lock 11. The money for the completion of the monument was raised by private subscription and the dedication of the monument was the occasion for a public ceremonial with a dedicatory address, by Hon. C. E. Hogg, Mayor John E. Beller receiving the monument for the town.

Forts Blair, Randolph and Point Pleasant

Governor Dunmore, under date of June 12, 1774, directed General Andrew Lewis to "*collect a body of men immediately; go down to the mouth of the Great Kanaway and THERE BUILD A FORT; and then if you have force enough to invade the Indian Country, do so."*

Before these orders could be carried out the Battle of Point Pleasant had ensued. The wounded of the army must be cared for and sufficient of the army must remain to protect and care for them while the majority marched on with General Lewis to Camp Charlotte.

So frail was the hastily improvised stockade that it was inadequate to withstand an attack but fortunately Captain William Russell and fifty Fincastle men were delegated by General Lewis to return to Point Pleasant and erect a fort. They arrived there November 11, 1774. Thus Captain Russell became the designer and builder of this small rectangular palisade, eighty yards long with block houses at two corners with cabins for barracks, which he called Fort Blair. It was erected upon grounds on the North Bank of the Kanawha as it emptied into the Ohio. Here in January, 1775, Cornstalk complying with the terms of the treaty at Camp Charlotte delivered a number of white prisoners.

On June 5, 1775, Governor Dunmore reported that the garrison at Point Pleasant had been ordered discontinued, but the Virginia Convention ordered that one hundred men should be hastened to Point Pleasant. Upon their arrival they found Fort Blair in ashes.

By whom or when destroyed, history does not record. On May, 16, 1776, Captain Matthew Arbuckle passed through Wheeling enroute to Point Pleasant where upon the ruins of Fort Blair he erected Fort Randolph. This fort was much larger than Fort Blair, called Fort Randolph in honor of Hon. Peyton Randolph of Virginia. It was from thence, garrisoned at expense of the Colony of Virginia, Captain Arbuckle continuing in command until the close of 1777. He was succeeded in command by Capt. Wm. McKee of Rockbridge County. In 1778 several were killed by Indians while outside the fort at work, including Lieut. Moore. In 1779, for a week Indians besieged the fort but to no avail except that they captured all the cattle. In 1779 prior to July 12, Ft. Randolph was evacuated after which it was burned by Indians. Capt. Andrew Lewis visiting at Point Pleasant in 1784 reported. There was then but little or no sign of the fort to be seen. In 1785 a third fort was built at Point Pleasant, on the Ohio River above the present First Street. Commanded by Colonel Thomas Lewis and from that year on the white man has never ceased to reside at Point Pleasant.

Participants of the Battle

No official roster having been preserved either by the Government or the State, the following list has been gleaned from the sources available after years of research by the writer:

Able, Jeremiah	Adams, John
Adkins, Parker	Adkins, Wilton
Atkins, Wm.,	Agnew, (Aggnue), John
Alexander, James Sgt.	Allen, James
Allen, Thomas	Alley, Thomas
Alden, Andrew	Allen, Hugh Lieut.
Allen, James	Alliet (Elliot) Robert
Alsbury, Thomas	Arbuckle, Capt. Matthew
Anderson, James	Anderson, Samuel
Andrews, Samuel	Arbuckle, John
Ard, James	Arnold, James
Arnold Steven	Armstrong, Geo.
Armstrong Thos.	Armstrong, Wm.
Arthur, John	Astle, Samuel
Atkins, Blackburn	Atkins, Charles
Atkins, Henry	Babbit, Ishmael
Baker, Martin	Barker, Samuel
Baker, Thomas	Baker, Markham
Baker, Samuel Ens.	Baily, John
Bailey, Campbell	Ball, James
Baret, Edward	Barton, Samuel
Basel John	Barkly, John
Bambridge, James	Barnes,
Barnett, James	Barnett, S. L.
Bates,	Baugh, Jacob
Boylstone, Wm.	Bazel, John
Bellew, Daniel (Canoe man)	Bell, Thomas
Bergman, Christian	Berry, Francis
Bishop, Levi	Blackburn, Arthur
Blackford, Joseph	Blair, Daniel
Blair Wm.	Blankenship, Richard
Bledsoe, Abraham Lt.	Blesly, Jacob
Blesly, John	Bojard, Abraham
Boh, Adam	Boh, Jacob
Boles, John	Boniface, Wm.

Borg, Francis	Boughman, John
Boughman, Jacob	Burney, Thomas
Bowen, Moses	Bowen, Reese
Bowen, Wm.	Bowles, Sgt.
Bowles, Robt.	Boyd, James
Boyd, Robert	Boyer, Henry
Boylstone	Boyles, Barney
Bradley, John	Bradley, Wm.
Brambradge, Jas.	Bramstead, Andrew
Breckinridge, Alex.	Breden, John
Breeze, Richard	Breeze, Robt.
Bradley, John	Brooks Geo.
Brooks, Thos.	Brown, Chas.
Brown, James	Brown, Low
Brown, Robt.	Brown, Wm.
Brown, Thos.	Brumfield, Humphrey
Brumfield, Solomon	Brumley, Thos.
Bryans, Shorgan	Bryans, Wm. Sgt.
Bryant, Wm.	Buchanan (Commissariat)
Buchanan Col. John	Buchanan, Wm. Ens.
Buford, Abraham, Col.	Bunch, Joseph
Buchnell, John	Burch, Richard
Burcks, Samuel	Burk, Thos.
Burk, John	Burnes, Thos.
Burnsides, James	Burrens, James
Burroughs John	Burton, Litton
Burtchfield, James	Buch, John Sgt,
Buch, Wm.	Buster, David
Butler, Joseph	Butler, Shadrick
Byrd, Richard	Byrne, Chas.
Calloway, Dudley	Cameron, Geo.
Cameron, Hugh	Campbell, Art.Maj.
Campbell, John Capt.	Campbell, Robt.
Campbell, Joseph	Campbell, Samuel
Campbell, Wm. Capt.	Canady, Thos.
Caper ton, Adam	Caperton, Hugh
Carlton, James	Carmack, John
Carney, Martin	Carpenter, John
Carpenter, Jeremiah	Carpenter, Solomon
Carpenter, Thomas	Carr, Geo.
Carr, John	Carr, Wm.
Cartain, James	Cartain, Joel

Cartain. John	Carter, John
Carther, Edward	Cary, Jeremiah
Casey, Wm.	Cashady, Simon
Cashaday, Thos.	Catron, Adam
Catron, Francis	Catron, Jacob
Catron, Michael	Catron, Peter
Catron, Philip	Cats, Roger
Cattes, John	Cavanaugh, Charles
Cavanaugh, Philemon	Cavanaugh, Philip
Cavanaugh Wm.	Cecil, Saul
Champ, Wm.	Chapline, Abraham
Chapman, John	Chapman, Richard
Chesney, John	Charlton, James
Christian, Wm., Col.	Clark, John
Clark, James	Clark, Samuel
Clay, Mitchell	Clay, Zekel
Clay, David	Clendenin, Adam
Clendenin, Alexander	Clendenin, Chas.
Clendenin, Geo.	Clendenin, Robert
Clendenin, Wm.	Clerk, John
Clifton, Wm.	Clinding, Wm.
Clinding, Geo.	Cloyne Nicholas
Cochran, Wm.	Cocke, Wm., Capt.
Coile, James	Coller, John
Coller, Moses Sgt.	Collet, Thos.
Collins, Richard	Condon, David
Conner, Patrick	Conner, Wm.
Constantine Patrick	Cook, David
Cook, Henry	Cook, John
Cook, Wm.	Cooper, Abraham
Cooper, Francis	Cooper, Leonard
Cooper, Nathiel	Cooper, Spencer
Cooper, Thomas	Copley, Thos.
Cornwell, Adam	Corder, John
Cormick, John	Cornwell, Adam
Courtney, Chas.	Cornwell, John
Cowan, Jared	Courtney, John
Coward,_____	Cowan, John
Cox, John, Capt.	Cox, Gabriel, Lt.
Crabtree, Wm. Scout	Coyl, James
Craig, John	Craig, George
Crain, John	Craig Wm., Sgt.

Cravens, James	Craven, Jos, Sgt.
Cravens, Robt.	Cravens, John
Crawford, John, Sgt.	Crawford, Bonard
Creed, Matthew	Crawley, James
Crockett, Joseph	Crisman, Isaac
Croley, Samuel	Crockett, Walter Capt.
Crow, Wm.	Crow, John, Sgt.
Cummins, Geo.	Curwell, Alexander
Cunningham ,James	Cundiff, Jonathan, Ens.
Current, Joseph	Cunningham ,John
Custer, Win	Curry, James, Capt.
Cutright, John	Cutlep, David
Dale, James	Culwell Alexander
Davis, Charles	Davis, Azariah, Capt.
Davis, Robert (scout)	Davis, Geo.
Davise, Jonathan	Davis, Samuel
Day, Wm.	Day, Joseph
Deek, John	Deal, Wm.
Deniston, John	Demonse, Abraham
Dickinson, John, Col.	Denton, John
Dingos, Peter	Dillon, ___ Lt.
Doack, Robt. Capt.	Divey, John
Doack, Samuel	Doack, David
Dobler, Jacob	Doack, Wm. Ensign
Dodd, James	Dodd, John
Dorherty James	Dorherty, John
Donaley, James, Sgt.	Dollarhide, Samuel
Donalson, JohnCol.	Donaley, John
Donalson, Thos.	Donalson, Robt.
Dooley, Thos. Lieut.	Donley, Jacob
Doss, Joel	Doran, Patrick
Daugherty, James	Daugherty, Geo., Sgt.
Daugherty, Michael, Sgt.	Daugherty, John
Douglas, James	Douglas, Geo.
Downy, John	Downy, James Sgt.
Drake, Ephriam	Drake, Joseph
Dulin, James	Draper, John, Lt.
Dunkirk, John Sgt.	Duncan, John, Sgt.
Dunn, John	Dunlap, Robert
Duttson, Philip	Dunowho, James
Eager, John	Dyer, Wm.
Eastham, Geo.	Eastham, Wm.

Edmiston (Edmondson) Wm.Lt.	Edgar, Thos.
Edwards, Jonathan	Edward, James
Elkins, Jesse	Egnis Edward
Elias, Thomas	Ellenborough, Peter
Ellison, James	Elliott, Robert, Capt.
Elswick, John	Ellison, Charles
English, Joshua	English, Joseph
Estill, Samuel	English, Stephen
Evans, Andrew	Evans, Evan
Ewing, ____ Jr.	Ewing, Alexander
Ewing, Samuel	Ewing, Robert
Fain, John	Ewing, Wm. Sgt. & Maj.
Fargison, Thos.	Fain, Samuel
Farley, Joh	Farley, Francis
Farmer, Nathan	Farley, Thomas
Fenquay, Isham	Feavil, Wm.
Ferrill, Wm.	Ferrill, Robt.
Fields, Wm.	Field, John Col.
Fielder, Wm.	Fielder, John Sgt.
Findlay, John	Findlay, Geo.
Fisher, Isaac	Fendlay, Robt. Sgt.
Fitzpatrick, Timothy	Fitzhugh, John
Flintham, John	Fleming, Wm., Col.
Floyd, John	Fliping, Thos.
Fowler, Jas. (scout)	Fourgeson, Thos.
Fowler, Wm.	Fowler, Samuel
Franklin, Wm.	Franklin, James
Freeland, John	Frazer, John
Frogg, John, Lt.	Friel, Jeremiah
Fry, Geo. Jr.	Fry, Geo.
Fullen, Chas.	Fry, John
Fullen, Daniel	Fullen, James
Gardner, Andrew	Fuls, Geo.
Gass, David	Garrett, Wm.
Gibbs, Luman	Gatliff (Gatlepp), Squire
Gilberts, Thos.	Gibson, Joseph
Gilkenson, Jas.	Gillihan (Gilliland) John
Gillespy, Thos.	Gill, Prisley
Gillman, Duncan	Gillass, Wm.
Gilmore, Jas., Capt.	Gilmore, John
Glascum, David	Givens, ___, Lt.
Glass Wm.	Glass, Samuel, Sgt.

Glenn, Davis	Glaves, Michael
Goldman, Edward, Lt.	Goff, Andrew
Goodall, John	Goldsby,____
Gorman, David	Gordan, Moses
Green, John	Graham, Benj.
Grigger, Michael	Griffin, Robt.
Grigs, John	Grigger, Peter
Grigsby,____	Grimp, John
Guillen, Edward	Guffy, James
Gullion, Barney	Guillen, James
Hackett, Thos.	Gurden, Michael
Hackworth, Wm.	Hackworth, Augustine
Hale, Edward	Haines, Lewis
Hale, Wm.	Hale, Thomas
Hall, Thos.	Hall, James
Hamilton, Isaiah	Hamilton, Francis
Hamilton, Jas.	Hamilton, Jacob
Hamilton Thos.	Hamilton, John
Hamrick, Thos	Hammond, Philip
Handley (Herrill) Robt.	Hamrick, Wm.
Hanee, Philip	Handley (Hensley) Sam'l.
Hanson, Wm.	Hansburger, Adam
Harlan, Silas	Harlan, Elijah
Harmon, Geo.	Harmon, Dangerfield
Harmon, John	Harmon, Israel
Harriman, Skid Sgt.	Harrel, Wm. Scout
Harris, John	Harris, Griffin
Harrison, Andrew	Harris, Stephen
Harrison, John, Lt.	Harrison, Ben., Capt.
Hart, Thos.	Harrod, James, Capt.
Hatfield, Andrew	Hasket, Thos.
Havens, James	Havens, John
Haynes, Benj.	Hayes, John
Hays, Chas.	Haynes, Joseph, Capt.
Henly, Wm.	Henly, Geo.
Herbert Wm. Capt.	Hensley (Hadley), Sam'l
Herrill, Robt.	Herd, Richard
Hendrix, Peter	Henderson, Sam'l
Henderson, Daniel	Henderson, John Lt.
Hays, Samuel (scout)	Henderson, Alexander
Hedden, Thos.	Head, Anthony
Hepenstahl, Abra.	Hedrick, Peter

Higgans (Higans), Peter	Hickman,___
Hill, ___, Capt.	Higgans, Philemon
Hill, Robert	Hill James
Hogan, Henry	Hobbs, Vincent
Holley, Wm.	Hogan, Wm.
Holston, Stephen	Hollway (Holloway), Richard
Homes, Lewis	Holwell, Walter
Hopton, Stephen	Hooper, Wm.
Home, Joseph	Hopton, Wm,
Howard, Henry	Howard, Charles
Hutchinson, Wm.	Hutchinson, Lewis
Huff, Peter	Huff. Leonard
Huff, Thomas	Huff, Samuel
Hughes, Ellis	Hughes, Davy
Humphries, John	Hughey, Joseph
Hunter, Robert	Hundley, John
Hynes, Frances	Hutson, John
Ingles, Joshua	Ingles, Wm., Major
Inglish (English), Jos.	Ingles, Thos.
Irvine, John	Inglish (English) Joshua
Jackson, Yerty	Isum, Wm.
Jenkins, Jeremiah	Jameson, John
Jewitt, Matthew	Jennings, Edmond
Johnson Arthur Capt.	Johns, Wm.
Johnston, Patrick	Johnston, John
Jones, John	Jones, Benj.
Jones, Wm.	Jones, Thos.
Keeneson, Charles	Kasheday, Peter
Kelley, Alexander	Keith, Samuel
Kendrick, James	Kelsey, John
Kennedy, Thomas	Kennedy, Ezekiel
Kenneson, Chas.	Kennedy, Wm.
Kennot, Zachariah	Kenneson, Edward
Kerr. Wm	Kerr, James
Kinder, Jacob	Kinder, George
King, James	Kinder, Peter
King, Wm.	King, John
Kincaid, David Jr.	Kincaid, David
Kincaid, James	Kincaid, Geo.
Kinsor, Chas.	Kincaid, John Serg.
Kinsor, Jacob	Kinsor Michael
Kishoner, Andrew Jr.	Kinsor, Walter

Kissinger, Andrew	Kishoner, Andrew Sr.
Knox, James	Kissinger, Matthew
Lapsley, John	Lammey, Andrew
Lashly, John	Larken, John Serg.
Lawrence, Henry	Laughlin, James
Learned (Lord) Lieut.	Lee, Sefinah
Lemaster, Richard	Lee, Zacarias
Lesley, John	Lesley, Wm.
Lester, Samuel	Lesley, Wm., Adj.
Lewis, Andrew, Gen.	Lester, John
Lewis, Chas., Col.	Lewis. Benjamin
Lewis, John Capt. of Botetourt	Lewis, John Capt. of Augusta
Lewis, Samuel	Lewis, John Pvt.
Librough, Henry	Lin, Adam
Litton, Solomon	Litton, Burton
Lockhart, Jacob	Litz, Wm.
Lockridge, Andrew Capt.	Lockhart, Queavy
Logan, John	Logan, Benj.
Logan, James	Logan, Hugh
Lord (Leord) Lt.	Long, Joseph, Ens.
Love, Philip Capt.	Love, Joseph
Lucas, Chas.	Luallen, Thos.
Lucas, Henry	Lucas, Chas. Jr.
Lucas, Wm.	Lucas, John
Lybrook, Henry	Luney, Michael
Lyman, Richard	Lybrook (Librough), Palser
Lyn, James	Lyle, John
Lyons, Wm.	Lynch,____
McAllister, Wm.	McBride, James
McBride, Joseph	McCallister, James
McCallister Wm.	McCandless, John
McCartney, John	McCastem, Wm.
McCarty, James	McClanahan, Absalom
McClanahan, Alexander, Capt.	McClannahan, John
McClanahan, Robt. Capt.	McAfee, Geo.
McAfee, James	McAfee, Robt.
McAfee, Samuel	McAfee, Wm.
McClintic, Wm.	McClure, John
McClure, Thomas	McCorkle, Wm.
McCoy, Wm. Lt.	McCune, Wm.
McCutchen, Wm.	McDonald, Daniel
McDonald, James	McDowell, Archibald

McDowell, M. Capt.	McDowell, Sam. Capt.
McElhaney, Francis	McFarland, Wm.
McFarland, Robt.	McGee, John
McGeehey, Samuel	McGinness, John
McGlahlen, John	McGuff, John
McGuff, Patrick	McKee, Wm. Capt.
McKinnett, Alex	McKinney, John
McKinsey, Hensley	McKinsey, Moredock
McLaughlin, Edw.	McMullin, John
McMullen, Wm.	McNiel, Peter
McNeal (Niel), John	McNiell, Daniel Lt.
McNutt, James	McNutt, Alexander
Madison, John	Monadue, Henry
Mann, John	Mann, Wm.
Marks, John	Martin, Brice
Martin, Christian	Martin, Geo. Sr.
Martin, Geo. Jr.	Martin, Philip
Martin, Wm Col.	Matthew, Geo. Capt.
Matthew, Sampson	Maxwell, Bazaleel
Maxwell, David	Maxwell, John
Maxwell, Thomas	Mayse, Joseph
Mead, Nicholas	Mead, Thos.
Meader, Israel	Mecrary, Thomas
Meek, Wm.	Messersnuth, Barnett
Messersnuth, John	Micalister, Wm.
Milican, John	Miller, James
Miller, Robert	Mills, John
Milwood, Geo.	Miner, Henry
Mitchell, James Capt.	Mitchell, James
Mitchell, Thos.	Moffat, Robt., Capt.
Moffat, George, Capt.	Montgomery, Jas., Capt.
Montgomery, Samuel	Moody, John
Moon, Abraham	Moor, Moses
Moor, Frederick	Moor, Wm.
Moor, John	Moor, Hugh
Mooney, Nicholas	Mooney, Frederick
Mooney, Hendly Ens.	Mooney, Hugh
Mooney, James	Mooney, John
Mooney, Moses	Mooney, Samuel
Mooney, Wm.	Morris, Wm.
Morrow, James	Morrow, James Jr.
Mullin, Thos.	Mungle, Daniel

Mungle, Frederick	Murry, John, Capt.
Murry, James	Myers, Wm.
Mercer, Hugh	Nail, Dennis
Nail, Thomas	Nalle, Martin Lt.
Nail, Thomas	Naul (Nowl), Wm. Capt.
Nave, Conrad	Neal, Wm.
Neaville, John	Neaville, Joseph
Neely James (Cadet)	Neely, Wm.
Neil, John	Nelson, John
Newberry, Joseph	Newell, James
Newland, Abraham	Newland, Isaac
Newland, John	Newman, Walter
Nicholas, John	Nickels, Isaac
Nowell, John	Noland, John
Null, Jacob	Null, John
Odear, James	Oguillen, Barnett
Oguillen, Duncan	Oguillen, John
Oguillen, Hugh	O'Hara, Chas., Capt.
O'Hara, Robt.	O'Hara, Wm.
Oharron, Henry	Olverson, Joseph
Ormsbey, Daniel	Overstreet, Wm.
Ower, Thomas	Owen, Robt.
Owens, David	Owler, Henry
Owler, John	Pack, George
Pack, Samuel	Packwood, Richard
Pain, Joseph	Parchment, Peter
Parsons, James	Pate, Jeremiah
Patten, John	Pauling, Henry, Capt.
Paulley, James	Paulley, John
Pawlings, Moses	Paxton, Samuel
Peary, Thomas	Pence, Jacob, Ensign
Perce, Thomas	Peregin, Molastin
Persinger, Jacob	Peyton, John
Petty, Benjamin	Pharis, Wm.
Peyton, Rowzie	Pierce, John
Pierce,___ Lieut.	Poage, Wm. Sgt.
Plunkenpel, Zacarias	Portor, Robt.
Poling, Mathew	Potter, Thos.
Posey, Thos.	Price, James
Preston, Wm.	Price, Rickard
Price, Reese	Price, Wm.
Price, Thomas	Priest, David

Pricket (Pucket) Drury	Priest, Wm.
Priest, Samuel	Prince, Wm.
Pright, John	Ranis, Robert
Prior (Pryor) John	Rains, Robt.
Ramsey, Josiah	Ratcliff, Wm.
Rapp, Frederick	Razor, Michael
Ratcliff, Matthew	Ravenscroft, Thos.
Ray, Wm.	Reagh, Archibald
Read, John Ensign	Reary, James
Reagh, John	Rediford, Benj.
Reburn, John	Reese, Andrew
Reed, Alexander	Reid, Thomas
Reid, Andrew	Richardson, Benj
Reynolds, John	Riley, John
Richardson, Wm.	Roberts, John
Roay, Joseph	Robertson, Wm., Lt.
Robertson, Jas., Capt.	Robertson, Tho., Major
Robertson, James	Robinson, Elijah
Robertson, Wm.	Robinson, John
Robinson, Hugh	Robison, Julius
Robison, Jas Lt.	Robison, Isaac
Robison, Wm.	Rogers, Andrew
Roe, ___, Capt.	Rogers, David
Rogers, Chesley	Rogers, Thomas
Rogers, James	Rollens, Richard
Rogers, Wm.	Ross, Tavener
Ross, Edward	Rucker, George
Rowen, Francis	Rue, Abraham
Ruddle, George	Rutheford, Benj.
Russell, Wm. Gen.	Sanders, James
Samples, Samuel	Salsbury, Wm.
Sappington, Dan'l	Savage, Samuel
Savage, John	Sayres, John
Sawyers, John, Col.	Scard, ___ Lieut.
Scails, Wm.	Scott, Archelaus
Scarbara, James	Scott, Daniel Capt.
Scott, Archibald	Scott, James
Scott, Geo.	See, Michael
Scott, Wm.	Seed, Francis
Sedbery, John	Sevier, John Gen.
Selby, James	Shain, John
Sevier, Valentine	Shannon, Sam'l.

Shannon, John	Sharp, John (scout)
Sharp, Abraham	Shaw, Henry
Sharp, Edward	Shelby, Isaac Lt.
Shelby, Evan Capt.	Shelby, Wm. Capt.
Shelby, James	Shillin, John
Shell, Arnold	Simpkins, Daniel
Shoatt, Emanuel	Simpson, James
Simpkins, James	Simpson, Wm.
Simpson, John	Skaggs, Zach
Skaggs, Reuben	Slaughter, ___, Capt.
Skidmore, John, Capt	Slaughter, Geo., Col.
Slaughter, Francis Col.	Smith, Daniel, Capt.
Smith, Bruten	Smith, Ericus
Smith, Edward	Smith, John
Smith, James	Smith, Moses
Smith, Mecagh	Smith, Wm.
Smith, Robt.	Sobe, Geo.
Smithers, Gabriel	Spratt, Isaac, Sgt.
Spicer, Wm.	Staffy, Michael
Squires, Uriah	Steele, Andrew
Stailey, Martin	Stephens, John, Lt.
Steele, John	Stephens, Wm.
Stephens, Thomas	Stephenson, Robt.
Stephens, Stephen	Sterns, Conrad
Stephenson, Hugh, Capt.	Steward, John
Stevens,___	Stewart, John
Steward, Walter	Stewart, John, Capt.
Stewart, Wm.	Stump, Michael
Stull, Martin	Sullivan, Sam'l
Sullivan, James	Swoop, John
Summers, Charles	Tate, Wm.
Tate, T., Lt.	Taylor, ___, Capt.
Tarney, Peter	Taylor, Isaac
Taylor, Daniel	Taylor, Wm.
Taylor, Sieltor	Torrence, Andrew
Teasy, Wm.	Thompson, Andrew
Thomas, Edward	Thompson, Robert
Thompson, Richard	Trent, Obediah
Thompson, Wm.	Trimble, James
Trimble, Isaac	Trotter, Richard
Trotter, John	Tyler, Isaac
Tucker, Wm.	Vallendingham, Geo.

Vails, John	VanBibber, Jesse
VanBibber, Isaac	VanBibber, Peter
VanBibber, John	Vance, Edward
VanBibber, Mathias	Vanhook, Samuel
Vance, Samuel Lieut.	Vaught, Christian
Vaught, Andrew	Venable, Wm.
Vaught Geo.	Vanhook, Samuel
Vaughan (Vaun), John	Waggoner, Henry
Waggoner, Andrew	Walker, Adam
Waggoner, Henry Jr.	Walker, James
Walker, Henry	Wallace, Andrew
Wallace, Adam Ensign	Wallace Robt.
Wallace, David	Walter, Michael
Wallace, Samuel Lt.	Wambler, Mitchell
Wambler, Geo.	Ward, James Capt.
Ward, David, Ens.	Warwick, Jacob
Ward, Wm. Sgt.	Washburn, Steven
Washburn, James	Watson, Jonathan
Watkins, Robt.	Weaver, Christian
Waugh,___ Cadet	Welch, James
Weaver, Michael	Welch, Thomas
Welch, John	Wells, Bazaleel
Welch, Thomas Jr.	Welsh, Christopher
Wells, Samuel	Wetzel, John
Whish, Richard	Whitley, Moses
Wetzel, Martin	White, Joseph
White, David	White, Wm.
White. Solomon	Whitton, Jeremiah
Whitticor, Joseph	Whitton, Thomas Jr.
Whitton, Thomas	Wiles, Robert
Wiley James	Wiley, Thomas
Wiley, Robert Jr.	Williams, David
Williams, Alden	Williams, James
Williams, Isaac	Williams, John
Williams, Jarrett	Williams, Philip
Williams, Mack	Williams, Rowland
Williams, Richard	Williams, Thos. Sgt.
Williams, Samuel	Williamson, David
Williamson, Aldin	Wilmoth, Wm.
Willis, Henry,	Wilson, Edward
Wilson, Benj.	Wilson, John, Capt.
Wilson, James	Wilson, Thomas

Wilson, George	Wilson, Sam. Capt.
Wilson, Wm., Sgt.	Wood, Adam
Wood, John	Wood, Archibald
Wood, Andrew	Wood, Jos., Capt.
Wood, James, Sgt.	Wood, Richard
Wood, Michael Capt	Workman, Daniel
Woolsey, Richard	Woodburn, James
Woodburn, Steven	
Young, John	

History of the Monument Building

In our research for information relative to efforts being made to erect a battle monument at Point Pleasant, the earliest record of which we have an account is a letter yet preserved, written by Hon. J. M. H. Beale, who, in 1848, represented that district of which Mason County, Virginia, was a part, in the lower branch of Congress, in which he says *"I have introduced a bill in Congress asking for $50,000 with which to erect a monument to commemorate the Battle of Point Pleasant."* As nothing came of it, it died in a committee room.

That amount of money in purchasing power, equal in value to twice that amount of money at the present time, only demonstrated the magnitude in which the battle was held when not so many years had intervened since that terrible struggle.

We find by reference to an old minute book preserved by Mrs. John Daniel McCulloch, that a monument committee had been organized in the year 1860. The exact date of organization is not given. The first meeting recorded is as follows:

Monument Association Rooms
Sep. 17, 1860

"The Regent being absent, Mrs. James Hutchinson, Vice Regent, called the association to order.

"On motion the minutes of the last meeting was suspended."

"The committee on By Laws reported series of laws by Mrs. Wm. Smith, Chair lady, & under discussion said By laws were adopted,& on motion the committee was discharged.

"On motion a permanent committee composed of Mrs. Charles Lewis, Mrs. Barlow, Miss Sallie Henderson, Miss Kimberling, Miss Till Stribling and Miss Sue Waggoner to collect historical facts connected with the Battle of Point leasant.

"On motion of Mrs. Smith, it is resolved this association will celebrate the anniversary of the battle, 10th of October.

"On motion it is resolved committee be appointed to see what will be contributed for a supper.

"On motion a committee composed of Sallie Lewis, Fannie, for the Flats, Miss Patrick Sehon for Mason City, Miss Stribling & Hall, upper part of town, Miss Jones & Miss Murdock lower end, Sallie Henderson and E. Smith, South Side Kanawha, Ginnie Neale & Maria Menager, Mercer Bottom.

"On motion it is resolved a committee of two be appointed to wait on Col. Beal and see if we can procure the Hall.

Signed, E. Smith Recording Secretary

M. T. Lewis Regent
Nov. 14, 1860"

There is left no written record of that supper given at Beal's Hall, but there are many living here yet who recall it as one of the greatest social events of the town up until that time, as there was gathered here all of the elite of the county. The money raised at that time by the supper was about $200.00, which was supplemented by $800,00 more in subscriptions, Mrs. John S. Lewis (Mrs. Mary T. Lewis) the Regent riding horseback over the county soliciting funds,

The society applied for a charter which was granted under the laws of the State of Virginia. The money was loaned to Mr. Peter Steenbergen Lewis, a descendant of Col. Charles Lewis killed in the battle, and was faithfully accounted for and interest paid until turned over to the Point Pleasant Battle Monument Commission provided for in 1901, by the State of West Virginia.

The only two surviving charter members of the original monument association are Miss Elizabeth Smith, of McCausland, and Mrs. J. D. McCulloch (Miss Sallie Lewis) of Point Pleasant.

We find in the above mentioned record book the following entry:

Monument Association Room
Nov. 14, 1860

"The Regent having called the meeting to order on motion of E. Smith, the historical committee is requested to wait upon, or otherwise communicate with all the early settlers of the county, that is practicable, to obtain all the information they can in regard to the *battle of the Point, and all other interesting events of the early Indian times.*

"On motion it is resolved, the monument be placed on the spot where the brave men who fell in the battle have so long lain unhonored, by vote was unanimously carried—affirmative Nannie Smith, Kate Murdock, Sallie Lewis, Sallie Henderson, M. J. Stribling, Ginnie Neale, Rose Barlow, Fannie Lewis, Eliza Waggoner, E. Smith—Negative.

"On motion it is resolved a fine of five cents be imposed on those who are not present by half after two o'clock, P. M.

"On motion it is resolved that this meeting adjourns to meet the first Wednesday in January."

It is well that the names of these patriotic women have been preserved to history, many of whom were descendants of participants in the battle. Sallie Lewis (Mrs. J. D. McCulloch) descended from Col. Charles Lewis; Sallie Henderson, the late Mrs. Jos. George, of Five Mile, descended from Samuel Henderson; Misses Sue and Eliza Waggoner descended from Gen. Andrew Lewis; Mrs. Charles Lewis was the mother of Mr. P. S. Lewis, a descendant to whom the first funds were entrusted; Mrs. Kimberling was the wife of Elijah Kimberling, for many years clerk of the county court; Fannie Lewis, wife of Judge John W. English, descended from Col. Charles Lewis, as did Miss Lizzie Sehon, of Mason City; Miss Hall was the late Mrs. B. J. Redmond, daughter of Hon. John Hall; Miss Jones is Mrs. J. W. Bryan; Maria Menger became the wife of Rev. George Lyle; Miss Till Stribling became the wife of Mr. Chap. Waggoner of Pleasant Flats: Mrs. Rose Barlow was the wife of a resident physician; Miss Kate (Beale) Murdock was the second wife of the late Col. C. B. Waggoner, Ginnie Neale now Mrs. Otis Stribling.

The Civil War breaking out, the efforts to erect a monument were put aside for the stirring incidents then agitating the minds of the people and no efforts were again made until the 100th anniversary of the Battle in 1874, when the proper celebration of the battle was taken up by Messrs. John Q. Dickerson, John D. Lewis, C. C. Lewis, Wm. Dickenson, of Charleston, P. S. Lewis, J. P. R. B. Smith, Judge John W. English, of Point Pleasant. These largely financed the celebration assisted by other of the most patriotic citizens of Point Pleasant and an effort was made to gather together as many as possible of the descendents of the Lewis's of that battle. In fact so little attention was paid by other descendants and so highly had the Lewis's honored the services of their sires that the proposed monument was spoken, of as the "Lewis Monument" and, for years, the writer, who was present at that celebration, scarcely knew there were other heroes participating worthy of being published in the school histories, there being no available books to be read and no one mentioned by word of mouth but the Lewis's.

All honor, however, to this family who honor their heroic dead. It was the most splendid palm they could place upon the brow of their ancestors to teach the world as they have done their descendants to revere the names of Andrew and Charles Lewis.

The first published agitation for the proper observance of the 100th anniversary of the Battle of Point Pleasant, we find in the Charleston Courier, reproduced in the Weekly Register of March 19, 1874, which we quote in part: *"It was at this place that occurred one of the bloodiest and severest battles in which the whites and Indians have ever engaged. On the morning of the 10th of October, 1774, an army composed almost entirely of Virginians, under the command of General Andrew Lewis, and numbering about eleven hundred men, was attacked by a largely superior force of savages under the command of the famous chieftain Cornstalk. The battle raged furiously the entire day, and ended in the defeat of the Indians, who throughout the battle, are said to have displayed the most determined bravery. The Virginia army sustained in this engagement a loss of seventy-five killed and one hundred and forty wounded."*

"Among the slain were Colonels Charles Lewis and John Field and eight subordinate officers, all of whom were of the best families of Virginia."

"The loss of the savages was never ascertained, as it was their custom to bear off and secrete their dead. Some twenty or more bodies, however, were found on the field, which the Indians had been unable to carry away."

"The wounded whites were placed within entrenchments, thrown up at the point of the confluence of the Kanawha and Ohio Rivers, and a garrison left there to protect them, the dead were buried

immediately outside of the entrenchments, though in a scattered manner. General Lewis then pursued his march northward."

"Finding our selves at Point Pleasant with considerable leisure and time, we proposed to an old friend and resident of the "Point" to take us to the graves of the heroes of the Battle of Point Pleasant. With a willingness to oblige which is a prominent characteristic of that gentleman, he readily assented, and in a few moments we found ourselves close to the junction of the two rivers, standing on tip-toe looking over a high bank on which we were standing completing the bounds. A few indentations or depression were all that indicated that within that small enclosure were buried some fifty or sixty heroes of the times that tried men's souls. The place was strewn with filth and refuse and seemed to be a general depository for the rubbish of the neighborhood. With a feeling of disgust at the cold neglect so plainly manifested by the authorities, not only of the governments of the States of Virginia and West Virginia, but of the county and city wherein rest these dead, we turned away."

The writer who signs himself "Virginiout," relating an interview with Mr. Andrew Darst, residing upon the extreme point where the rivers meet, who not only exhibited a grind stone, cannon ball, and shovel, taken from an old well that had been within the fort, but he exhibited the site of the old magazine long since gone over the bank and the site of the cottage wherein Cornstalk was murdered.

Quoting further from article of date above given, Mr. Darst said in that published interview: "About 1832 thar came by here an old man who had been here in Injin times. Some folks were wondering whar Cornstalk had been buried. The old man said he knowed, and if they'd follow him he'd show 'em. So he took 'em out to a ditch just back of that drug store you see there, (2nd and Viand Streets) told them to dig in at a certain place and they'd find Cornstalk about four feet underground. They dug in there and sure enough they found him. They then took him up and buried him in the Court House yard."

"The spot of land here on the point was once a big Injin grave yard, and if you will take the trouble to look over the bank where it has been washed you'll find bones a plenty. All of 'em's across beads and trinkets among the bones."

Acting on the suggestion we took a look over the bank and discovered many fragments of bones which were lying loosely on the soil or projecting from the face of the bank. After sauntering around a few moments longer we bade "Andy" farewell and walked off to take a look at the town."

"The heroes of Bunker Hill have their monument to commemorate their deeds, but the brave little band sleeping so silently on the bank of the Kanawha, have nothing but an old decayed, worm eaten fence to mark their graves. Point Pleasant and Bunker Hill, were each fought in the same cause, and those acquainted with the history of "Dunmore's war" will not contradict the assertion that the battle of "Point Pleasant," was really the first battle of the Revolution."

The Weekly Register of May 17, 1874, editorially comments on the importance of the Battle of Point Pleasant and quotes again from the Charleston Courier, as follows:

"Is there any event connected with our past history which so closely affects the people of the Valley as the Battle of Point Pleasant, where Virginians bared their breast to protect it from invasions? While Eastern Virginia had her Yorktown, West Augusta had already purchased a victory at Point Pleasant. To no event transpiring within the limits of our State has ever attached the importance and grateful recollections as has to the Point Pleasant battle. It is well suggested then that the people all along our Valley take some steps to celebrate the one hundredth anniversary of this event at Point Pleasant in October next. Our neighbors in Mason will readily adopt the suggestion, as well as all other counties that feel an interest in preserving afresh both the memory of the gallant dead and their resting places."

"For many reasons the Mason County people should take the lead in this matter, and we feel confident they will. Let every community then from the Ohio to the Greenbrier, fall into line and adopt some harmonious action to fitly celebrate the day, and to raise suitable funds to remove the disgrace of the neglected graves. There is not a superabundance of time, and we predict a prompt response from Mason. Who will take the initiatory for a grand celebration of this event, which if of all others the one great shrine which every creed, every political faith and every class in the State can pay their homage."

A correspondent from Mason County to the Charleston Courier contributed the following:

"There is considerable talk just as this time about our centennial anniversary and a good deal of patriotic feeling is being exhibited in that direction. History records that on the morning of the 10th of October, 1774, there was fought at this Point one of the severest and most hotly contested and bloody battles between the whites under General Lewis and the Indians under command of the great warrior, Cornstalk, that ever took place in the early times of this country. It is in fact, claimed that this was the first battle of the Revolution, and for freedom, from the British yoke. On the 10th of October, 1874, one hundred years will have elapsed since that memorable battle, in which the troops under Gen. Lewis achieved such a triumph."

On Tuesday, May 26th, the Directors of the Second Annual Mason County Fair decided to hold their Fair on October 6th, 7th, 8th, and 9th, but no mention is made of the observance of the 10th, the anniversary of the Battle. Plans, however, were going forward from Charleston, as the Charleston Courier, in its last issue of May 18, 1774, gives the following:

"The idea of the Centennial celebration at Point Pleasant is a very happy one. It is an event in which every true West Virginian should take pride. Our state embraces a large boundary of territory of "West Augusta," whose sons rendered themselves so famous in the days that "tried men's souls," and to whom the great Washington looked for raliance when all others should fail him,"

"Many descendants of the participants in the famous Indian battle at the Point are now living in this, State. In the counties of the Greenbrier Valley as well as in the Kanawha Valley are living those who bear the name and through whose veins run the blood of the Captain of the Virginia forces, Andrew Lewis, as well as those who descended from the brave men that followed him in that remarkable campaign. The result of the battle at the Point saved all the Virginia frontier from the invasion of the Indians. If Cornstalk had been successful who can imagine the fearful desolation that would have been wrought from the Ohio to the Alleghenies."

"Is, it not a little remarkable that while this battle should have become so famous in history, that so little should be known of the particulars of the fight? While history is silent, we have traditions that should be gathered, and the most authentic ones be placed in some shape as to be reliably transmitted to posterity. There are many households of West Virginia, where stories of grandfather's experience in the battle of the "Pint" are related to day, and many of them told by those who have heard the relation from the lips of the veterans himself. What a pleasant task then for someone to collect these traditions and weave history from them."

*****

"Just as the Battle of Point Pleasant was the prelude to the war of Independence, so let the celebration at the Point in 1874 be the prelude to the grand affair to come off at Philadelphia in 1876, and let every West Virginian, and every Old Virginian, and everyone who sees proper to join us, take part in the jubilee on the 10th of October next."

To further stimulate the interest in the Battle Celebration, the Register, on June 25th, copied from Nile's Register, of May 3, 1817, an account of the battle and in the issue of August 27, 1874, the Register copied De Hass' History and Indian Wars in West Virginia, the account in full of the Battle of Point Pleasant. The Register of October 8, has failed up until that time to give any program or details of the celebration, but, in speaking of the Fair then in session, says:

"The Fair will close on Friday evening with a grand ball at Beale's Hall. On Saturday the Centennial Celebration will come of."

The issue of the Weekly Register of October 15, 1874, gives the following detailed account of the Celebration; written Oct. 10th, 1874:

"The Centennial celebration of the Battle of Point Pleasant is now over. Just one hundred years ago tonight, brave men and true were mourning over the dead, and ministering as best they could to the wounded and dying. Let us as best we can, look back upon the day that has just been closed by the setting sun of the 10th day of October, 1874, and tell our readers what has been done. Many an eye looked out anxiously this morning to see what was to be the prospect for a beautiful day. For one I was sadly disappointed and feared that the Heavens would soon be sending down the rain.

"How anxiously we watched every appearance indicating like a breaking away of the lowering clouds. Soon after an early breakfast, the clouds began to look thin, and then spot after spot of blue sky was seen. Anxiously did the eager gathering crowd, look for the promised published programme. About 9 o'clock A. M. the Register office sent out the first, which were eagerly seized by the hungry crowd; then another and another handful of programmes were distributed, so that before the hour of 10 A. M. all seemed to be posted as to what was to be done. About 10 o'clock the Company of Cadets from the University o£ West Virginia, at Morgantown, were formed in line by their Captain, H. H. Pierce, in front of the Kline House, near the wharf-boat, on the Ohio, and waited to receive the Knights of Pythias, from Gallipolis, Ohio, accompanied by the Gallipolis Brass Band. Soon the Knights came marching up, splendidly dressed, and a fine looking body of men they were passing in front of the Cadets, they halted on Main Street. The Cadets, moved in column of fours up to Main Street, then wheeling to the left, were halted opposite the Court House—the site of which is supposed to have been on the line of battle as it was formed, just one hundred years ago today. Here let us give the programme as follows:

Centennial Celebration of the Battle of Point Pleasant

Order of Exercises
Procession to form in front of Court House at 10 A. M. in the following order: Mayor, Orator, and Committee of Arrangements.
State Cadets
The Clergy
Relatives. Music
Knights of Pythias and other Orders
Distinguished Guests
Citizens
Funeral Procession
Escort of State Cadets

Re-interment of the remains of the heroes who fell in this battle, with becoming ceremonies at 3 o'clock p. m.

Under the effective Marshals who had been on duty at the Fair Grounds for the last four days, the column was formed— The Cadets were headed by their own drum corps; the Knights of Pythias by the Gallipolis and Point Pleasant Brass Bands combined, whilst the

Ravenswood Brass Band marched up the side walk and waited for the formation of the column, after which it took the place assigned it.

Just before 11 A. M. the column was put in motion and marched in the order assigned, to the Fairground, where more than a thousand people were found awaiting the arrival of the column. So densely crowded was the amphitheater before the head of the column reached its front that it was with the utmost difficulty that the Committee of Arrangements could clear away space enough for the Company of Cadets. A stand for the speakers had been erected just opposite the center of the amphitheatre. This stand was occupied by the following persons: Col. Lewis Ruffner, Col. C. B. Waggener, Col. Benj. H. Smith, Capts. H. H. Pierce, Commanding the Cadets, Geo. C. Sturgess, Corresponding Secretary of the Historical Society of the Board of Regents University of West Virginia, J. W. Screntz, Treasurer of the same, Dr. Thomas Creigh, of Greenbrier County, Dr. S G. Shaw, President of the Centennial Society, F. A. Guthrie, Attorney at Law, and member of the Committee of Arrangements, Jno. E. Timms, Attorney at Law, Secretary of the Mason County Agricultural Society, Col. (Dr.) A. R. Barbee, G. W. E. Mitchell, of Portsmouth, Ohio, John D. Lewis and Jno. Waddell, who was wearing the shot pouch and powder horn carried by his father, Alexander Waddell, in the Battle of Point Pleasant. The Clergy occupying the stand were Father Francis Guthrie, one of the Pioneer Methodist Preachers of the Kanawha Valley, Revs. S. E. Lane, T. H. Rymer, T. H. Lacy, G. C. Wilding, and W. E. Hill. The exercises were introduced with a prayer offered by Father Guthrie which was full of thanksgiving and praise, then the orator, Col. Ben Smith, was introduced by Mr. Timms. He commenced reading his well-written and interesting address at 12 o'clock and 22 minutes, just five minutes after the 13th gun of the salute was fired by the Artillery Company from Gallipolis, Ohio. This occupied about thirty-five minutes. The speaker took his seat amid deafening roars. The following resolution was offered by Dr. Barbee:

Resolved, that the thanks of this audience be returned to Col. Smith for his interesting address, and that, with his permission, it be published in full in the Point Pleasant Register.

This resolution was carried without a dissenting voice.

After this, the following preamble and resolutions were offered by Rev. W. E. Hill:

Whereas, just one hundred years have passed by since the Battle of Point Pleasant was fought and won.

2. In this battle there was displayed gallantry of such character, as to merit a lasting monument.

3. It is the opinion of some, whose opinion is worthy of respect, that this battle bore an important relation to the war of the Revolution, by which the original thirteen colonies gained their independence.

4. The Battle of Point Pleasant hastened the material prosperity of this and other States, by the sacrifice of noble blood, therefore be it Resolved.

1st. That a committee of three with power to engage others, be appointed to solicit contributions for the purpose of erecting a monument and purchasing the ground round about the spot where the remains of our heroes now repose.

That, this committee be empowered to raise a subscription on the ground to-day; to write to the descendents of the brave men who were engaged or fell on the field of Point Pleasant, asking them to aid in this work by contributions; to ask the Legislatures of Virginia, West Virginia, Kentucky and Ohio, to make appropriations to this work; and to request also the Congress of the United States to make an appropriation to the same end.

2nd. That this monument be erected within the next twelve months, and of West Virginia marble.

3rd. That it be unveiled on the 10th of October, 1875.

4th. That the committee be empowered to arrange for funeral oration and an historical address on the occasion, and to make such other arrangements as may be necessary to gather together the military organizations of the State; the various secret societies of a benevolent character; the legislatures of the State, etc.

Mr. Hill introduced these resolutions by a motion to resolve the vast audience into a Monumental Centennial Organization. After the reading of the resolutions a motion was made to adopt. Pending this, Dr. Creigh arose and asked to be allowed to speak on the question. Permission was granted, and the Dr. perfectly thrilled those within reach of his voice. After the Doctor's eloquent speech, the motion to adopt the resolutions was carried with but one single dissenting voice, whose "no" was followed by cries "of "Put him out!", "Knock him down!" etc.

Mr. Mitchell, of Portsmouth, Ohio, was then introduced and made a short speech, which could not be heard very far off, owing to the noise of the moving crowd and the low pitch of voice and its effectiveness was marred to some extent. Loud cries were heard for (Walker). It was announced that Mr. Walker was at the Point and had been sent for, but could not get here for some time.

A cry for Sturgess brought that gentlemen to his feet, and he made a very happy address.

The President, Dr. G. S. Shaw, announced as a temporary committee to wait upon the crowd, to solicit contributions for the monument, viz: E. L. Neale, Dr. C. T. B. Moore, and F. A. Guthrie. The latter gentlemen being a member of the Committee of Arrangements, suggested Rev. W. E. Hill, as his substitute. Recess was taken and ample provisions were made to "fill the inner man." Many families gathered in groups about the grounds, in picnic fashion, and ate their dinner whilst a roast ox was served up at the public table. During the recess the committee raised by subscription about six hundred dollars. One gentleman subscribed two hundred dollars in cash on two papers, and we do not think he intends to stop at that if more is necessary from him, to erect the monument. There was such a dense crowd and such hurrying to and fro that it was almost impossible to get the attention of the people long enough to get them to subscribe, or we doubt not, more than a thousand dollars could have been raised.

After dinner the crowd was called together to listen to Hon. Henry S. Walker, who delivered a most appropriate and thrillingly eloquent address. We would not attempt to given even a synopsis of it, so carried away were we with its effect upon the people that we could not take a note but stood, feeling with delight its effect upon our self and watching the feelings of others as their animated countenances told that the touch of eloquence was forcing the tell-tale blood to their faces. Frequent outbursts of applause interrupted the speaker and a hearty vote of thanks was returned for his eloquent address. We must say one thing about Mr. Walker's address; it was written and written too in a few hours, for he was captured as he was aiming to pass the Point. In this case captured property proved to be "A No. 1".

After the address by Mr. Walker, the procession was reformed in the same order and took up the line of march from the point at the head of Viand Street. The column received the Hearse and Casket containing the remains of some of the heroes of Point Pleasant that were killed in the battle. These were exhumed on yesterday and today, under the supervision of the Committee, Dr. Barbee Superintending in person. Here the Cadets with reversed arms and muffled drums took their position as an escort. The column moved down Main Street, to the Kanawha River and filed to the right, where the bones of our slain heroes were re-interred with military honors. At the grave the beautiful burial service of the Church was read by the Ministers present in the column.

As the procession was moving down Main Street, first the Court House Bell, then the bell of the M. E. Church, South, were tolled, whilst the minute gun was fired by the Artillery Company. The drums were muffled and the band played an appropriate piece, thus giving solemnity to the exercises.

Just before the benediction was pronounced, a vote of thanks was returned to the Morgantown Cadets, to the Knights of Pythias, Band and Artillery, of Gallipolis, Ohio, to the Ravenswood Band, and all others who had aided in the Centennial Celebration.

The crowd then dispersed, the Cadets marched to the Kline House, where three rousing, hearty cheers were given them by all present; the Knights took up their line of march toward their homes at Gallipolis, and the other organizations went also to their homes. The Cadets took the steamer Clara Scott for Charleston.

Thus ended the First Centennial Celebration of the Battle of Point Pleasant. We say in concluding our description of it, from morning till night; each one that had a given part to perform, vied with the other as to which could do it best. All acted well their parts.

There may have been, but we did not see, a single drunken man on the ground.

The Point Pleasant Brass Band has done better than its most sanguine friends had hoped for it, both during the celebration of today and the three days of the Fair. May it still continue to improve—

we can stand the hum drum of practice for the sake of such a treat as they have given us in the last few days.

Let us all now go to work earnestly and determinedly to make the "Unveiling of the Monument" as decided a success as the Celebration of today—but let us make it wider in its extent. Let us make it State and National. Come up, one and all with what you can do with money and influence and we shall have the pleasure of chronicling at the end of another year, the success of the enterprise inaugurated today. There will be some "croaking" as a matter of course—some men grumble even at the wisdom and benevolence of the Infinite God—but let us, who are determined to succeed in the enterprise before us, turn a deaf ear to all croaking, and the more they croak, the more determined let us become. One hundred years ago was a great historical epoch of Point Pleasant. Today has been another. Let one year from today be another. Who dares say "nay?" What citizen of Mason County, or West Virginia, or Virginia, or Ohio, or Kentucky, or the United States, could refuse to aid in doing honor to the heroes of Point Pleasant?"

BRIEF MENTION

"In the midst of the throng of the Centennial celebration, we noticed many of the direct descendants of the warriors of one hundred years ago and will recall the names of them as far as we can: There were the Easthams, the Somervilles, Jas. Arbuckle, Jr., of Greenbrier, John D. Lewis, of Kanawha, the Lewises, of Mason. Mrs. Agnes Sehon, who had two grandfathers in this great battle, (Col. Charles Lewis and Col. John Stuart,) who is also the first representative of four living generations who were upon the ground and who are lineal descendants of the two pioneers—Cols. Lewis and Stuart. The fourth generation was represented by her great grandchild, little Grafton Tyler, who is now some three or four years old. Mrs. Sehon was probably the only person on the ground that could say as much— John Waddell, of Ohio, was also present and had swung around his shoulder the powder-horn and bullet pouch, carried by his father in the Battle of Point Pleasant on the 10th day of October, 1774. The Hannans, the Clendennins, the Millers, of Mason

County, the Clendennins, the Hannans, the Millers of Ohio. There were a number of others present whose names we did not ascertain."

On October 22nd, the Register published the speech of Dr. Thos. Creigh, of Virginia, delivered on the occasion of the anniversary of the battle, which we quote in part:

"I am glad I am here because I witness a scene, (and I appeal to the best and oldest historians here present for the truth of the remark, that such a scene of moral sublimity, except the signing of the Declaration of Independence, has never been presented to the people of these United States as is presented here today.) And what is that scene? I see around me some two thousand people with the descendants of the heroes of the Battle of Point Pleasant, to the third and fourth generation, on this 10th day of October, 1874,— under a bright October sun, one hundred years after the battle,— assembled on the battle-field, following the lofty instincts of our nature, to gather the bones of their ancestors, place them in a metallic coffin, catch the inspiration of their ever living virtue and valor, and determining to place a high and enduring monument to their memory. Yes sir, to erect a monument high and lofty on the banks between the Great Kanawha and Ohio, to overlook these two great rivers, the music of whose waters will mingle with the names forever, where the passengers on board your vast merchant steamers, sailing on these great commercial highways, shall see it and as they pass by uncover their heads and toll from the bell a requiem to their memory, and where the valiant youth of our country shall in all future time come to worship at this shrine, study their character, imitate their virtues and be inspired by their lofty deeds of patriotism, and where boys and girls in happy bands shall come for long centuries and cover this marble column with the cypress and the vine, and the immortal flower."

"Yes, sir, build this marble column to their memory, for they were "tall and grand" old warriors. Do you know why I say "tall and grand?" they are not original terms with me. I will tell you where I got them. Old Pool, a colored man, was the body servant of Col. John Stuart, of Greenbrier at the battle and witnessed the fight at Pt. Pleasant, and took part in it. Old Dick Pointer, another colored man, was the hero of Donnelley's Fort, near Lewisburg, Greenbrier County, and for his bravery, was freed by the Legislature of Virginia, and received a pension. Col. Ben Smith, our orator, was no doubt a member of the Virginia Legislature at that time. Old Pool and Old Dick were talking over their battles in Lewisburg one day when I was a school boy, and we school boys were all standing by and listening. Pool and Dick became very much excited in telling what each had done. Dick says the Indian is taller than the white man for I killed Indians as high as the court house. No, says Pool, if you could have seen Mas. John and Charles and James, in the fight at the Point, when fire flew out of their eyes like the fire out of their guns; they were just as tall and grand as the old trees on Kanawha. That is the reason why I say they were "tall and grand old warriors."

"But, sir, history informs us that there was a man by the name of George Washington, who had a high opinion of the companies of these Point Pleasant, warriors, for he said in a dark hour of his campaign to his wearied and dispirited army on the plains of New Jersey, "only give me the men to place the standard of my country on the mountains of West Augusta and I will call around me the men who shall make my country free. These "tall and grand" warriors were West Augusta men, and Washington knew them."

"Yes, build a monument of enduring marble to the memory of those old grand warriors, for you may look down the long picture gallery of history and you will find no brighter or grander names than the men of 1774 and 1776. Nor let us forget their characters, or their great principles of civil liberty, or insult the spirit of liberty."

While the Register of December 10, 1774, gives the following account of the committee:

The Point Pleasant Monument Association held their first meeting in the law office of John W, English, Esq., on December 4th, 1874. All the members of the Committee, viz: W. E. Hill, F. A. Guthrie and John W. English were present. On motion, John W. English, was called to the chair; and on further motion, was made permanent Chairman. On motion, C. E. Hogg, was elected Secretary, and T. Stribling, Treasurer. On motion, the Committee was ordered to inquire into the title of the land on which the monument is to be erected. On motion, the Committee was directed to see Drs. Shaw and Moore with reference to subscription papers and also ascertain how much money is in their hands belonging to the Association, and to pay the same to the Treasurer. On motion, the Association adjourned to meet Thursday evening, December 17th, 1874."

While no report has been preserved of the Monument Association, founded on October 10, 1874, the work of procuring funds was taken up by the Mason County Representatives in the Legislature of West Virginia, Hon. Edmund Sehon, descendant of Col. Charles Lewis introducing the bill in the lower house, while Hon. P. C. Eastham, descendant of George Eastham, of the Battle of Point Pleasant, introduced the bill in the upper house. On Feb. 25, 1875, the Legislature passed a bill carrying an appropriation of $3,500.00 to aid in the purchase of land and the erection of a monument in commemoration of the Battle of Point Pleasant, the President and Secretary of the Monument Association to have charge of the erection of said monument, the parties investing the money with approved security, awaiting assistance from other states. No further action was taken until Feb. 26, 1897, when the Legislature adopted a Joint Resolution by which Governor Geo. W. Atkinson appointed Judge John W. English, Dr. A. R. Barbee and Judge F. A. Guthrie as custodians of the fund appropriated by the Legislature.

The matter again lay dormant and no effort was made either to collect the funds or secure further appropriations.

That the State and Point Pleasant was not free from censure for their dereliction of duty, we quote in part from the Kingwood Argus of June 29, 1899, copied in the State Gazette July 4th, of that year:

"We were at Point Pleasant and visited the graves of the almost forgotten dead who fell in that memorable battle and we were surprised and indignant to find the place almost surrounded by stables and hog pens and lying along a back alley with not a mark of any kind to designate the spot; not even a fence or wall around the place and no one could find it without a guide who knew just where it was. It was only a very small plot of ground, in someone else's back yard, with stables on two sides of it and a garden on another side and the only way to get to it is down a dirty alley.

Nearly a hundred pioneers of that section who fell in that battle, fighting old Cornstalk for possession of the beautiful land along the

Ohio River lie buried there, unmarked and almost forgotten. It is a burning shame and disgrace on the town to allow it.

We went up to a newspaper office and made a vigorous kick about it and learned that money had been appropriated by the State and also quite a sum raised by the ladies of Point Pleasant to erect a monument to these heroes, dead defenders of our country. Now let justice and decency compel a disposition of this matter. The State or the town should take charge and secure some contiguous ground to the resting place which cannot be called a cemetery or even a graveyard, as it is now, and make a little park out of it with a fence around it and erect a handsome monument on the center of the site and make a decent way to get to it by removing some of the adjoining stables and hog pens."

The State Gazette appended the following editorial comment:
"We think the suggestion that the park and monument should be contiguous to the resting place of the dead heroes and should include it as well as the site of the old fort is the correct solution. The Argus will no doubt be surprised to learn that there are suggestions now made that the monument be placed away up on the Ohio bank, twelve squares from the site of the old fort and the grave of Col. Lewis and others, and suggestions that it be placed back on the hill overlooking the town."

There is no mention of the celebration of the anniversary of that year 1899 save the local newspaper account that,

"Today, October 10, 1899, is the one hundred and twenty-fifth anniversary of the Battle of Point Pleasant, fought between General Andrew Lewis and Cornstalk, the sachem of many nations and no citizen evidenced any interest save Col. G. B. Thomas, the Postmaster, who decorated the Post Office with flags."

No further agitation of the subject appeared in the local newspapers save that of the State Gazette of April 21, 1890, urging the organization of a Chapter of Daughters of the American Revolution and Sons of the Revolution here, looking forward to proper recognition of the Battle of Point Pleasant in which it said:

"Here was fought the first battle of the Revolution and why should not this town and county boast of the largest patriotic organizations in the State."

No further steps were taken at Point Pleasant looking to a monument appropriation until February 11, 1901, when Mrs. Livia Simpson-Poffenbarger issued a call for the organization of a Chapter of the Daughters of the American Revolution which is of date of Feb. 14, 1909, reported as follows in the State Gazette:

"A sufficient number of ladies met at the home of Mrs. George Poffenbarger yesterday to organize a Chapter of the Daughters of the American Revolution. As soon as the requirements are duly met, a Charter will be granted. This is a most commendable move and should meet with the support and best wishes of the entire town."

At this meeting it was explained that the chief motive in organizing this patriotic society was that an organized effort might be made to secure funds for the erection of a Battle Monument at Point Pleasant and the recognition of the battle as that of the first Battle of the Revolution.

On Feb. 26, 1901, a call was issued for the organization of a Chapter of Sons of the Revolution and the State Gazette of that issue said editorially:

"This is a move in the right direction. This is the historic spot of the first battle of the Revolution. In order that history may accord us that place with due credit, we must first show that Point Pleasant appreciates this fact. If the spot is to be properly marked and receive from the National Government the appropriation and recognition for a splendid monument that the battle deserves, we must first show that the memory is dear to us."

On Feb. 29, 1901, the Daughters of the American Revolution were formally organized and the name selected was that of Col. Charles Lewis, named for one of the best beloved heroes of those who fell at the Battle of Point Pleasant. At that meeting the Daughters in conformity with the statement of Governor White that he would appoint one man outside of Point Pleasant and two resident members of the commission to look after the funds, the ladies recommended V.

A. Lewis of Mason and P. S Lewis and C. C. Bowyer of Point Pleasant, but the Governor later decided to appoint but one man in Point Pleasant and the Commission named was John P. Austin, C. C. Bowyer and V. A. Lewis. On March 11, 1901, Mr. Joe Friedman not only presented the Col. Charles Lewis Chapter the money with which to pay for their charter, but also for the purchase of their record books and proffered when a monument was completed to donate a splendid band and Speaker's stand.

The State Gazette of March 11, 1901, says:
"The new committee to be appointed should first secure the grounds. This would be the beginning looking toward the end. Then the old buildings could be cleared away, grading done, grass sown, trees set out and the grounds beautified. These all take time to bring them to perfection. There is sufficient money all ready subscribed, together with what could be secured, by private subscription to do this much handsomely. The government could then be presented the ground as a National Historic Park and the War Department under the head of Rivers and Harbors could be induced to grade the banks bordering on both rivers and they would then be forever taken care of. Besides, its historic significance, it is in point of beauty of location the most desirable site in town. The view is splendid from both rivers. The view from the surrounding hills is perfect and it would give strangers a different opinion of the town from the ragged appearance it now has from rail and river."

On April 18, 1901, the newly appointed Monument Commissioners gave bond before the Mason County Court with approved security and when they had met for organization, John P. Austin was elected President and C. C. Bowyer Treasurer and V. A. Lewis Secretary.

The issue of May 28, 1901, of the State Gazette says:
"The Battle Monument Commission held a meeting at the Merchants National Bank Saturday last. The members composing the commission Hon. John P. Austin, President, Hon. V. A. Lewis, Secretary and Hon. C. C. Bowyer, Treasurer, together with other citizens and a State Gazette Reporter went down to the Kanawha point where had stood the old fort and where some of the heroes of

the Battle of Point Pleasant were buried and made a careful inspection of the grounds. The public seem generally united in the belief that this is the proper place to erect the monument and it might be said that the property bounded by Main and First Streets and the two rivers will be purchased shortly by the Commission, provided the owners of the property do not demand too exorbitant a price."

On Decoration Day, May 30th, 1901, for the first time a public memorial exercise was held, whereby the graves of the heroes of the Battle of Point Pleasant were decorated, in charge of the D. A. R, and G. A. R. societies of the town. A large concourse of people attended the exercises. The State Gazette of June 18, 1901, records that *"John D. McCulloch had given an option on his property on the monument site for $1,000 00; C. H. Varian $1,200.00; Geo. T., Chas. and Henry Stone $3,000.00; Thos. Durst $600.00, a total of $5,800.00, which includes all the contemplated territory needed except the Geo. Comstock property, upon which a price had not been agreed."* Later Mr. Comstock's property was secured at $2,200.00.

From the issue of August, 1901, of the Charleston Daily Mail's report of the Monument Commission, held at that place we glean the following:

"Hon. V. A. Lewis reported that the Commission had about $11,000.00 in the treasury, but that the work, as planned would necessitate the expenditure of $25,000.00 more."

Speaking of the Battle of Point Pleasant, the Daily Mail quotes Mr. Lewis as follows: **"All careful, painstaking, thoughtful historians have regarded it as the first in the series of the Revolution which gave the continent to liberty. It was the chief event of Dunmore's War."**

On August 29, 1901, the State Gazette announced that the Committee had decided to commence clearing the grounds at once and that paper made the first appeal for the Celebration of the Battle:

"It is the intention that the clearing of the grounds shall be completed by the anniversary of the great Battle of Point Pleasant, Oct. 10, 1774."

"The significance of the battle has not been wholly overlooked. Thousands know of its importance and it remains for Point Pleasant herself to appreciate her relation to history and demand from the State and from Congress the substantial recognition due this spot. Our citizens should join in one glorious celebration of this anniversary October 10. We trust that there is enough patriotism in the town to observe it. If in no other way, let it be one grand union picnic. The weather will be fine and all can come together at least in the spirit of patriotism and good fellowship".

Mrs. Poffenbarger, editor of the State Gazette, not only issued a call for a citizen's meeting on Thursday night September 5th, looking toward the celebration, but she had secured the cooperation of Col. J. P. R. B. Smith and, at that meeting donated the services of her paper to advertise the meeting, supplemented by a subscription secured by her of over $200.00 with which to begin the work. The paper of that issue contained the following full page advertisement, besides the names of the donors of cash:

127th ANNIVERSARY
The First Battle of the Revolution
to be celebrated at
POINT PLEASANT, W. VA.
Thursday Oct. 10th, 1901.

Great National Speakers will be present. Entertainment for the people, excursions on all railroads and steamboats will be arranged for.

The Old Log Mansion built in 1796 that has lived in three centuries will be used to exhibit the greatest lot of Historic Relics ever brought together in West Virginia, outside the Historical Society at Charleston.

EVERY ONE INVITED

The monument Park and Court House yard will make fine picnic grounds. Watch this space for attractions as they are secured."

As a result of the meeting at the court house committees were organized and Mrs. Poffenbarger participated in the work of all the committees. The issue of September 19 shows an additional subscription, making a total of $409.00, besides generous subscriptions, of exhibits for the museum. The children of the public schools contributed $8.50 to be used in decorating a wagon for the parade. The newspapers of the country stood up and took notice of the big celebration and helped advertise it.

In the issue of Oct. 10th, The State Gazette announced the presence of distinguished visitors, among whom was Gen. C. H. Grosvenor of Ohio, faithful advocate for an appropriation from Congress to commemorate the battle. Virgil A. Lewis, in an article published in the State Gazette of that date, said:

"After all, even though it be here, is it best to assert without reference to the proof that the Battle of Point Pleasant is the first battle of the Revolution and then array against us the whole of New England where the people are jealous of the claims of Lexington. It is easy to make assertions, but to examine hundreds of volumes and obtain records from both Europe and America in proof of the same, is quite another thing. Do not throw the burden of proof of this matter on a committee before a Congressional Committee."

The State Gazette of October 17, 1901, announced that the Mansion House had, been turned over to three ladies who had accepted it as a headquarters for the Col. Charles Lewis Chapter D. A. R. Also that work on Tu-Endie-Wei Park had been discontinued for want of funds and made an appeal that the Commission set out trees on the edge of the Park or permit the citizens to do so. Also the list of subscribers to the expense of the Celebration. While the following is the published account of the big celebration:

THEY CAME
From Every Direction
Ten Thousand People Celebrated the 127th Anniversary of the

First Battle of the Revolution
Tu-Endie-Wei Park

On last Thursday the good citizens of Point Pleasant celebrated the 127th anniversary of the Battle of Point Pleasant, the first battle of the Revolution.

It only needed for our people to arouse themselves and make the effort to have one of the biggest celebrations ever held in the state. Beside our people, who were for the most part upon our streets, enough more swelled the crowd until we had fully ten thousand celebrating. Heretofore, when we had any demonstration in the town, the crowd was from the Ohio River landing to the Court House. This time the streets were crowded from the Court House to the Kanawha River, with fully five thousand people upon the Park.

The K. & M. Railroad ran a dollar excursion from Athens to this place and Point Pleasant can never forget the kindness of that road. When we solicited them for a cheap rate they replied if it would be any accommodation to Point Pleasant and they only made it pay expense of running the train they would give it to us to show to Point Pleasant the kindly feeling of that road toward our town. They not only gave us just the service we asked for but they put out 15,000 attractive band bills and advertised their rates in the newspapers along the route, and when they came in here they brought us not only the Nelsonville and Middleport bands, but they brought a big train packed with people from Athens and way stations. They brought us Gen. Chas. H. Grosvenor, one of the stalwart Sons of the Revolution who came to address our people and promote the success of the day. The K. & M. brought us a train of eight or ten coaches from Charleston that had standing room only and while the excursion was profitable to the K. & M., and we are glad it was, we must not forget that it was run wholly to compliment Point Pleasant. The conduct of the K. & M. was greatly in contrast to that of the Ohio River Division of the B. & O. R. R. who were importuned by letter, in person, and by telegraph, to give us a rate, but of no avail, and notwithstanding full fair was charged, that road brought in crowds of people with a crowded train from the north and standing room only coming in from the south end. Steamboats brought in excursions and hacks ran between here and Gallipolis while six hundred persons crossed the

Kanawha Ferry and as many more had to be ferried in private boats in harbor. The farmers came in carriages, buggies, expresses, big wagons, horseback and on foot, any way so they came, and they came as a multitude.

"Notwithstanding the rain, the night before, which was just enough to lay the dust, the sun shone out about eight o'clock and the day was ideal."

"Never before did the old town wear such a gala dress. Old Glory and buntings galore waved from every residence and business house. There was neither the difference of politics or religion nor even the distinction of secret organizations to mar the occasion, but all came together upon a common level for one grand glorification of the celebration of the battle, the farthest reaching in its effect of any battle ever fought upon the American Continent—the first battle of the Revolution—the battle that broke the power of the red men in America; the battle that brought the treaty that enabled civilization to march on to the west and southwest and great northwest territory; the battle that resulted in ceding to Virginia and thence to the colonies the great Northwest; that battle that defied at its close Tory misrule, the first battle ever fought after the tea had been thrown overboard at Boston Harbor the preceding March. The Boston Port Bill, of May, 1774, the signal for actual conflict had been passed. The House of Burgesses, of Virginia, had declared the first of June of that year to be *"A day of fasting, imploring the Divine interposition to avert the heavy calamity which threatened destruction to their civil rights and the evils of a civil war."* Massachusetts had passed resolutions deploring the oppression of Great Britain. Patrick Henry had made his famous speech before the House of Burgesses of Virginia, declaring that *"The war is inevitable, and let it come,"* and asked *"Is life so dear or peace so sweet as to be purchased at the price of chains and slavery?"*

England, too, recognized before the Battle of Point Pleasant that the war was inevitable and determined to keep the colonists so busy defending themselves from hostile Indians armed with English muskets and English ammunition, that they would have no time to think of the wrongs inflicted upon them by the mother country. Great Britain never had a better tool than Lord Dunmore, the Tory Governor of Virginia, as his subsequent conduct proved. Hence, the

Battle of Point Pleasant, (in which Lord Dunmore intended the flower of the Colonial Army of Virginia to be destroyed but which, victorious to his surprise) became the first battle in which the blood of patriots was spilled upon American soil for the cause of National Independence, and was so credited by Alexander S. Withers, in his chronicles of Border warfare, later by Bancroft, the Government historian, by President Roosevelt, in his "Winning the West," and by many other historians, of repute.

Is it any wonder that we point with pride to this battle and invited the whole country to celebrate with us?"

At ten o'clock the parade began to form on First Street and it was of such magnitude that it took Col. J. P. R. B. Smith, the Grand Marshall of the day, and his corps of splendid assistants, an hour to get them all in line ready for march. It was headed by James Somerville, of Pleasant Flats, dressed as Uncle Sam, (and in face and figure he is typical of the figurative head of the nation,) all the city fathers, except Mayor Somerville, who acted as a marshal, were in the parade in carriages, The fire department were out with their wagon decorated. There were floats galore, put in by the business men of the town, vying with each other to see which could make the finest display. The three splendid bands, Cheshire, Middleport and Nelsonville, discoursed sweet music along the route and the children of the white schools marching in line wearing boutonnieres of national colors, waving flags, which little girls representing the states and territories, and the colored children on a wagon beautifully decorated made the prettiest parade ever seen in Point Pleasant.

What might have been a serious accident, but proved to be a fortunate escape, occurred when a wagon with 103 children on it passed over a culvert on 14th Street. The culvert went down and the top of the wagon was separated in the lunge from the platform and the children were precipated to the ground. Fortunately no one was hurt and the procession preceded down Main Street to First, the children falling in line with the others in the line of march, where they disbanded. Three open air concerts were given from 1 to 2 o'clock when the speaking began from a platform at the grounds recently purchased as a site for a monument yet to be erected. The grounds are situated at the junction of the Kanawha and Ohio Rivers, without doubt the most beautiful site for a park on the Ohio River.

The large audience was called to order by Col. J. P. R. B. Smith, who called our distinguished fellow townsmen, Hon. C. E. Hogg to the chair. Mr. Hogg in his usual pleasing manner did the honors of the occasion with credit to himself and to Point Pleasant. Mr. Hogg then introduced Mrs. Livia Simpson-Poffenbarger, Regent of Col. Chas. Lewis Chapter of the Daughters of the American Revolution, who had been designated by her Chapter to dedicate and name the park which she did in a short-address, as follows:

"Mr. Chairman, Ladies and Gentleman:

It has been deemed fitting and appropriate, that, by some means this beautiful and historic spot of ground be dedicated to the noble purpose for which it has been purchased, and given a name by which it may be known in the future. The important duty has not been sought by the organization I have the honor to represent. I wish to emphasize the fact, without going into explanation or detail, that it has been rather thrust upon us. We are simply doing that which has been denied to others who have been invited to do it, by their situation and present circumstances. We have accepted the trust and assumed the duty in the absence of others who might, and we sincerely believe, would have preformed it better.

However, I wish to premise that it is not at all inappropriate that the Society of the Daughters of the American Revolution perform this most important function. Ours is purely a patriotic organization and our work is carried on in the name of patriotism and inspired by love of country. The objects and purposes of our society are set forth in our constitution, Article 1, as follows:

(1) "To perpetuate the memory of the spirit of the men and women who achieved American Independence, by the acquisition and protection of historical spots, and the erection of monuments; by the encouragement to historical research in relation to the Revolution and the publication of its results; by the preservation of documents and relics and of the records of individual services of Revolutionary soldiers and patriots, and by the promotion of celebrations of all patriotic anniversaries.

(2) To carry out the injunction of Washington in his farewell address to the American people, "To promote as an object of primary

importance, institutions for the general diffusion of knowledge," thus developing an enlightened opinion, and affording to young and old such advantages as shall develop in them the largest capacity for performing the duties of American citizens.

(3) To cherish, maintain and to extend the institutions of American freedom, to foster true patriotism and love of country and to aid in securing for mankind all the blessings of liberty."

"Another thing I wish to impress upon all here today is the fact that ours is the only society professing to be founded exclusively upon our Revolutionary struggle that recognizes the Battle of Point Pleasant as a part of the war for American independence. Reputable historians, including Bancroft, President Roosevelt and others have asserted that it was the initial, the first battle of the Revolutionary war. Moreover, they have produced the indisputable evidence upon which the assertion is based. What the consensus of American opinion will be as the years shall roll on and historical research shall bring to light the whole truth, we cannot say. If the verdict shall be the affirmative of that proposition then the first battle shall not be lacking in display of heroism and patriotism, exhibited in the midst of an almost interminable wilderness and hand to hand with a savage and at the same time valorous foe."

"The memory of that great struggle, will, we think, be well and fittingly preserved upon these grounds. A splendid and enduring monument is to be erected commemorative of the battle. On some part of it will be a bronze statue of the heroic Andrew Lewis, the commanding general. On it will be inscribed in imperishable letters the names of the brave Col. Chas. Lewis and Col. Fields and all those who fell with them in defense of liberty and the homes of our race. On these grounds will be laid down and preserved the outlines of old Fort Randolph.

Without some reference to the stubborn foe which drew the brilliant flash of fire from the steel of these heroes, in the shades of primeval forests, far from the abode of any white man, this history written in grounds, stone, marble and bronze would be incomplete. The red men were fighting for their homes and hunting grounds. From their standpoint, their conduct was patriotic. They were defending the graves of their fathers."

To the end, therefore, that history, as far as possible, may be fully preserved and patriotism, in its broadest sense may be recognized, it has been decided to give this park the oldest —first name it has ever been known to possess—its Indian name. By authority of the Monument Commission appointed by the Governor of this state, and in the name of the Society of the Daughters of the American Revolution, we now dedicate this park, the property of the State of West Virginia, to patriotism and the preservation of history and name it "Tu-Endie-Wei Park," which signifies in the Shawnee tongue "the mingling of waters," this being the junction of two rivers."

Mr. Hogg next introduced Col. Bennett H. Young, of Louisville, Ky., who had been previously invited to address the Assembly and no happier selection could have been made. The people as a unit fell in love with the man. He talked directly to their hearts and we fortunately secured his speech which is reproduced in this issue of the State Gazette. Col. Young also loaned, for the occasion, his pioneer suit, which consisted of a hunting shirt and flint lock gun which had belonged to Daniel Boone, which he had completed by the addition of a "long knife," leather breeches and a coon skin cap. Herman Snyder was selected to wear the suit, being smooth shaved and corresponding in weight and height to Daniel Boone.

Col. Young was followed by our poet laureate, Louis Reed Campbell, who recited in splendid style his poem, written for the occasion:

OUR HEROES

Grave by grave, where the rivers meet,
and gently flow.
The patriot sleeps, and by his side,
a vanquished silent foe.

Year on year with,
wondrous swiftness glided by.
And yet no stone was reared,
where brave men dared to die.

Time's hand was in the game,
that drove the Indian from his land.
In it the shadow of a wrong,

that greed could not withstand.

More than a century gone,
ere right doth o'er wrong prevail.
Alike we honor, now, who faced,
The feathered shaft and rifles' deadly hail.

Departed chieftain of a mighty race,
so soon to disappear!
What does the future hold,
save memory, softened by a tear?

For even now adown
the changing slope of fleeting time
The painted warrior glides away,
to leave no trail behind.

No power can dim the luster now
of that victorious band,
Who fought and fell and fired again
where now we stand.

If fairness to the foe is due,
what honor must be theirs,
Whose names too sacred for a eulogy,
drift upward with our prayers."

The following is taken from the Point Pleasant Observer of October 17, 1901:

"TU-ENDIE-WEI PARK."

A Great Outpouring of the People at its Dedication Last Thursday.
A Gala Day for Point Pleasant

"We have not space to tell of the big celebration on Thursday the 10th. This means that if we were to take up every inch of space in the whole paper we could not tell all about it. So we will have to tell a little about it and let the rest go."

"Day dawned bright and clear with never a cloud to remind one of the little sprinkle of the night before. The town was profusely decorated with flags and bunting. The first signal of the coming dawn was announced by the watchman on the site of Old fort Randolph, who was in charge of the relics, firing the morning gun. Immediately after this the church bells begun to ring, say at 5 o'clock, and the mill whistles and those of the steamboats began to blow until not only everybody in town, but everyone within five miles of the town, was wide awake.

By eight o'clock, the country people were pouring into town in streams from every direction. All roads led to Point Pleasant and all roads were full. At half past nine the trains began to pour their loads into town and by 10 o'clock the crowd was variously estimated from 6,000 to 10,000 people. At 10 o'clock Col. J. P. R. B. Smith began to form the huge mass of people into a line of march and even with his able assistants it was a Herculean task. Finally the parade was formed and headed by Col. James Somerville and a platoon of police followed by Grand Marshall J. P. R. B. Smith, the large procession moved over the principal streets of the town and at last ended at the beautiful park at the junction of the two rivers."

"The parade consisted of the town officers in carriages, citizens in carriages, citizens on horseback, people on foot, the children of the public schools, both white and colored, some in wagons and some on foot, with three brass bands, interspersed at regular intervals, and all interspersed With display made by our merchants until the whole presented a scene of beauty. Merchants from other towns who inform the newspaper people of Point Pleasant that it does no good to advertise here were also glad to have a place in the big parade and were not ashamed to be the lustiest howlers for Point Pleasant's big day."

After the people had gotten something to eat they again assembled at the park and were called to order by J. P. R. B. Smith who called Hon. C. E. Hogg one of this district's distinguished ex-congressmen to the chair. Mr. Hogg after a short but eloquent address introduced Mrs. George Poffenbarger, Regent of Col. Chas. Lewis chapter of the Daughters of the American Revolution who, in a short address, and by authority of the Monument Commissions named the beautiful plot of ground "Tue-Endie-Wei" Park, "Tue-Endie-Wei" in the Shawnee language meaning "the mingling of the waters."

Chairman Hogg next introduced Col. Bennet H. Young of Louisville, Ky., after which Louis Reed Campbell recited an original poem written for the occasion entitled "Our Heroes." Next followed Gen. Chas. H. Grosvenor of Ohio, who delivered a characteristic Grosvenor address. The program of the day was concluded by the burial of the remains of "MAD ANN BAILEY," which had been disinterred from their resting place of 76 years and brought here for burial, thus carrying out her desire, expressed more than three quarters of a century ago, to be buried on Virginia soil."

"The museum contained large number of historic relics which held the interest of the vast crowd from early morn to the leaving time of the late rain and steamboat in the evening."

The Huntington Advertizer of October 11, 1901, said:

"The Huntingtonians who visited Point Pleasant yesterday returned last evening happy over the exercises of the day."

"It was the proudest and most memorable in the life of that historic community. Amid an assembly of ten thousand persons, many of whom had come half way across the continent to be present, the beautiful grove at the junction of the Kanawha and Ohio Rivers, was forever dedicated to the memory of the gallant Virginians who, one hundred and twenty-seven years ago, gave to the world the first manifestation of that valor, which in after years, broke the power of Great Britain and made this continent the abiding place of civil liberty."

"No spot in the Ohio Valley is so full of historical significance as the old town of Point Pleasant. No spot will be more beautiful when the towering granite shaft, to be erected at an estimated cost of forty thousand dollars, shall greet the eye of the stranger as he approaches this true cradle of American liberty."

Quoting from the Gallia Times of October 9th, we find.

"Much interest is being taken by the Point Pleasant people in the coming anniversary of the Indian battle fought there. This was on October 10, 1774, or 127 years ago, and, on this day the power of the Red Men in the Kanawha and Ohio Valleys was wrested from them. The day should long be remembered and we believe will be fittingly celebrated by our neighbor city."

The Gallipolis Journal of October 9th, said:
BATTLE
of Point Pleasant will be
Celebrated on Thursday next

"Our neighbors across the river are making extensive preparations for the celebration of the Battle of Point Pleasant, the first conflict of the Revolution, on Thursday Oct. 10. It was in 1774 that the most desperate Indian battle on record was fought between the confederated Indian tribes, under the celebrated chief Cornstalk and the Virginia Militia under command of Gen. Andrew Lewis."

"There will be a relic display and a big parade. The old log mansion that has stood in three centuries will be among the other relics of primitive days. Gen. Grosvenor and Col. Bennett Young, of Louisville, one of Kentucky's most magnetic speakers, will be present at the celebration. The remains of Ann Bailey, the heroine of the revolution, have been disinterred and will be consigned to their new resting place on Thursday. There will be three bands and a most interesting program and the 10th promises to be an eventful day at Point Pleasant"

The following is from the Weekly Register, of Point Pleasant, W. Va., under the date of October 17, 1901:

THE CELEBRATION
Of the One Hundred and Twenty-Seventh
Anniversary of the Battle of Point Pleasant
Thousands of Visitors Within our Gates
The Celebration a Success in Every Particular and the day will be
long remembered by all present.

"Despite the cloudy weather and rain of Wednesday, Thursday morning, October 10th, 1901, dawned with the old Sol and a twinkle in his eye, to the gratification of the committees in charge and the citizens of our little city in general for clear and favorable weather meant for the celebration of the first battle of the Revolution, (fought at Point Pleasant on October 10, 1774, between the whites under command of Colonel Charles Lewis, and the Indians,) unbounded and unprecedented success.

The committees in charge of this, the 127th anniversary of this great battle, have been earnest workers to accomplish this end, and deserve much credit for their untiring efforts.

The genial Marshall in chief, Colonel J. P. R. B. Smith and his assistants, hand-led the big parade which was formed in the first ward in a manner creditable to a general with an army of 100,000.

In the parade was a representation of all our business people, the children of our public schools turning out in full, dressed in national colors, companies of horsemen, the fire department, the hook and ladder company, and everything and everybody to make up a grand trades display the like of which has never before been seen in Point Pleasant."

"To say the town was gaily decorated with bunting, flags, &c, is not necessary, for the emblem of our great nation was never so profusely displayed as on this occasion."

"The park at the confluence of the Ohio and Kanawha Rivers where the monument to commemorate this great battle will be erected, has been put in the best proper shape, and was thronged with visitors and sightseers throughout the day."

"The old house, considerably over a hundred years old, which was converted into a museum and filled with relics, was the most interesting feature of the occasion."

"The ladies in charge of the museum are commended by our citizens and visitors upon the manner in which this "relic store" was conducted, and the courtesies accorded all."

"A collection of relics, such as Indian implements of warfare, old pictures, dishes, dresses, jewelry and many other articles too numerous to mention, are not seen by one generation more than once, and one who missed this treat is at loss to know or conceive the manner in which these old settlers lived and had their being. Bands of music delighted the visitors and the day was one of joy from morning until night. The crowd was orderly well behaved and jolly. No congregation of human beings had a more joyous time for one day, than did this one."

"After the parade, which moved at noon, and which was never surpassed as a trades display in this place, had disbanded and the throng of people had dined, the speaking at the park began."

"Hon. Chas. E. Hogg, one of West Virginia's most eloquent orators, had charge of the ceremonies at the speaker's stand, and his introductory remarks were well received. Mr. Hogg never fails to please and enlighten his hearer, and at the conclusion of his remarks introduced Mrs. Judge Poffenbarger, who opened the speaking with an address listened to by the throng of people with marked attention, and which was eloquent and instructive."

"Col. Bennett Young, of Jessamine County, Kentucky, member of Congress from his district, was introduced and to say his address was eloquent, logical and interesting, is but a trifle, for the marked attention of his hearers was undisturbed. He is a fluent speaker and one would never tire listening to him."

"Next to be introduced was Mr. Lewis Reed Campbell, who recited a beautiful poem, entitled "Our Heroes." This was one of the most beautiful, and being prepared as it was, only a few hours before the hour for delivery, places our young friend at the maximum. The manner in which this beautiful poem was delivered was pleasing in the extreme and delighted the immense crowd who listened with marked attention."

"Gen. Chas. H. Grosvenor, of Ohio, was next introduced, who made, as all know, an address second to none. The General is one of Ohio's influential and honored sons, and when he appeared on the speaker's stand, a smile of pleasure and gratification covered every face in the audience. General Grosvenor's remarks were listened to attentively, and his eulogy to our martyred President, was pathetic. Concluding his remarks, General Grosvenor said it would be well for Great Britain, had she a commander like "Cornstalk" at the head of her forces in South Africa, which was met with a round of applause."

"Space and time will not permit us to report this celebration as we would like to, but those who were here had a good time, enjoyed themselves and left our little city with the wish to soon return."

"The short-comings of our report of this big day are attributed to the absence of the editor in chief and had he been at the helm, our "chases" would not have held the flow from his pen and our "machines" would have been sorely overtaxed."

The Mail Tribune, Charleston, W. Va., Oct. 12, 1901, says:

"POINT PLEASANT Celebrates Important Anniversary Remarkable Demonstration in Honor of the Famous Battle Col. Bennet Young, of Ky., and Gen. Grosvenor, of Ohio, Principal Speakers"

"Point Pleasant, W. Va., Oct. 10th, 1901 was the proudest and most memorable in the life of this historic community. Before an assembly of 10,000 persons, many of whom had come half way across the continent to be present, when the beautiful grounds at the juncture of the Kanawha and Ohio Rivers was forever dedicated to the memory of the gallant Virginians, who, 127 years ago gave the first manifestation of that valor which, in after years, broke the power of Great Britain and made this continent the abiding place of civil liberty."

"No spot in the Ohio Valley is so full of historic significance as this old town of Point Pleasant, and no spot will be more beautiful when the towering granite shaft to be erected at an estimate of $50,000.00, shall greet the eye of the stranger as he approaches this true cradle of liberty."

"Gen. Chas. H. Grosvenor, of Ohio, in his speech, said in part:

"It is pleasant on this October day to reflect that here on the banks of the beautiful Ohio, then so remote from the center and homes of our ancestors as to be terra incognita to the people of our country and of the world there should have been struck that which turned out to be the first great blow for American Independence and American Liberty. Figure it as you may, the battle whose anniversary we here today celebrate, was the first real blow of the Revolutionary War. Nobody so understood it. Grant that, who understood what was to flow from Lexington or Concord or even from Bunker Hill? What was the name of the man who foresaw when the spring time grass of Massachusetts was reddened with the blood of patriots at Lexington that the blood was to sanctify the soil and result in the rights of the people for self government? Lord Dunmore was loyal to the source from which he derived his official dignity and official position. He was however, as appears by the records, not quite the open manly frank man that Americans love to recognize and honor. When he came to the mouth of the Big Hockhocking River, under promise to join the troops that he supposed were subordinate to him, he failed to join them for the manifest purpose of weakening their forces and thus enable the Indians to overcome the settlers. While he was not acting that manly, open and above-board part which Americans love to honor and recognize, but if the reports are true and conclusions are allowable, Lord Dunmore was guilty of an act of the basest treachery and a manifest purpose of the most inhuman outrage. But it cannot be lost sight of that even in this, shameful as his conduct was, he was acting in furtherance of his purposes to aid the government to which he owed allegiance. It may be that in his horoscope he saw the coming of the overthrow of British power in the colonies and the organization of a new government and the stripping of the British Crown of all it held so dear in the United States. However, much we may condemn, from the standpoint of our own sympathy, all and singular in their behalf, there is nevertheless more or less of mitigation of wrong and treachery and double dealing in the fact that he was doing it all in behalf of the country and sovereignty to which he owed allegiance. The colonies were proposing to fight for mitigation of the wrongs of unequal and unjust taxation and the refusal to them of the right of representation in the British law making body and yet out of that little movement which I have shown was only for the mitigation of wrong, came this the great idea, so suddenly developed, of independence, and from it has come all the glory of a mighty and united country."

While William Hunter, an eminent Ohio writer, of the Chilicothe Advertiser, says:

"It give us pleasure to note that the Battle of Point Pleasant is called the first battle of the Revolutionary War by those who are celebrating the anniversary, although questioned by New England historians who seem to believe that the whole war was fought in a radius of twenty miles of Boston, and the most has been made of every little skirmish in that region, while the battles in the Western country are not even mentioned."

State Historian V. A. Lewis again says, in the West. Virginia Historical Magazine, of the battle:

"It is the greatest event in the colonial period and stands just at its close. With it the Revolutionary Period begins. Hence the battle is as it were the connecting link between two of the great periods in all American History. Closing as it does the one, and opening the other.

Edward Ingle, writing in the Manufacturer's Record, in November, 1901, on the Preservation of Virginia's Antiquities, says:

"Andrew Lewis, not a Virginian, but yet a type of the rearguard of the Revolution, fought successfully at Point Pleasant in 1774, that which was really the first battle of that struggle and a battle far reaching in its significant results."

While a bill introduced by Senator Scott passed the Senate in 1905, carrying an appropriation, Senator Scott wrote and offered his personal check for one thousand dollars with which to erect the monument if the commission would abandon the idea of securing aid from the National Congress. A hasty conference of friends of the movement was held and the offer declined, as the agitators of the monument building were not only anxious that the Government should appropriate adequate funds, but that it should officially recognize the battle as one of those of the Revolution; so the offer of Senator Scott was politely declined. Congressman Hughes pressed the passage of the bill at that time in the lower house of Congress. Hon. J. T. McCleary, Chairman of the Committee to which the bill was referred, wrote a letter to Mr. Hughes, as follows:

"As I advised you yesterday, the committee adopted a policy more than a year ago as its policy for this Congress, that of making no appropriations for monuments to be erected outside of Washington."

The monument commission assisted by Mrs.. Poffenbarger, then hastened to Charleston, where the Legislature was then in session, and the Charleston Mail gives, in part, the following:

"Mrs. Livia Simpson-Poffenbarger arrived here Thursday from her home at Point Pleasant, to aid in securing an appropriation for a Point Pleasant Battle Monument. She has attended a part of two former sessions of the Legislature for the same purpose. When seen by a Mail reporter in the office of her husband Judge George

Poffenbarger, of the Supreme Court, she said in response to the question, when asked what the prospect for an appropriation is:

"It is the first time I have ever believed we would get an appropriation, when it was asked for. I believe now we are going to get it. We expect to get a recommendation for an appropriation through the Joint Finance Committee, and if we get a favorable report from the committee we have "crossed the Alps" for there is positively no opposition to it this year outside of whether or not there will be available funds."

"What amount have you asked for, Mrs. Poffenbarger?"

"I had a most courteous hearing before the committee who had previously heard the members of the Monument Committee and I asked for $25,000.00, payable $5,000.00 annually."

"But can the state make an appropriation covering five years?"

"No, but they can for two and the appropriation may be for a monument not to exceed $25,000.00 expense to the state of West Virginia, $5,000.00 of which is available now and $5,000.00 next year, and the rest may be implied, as in the case of the appropriation made for the West Virginia Hospital at a cost of $80,000, $10,000.00 of which was available when appropriated."

Here followed the history of the effort made for the erection of a monument.

Mrs. Poffenbarger telegraphed her paper:

Charleston, W. Va.,
February 28, 1905. The State Gazette—

The Senate at 6:30 P. M. passed an amendment to the Appropriation Bill of $2,500.00 for this year and $2,500.00 for 1906. The bill still has to go back to the House for concurrence and if it fails there, will go to a conference committee."

The amendment was offered by Senator E. S. McCown, of the Fourth Senatorial District. His speech was one of his best efforts while Senator Darst worked heart and soul for the appropriation. The amendment failed to pass the house, but was saved in the Joint Conference committee where by herculean work the building of a battle monument at Point Pleasant was assured. The state had once again assumed the responsibility and every year since the

Legislature has appropriated money with which to build the monument. Except this appropriation for 1906 and 1907, all has been vetoed except that of $1,000.00 made in 1909, because of lack of funds as announced by Governor Dawson.

Feb, 15. 1906, Hon. James A. Hughes, who was pressing Congress for an appropriation for funds with which to build the monument wrote as follows from Washington:

Mrs. Livia Simpson-Poffenbarger
Point Pleasant, W. Va.

I am in receipt of a letter from Mr. Austin who states that it is the opinion of the Monument Committee of your place that the amount asked for be reduced from $50,000.00 to $10,000.00."

"The amount carried in the bill does not amount to anything as the committee would only appropriate such an amount as they saw fit and would be governed by the wishes of the committee. I will introduce another bill carrying $10,000.00 instead of $50,000.00 as in the present bill. I had a talk with Mr. McCleary and he told me that the committee still had under consideration the advisability of whether they would make any appropriations outside of the City of Washington. So far, they have not come to any conclusion. I had a talk with Senator Scott in regard to this appropriation and he doubted very much whether they would make any appropriation outside the City of Washington and he advises that this monument should be erected and that it should be done by private subscription and in addition to what the State had already appropriated he said he would be glad to head the list with a private subscription."

"Now I want to advise you frankly about this, if the Library Committee of the House refuses to make any appropriations for monuments, outside of the City of Washington, I think it will be useless to press the matter further, and I think it would be well to consider the suggestion of Senator Scott.

I will be glad to hear from you in reference to the matter.

Very truly yours,
J. A. Hughes."

To the above letter, Mrs. Poffenbarger replied:

"We do not ask that the Congress of the United States build the Battle Monument at Point Pleasant because the funds cannot be raised by private subscription or secured as an appropriation from the State of West Virginia, but because we want the Government to officially recognize the battle as it was in truth, a battle of the Revolution, indeed, the First Battle of the Revolution and no matter how insignificant the approbation, if the bill correctly states its status we will be content to raise the money necessary as best we can, although we want as large an appropriation as we can get. While we appreciate the generosity of Senator Scott, should he donate the entire amount necessary it would fail in our main purpose of having the government officially credit the battle the honor it deserves and we will have again to decline his offer and insist that you both press the matter before Congress so vigorously as to ultimately bring the desired result. Again thanking you and Senator Scott for your past efforts and expecting renewed zeal, I am

Very truly,
Livia Simpson-Poffenbarger"

That the Congress of the United States was still importuned is evidenced by the fact that on December 4, 1907, Senator N. B. Scott introduced Senate Bill 160 which was favorably reported February 17. 1908, **without amendment, as follows:**

"A BILL to aid in the erection of a monument or memorial at Point Pleasant, West Virginia, to commemorate the Battle of the Revolution fought at that point between the Colonial troops and Indians October tenth, seventeen hundred and seventy four,"

An identical bill was introduced in the lower House of Congress by Hon. James A. Hughes.

A Telegram, as follows, brought the first intelligence to Point Pleasant that the bill had passed both branches of Congress:

Mrs. Livia Simpson-Poffenbarger,

Congress appropriated $10,000.00 for a battle monument at Point Pleasant.

Congratulations,

James A. Hughes.
Washington, D. C.

The Monument Commission got busy and realizing that the introduction of new methods of monument building, lasting as the pyramids of Egypt, had been introduced, by which the monument could be built with the money available, a contract was let for the monument at a cost at the factory of $15,000.00. The shipment and erection of which would make a total cost of $16, 000. The monument to be built of Balfour granite and the statue thereon to be of Westerly granite. The shaft is an obelisk with a base twenty-four feet square, the height to be eighty-two feet. The statue is to be that of a colonial soldier of the primitive Virginia style, dressed in hunting shirt, coon skin cap, leather breeches and long rifle. The whole to be completed for the unveiling of the monument on the One Hundred and Thirty-fifth anniversary of the Battle of Point Pleasant, October, 10, 1909.

The Monument Commission on June 10, 1909, issued the following announcement:

ATTENTION CITIZENS

A general invitation is extended for a citizen's meeting at the Court House at Point Pleasant on Thursday June 10th at 8 P. M. to make preparations for the celebration of the Battle of Point Pleasant, the unveiling of the monument and Home Coming Week, under the auspices of the Mayor and Civil Authority of the town of Point Pleasant, and interested citizens of the town, county and state.

Signed,
John P. Austin
President of the Monument Committee

There was a large and enthusiastic meeting held in response to the call. Judge John Lamar Whitten, Mayor of the town, who presided, was elected as the permanent chairman of arrangements for a West

Virginia Home Coming Week, Celebration of the Battle and Unveiling of the Monument, October 7-8-9-10, 1909. The others appointed to further the success of the proper observance of the battle were the following Committees in charge of the Celebration.

Organization

Chairman-- Mayor John L. Whitten.
Secretary-- E. Jacob Somerville.
Asst. Secretary-- Warren O. Whaley.
Grand Marshall-- Col. John P. R. B. Smith.
Assistants-- Lewis C. Somerville, Peter Higgins Steenbergen, Edward Barto Jones.

Committee at Large

Hon. John P. Austin, President Monument Commission

Monument Commissioners

Hon. V. A. Lewis
Mr. C. C. Bowyer Mayor
Judge John L. Whitten
Col. John P. R. B. Smith
Mrs. Li via Nye Simpson-Poffenbarger

Finance Committee

Joseph Friedman, Chairman,
Peter Higgins Steenbergen, Edward E. Thomas, Peter S. Lewis, Griff T. Smith, Tol Stribling, Hon. J. Samuel Spencer, John G. Stortz, **Point Pleasant.**
R. J. Patterson, **Maggie.**
William R. Thompson, **Huntington.**
Charles Cameron Lewis, Jr., Ex-Governor Wm. A. McCorkle, Hon. Jno. Q. Dickenson, **Charleston.**
Ex-Governor A. B. Fleming, **Fairmont.**

Invitation Committee

Governor Wm. E. Glasscock, Senator Stephen B. Elkins, Senator Nathan B. Scott, Hon. James A. Hughes, Judge Ira E. Robinson, Judge George Poffenbarger of **West Virginia**.

Col. H. R. Howard, John E. Beller, Robert E. Mitchell, B. H. Blagg, Andrew Lewis Boggess, Charles C. Lewis, H. Green Nease, Hon. George W. Cossin, James M. H. Beale, Hon. J. Samuel Spencer Judge John W. English, Judge Wm. A. Parsons, **Point Pleasant.**

Hon. E. O. Randall, **Columbus, Ohio**

Hon. W. Sidney Laidley, William Burdette Mathews, Charles C. Lewis, Sr., John Q. Dickenson of **Charleston**

General Charles H. Grosvenor and Hon. Jerry Longfellow Carpenter, **Athens, Ohio.**

Hon, Edmond Sehon, Dr. Lewis V. Guthrie and Louis Sehon Pomeroy, of **Huntington.**

Trades Display

Robert J. Heslop, Charles K. Blackwood, Charles E. Jones, David S. Snyder, James Walter Winden, Mark Shiflet, Horton Roseberry, Joseph W. Rhoades, Will Filson, John C. Franklin, Ed. Lawhead, H. H. Henry, C. Frederick Hess, Captain C. Homer Varian, Robert Kiger, James Stephenson, George Miller, John Wells, Geo. W. M. Hooff, Alexander B. McCulloch, James Cavanaugh, James B. Tippett; F. B. Tippett. Lemuel Shiflet, Hugo Juhling, Jr., Bertram L. Burdette, Frank Fadley, Enos B. Thomas, H. W. Ellis, Dr. Ed McElfresh, Jacob P. Hetherington, L. J. Coley, Peter C. McDade, W. A. Williams, Harry M. Langley.

Decoration and Speakers Stand

Frank Filson, B. Franklin, Jr., Charles Russell McCulloch, Wm. H. H. Gardner, J. Floyd Burdett, S. Waldo Swisher, Alonzo Walker, Enos, C. Winger, John W. C. Heslop, Ed A. Arrington, Edward W. Craig, Geo. P. Gardner, Wm. Tully, John Love, Sam'l Lutton,- Fredrick Capes, Charles Dashner, G. E. Mathews, Mesdames Harry E. Burnside, Wm. Steenbergen, Robert E. Mitchell, Edward McElfresh, Rush H. Burnside, Edward J Burnside, Lem Shiflet, Samantha J. Baum, Wm. Steinbach, Mrs. M. Friedman, Mrs. Kate Williams, Mrs. J. W. English, Mrs. Robert P. Lynch, Mrs. Ella Fenton, Mrs. Horton Roseberry, Mrs. E. H. Woelffel, Mrs. Wm. Kenny, Mrs. E. H. Armstrong, Mrs. H. A. Barbee, Mrs. James B. Tippett, Mrs. Wm. C. Stortz, Mrs. J. F. Burdett, Mrs. B. Franklin, Jr., Mrs. George Comstock, Mrs. Joseph H. Holloway, Mrs. Ashabel Hughes, Misses

Edith Tippett, Maud Kisar, Reba Beale, Hattie Price, Mary Lewis, Venie and Jessie Thomas, Mrs. Homer Smith, Mrs. E. B. Jones, Mrs. Wm. E. Hayman, Mrs. W. C. Whaley, Mrs. Tol Stribling.

Advertising Committee

Homer Smith, Dr. W. P. Neale, Marcus Friedman, Warren C. Whaley, Charles C. Lewis, Edward C. Berridge, Dr. Ed. McElfresh, John F. Lewis and James B. Tippett.

Entertainment Committee

Griff T. Smith, Howard L. Robey, Lesley L. Neale, Geo. C. Somerville, Dr. Frank V. Butcher, Ed Filson, Wm. Steinbach, Howard Long, Geo. W. Long, John L. Hutchinson, E. H. Woelffel, W. W. Riley, R. P. Liter, Lem Shiflet Jr., **Point Pleasant.**

John D. Lewis, Phil Walker, John Baker White, **Charleston**.

Lycergus N. Knight, **Maggie**

M. G. Tyler, H. E. Spilman, Dr. Richard Stone, **Spilman**

Dr. Charles Petty, **Hartford.**

Mesdames John Samuel Spencer, Charles Clendenin Bowyer, John L. Whitten, Charles C. Lewis, John Daniel McCulloch, H. Green Nease, John W. C. Heslop, L. J. Williamson, Rankin Wiley, John McCulloch, Frank Filson, Wm. P. Neale, Peter Higgins Steenbergen, Hiram R. Howard, J. H. Wade, Jackson Lee Pannel, Charles Russell McCulloch, James W. Windon, Patrick F. Ryan, John P. Austin, Robert P. Liter, Howard L. Robey, E. Barto Jones, Joseph Friedman, E. B. Sisler, B. Franklin, Jr., E. E. Thomas, Mary Margaret Bryan, Homer Smith, Ben Franklin, Sr., S. W. Swisher, Walter Lincoln; Misses Josephine Howard, Irene Bowyer, Lillie Lee Hogg, Elizabeth Harding Hogg, Julia Polsley, Ada Gilmore, Cornelia Smith, Veva Haptonstall, Margaret Lynn Neale, Gertrude Howard, Edith Tippett, Venie and Jessie Thomas, Kate Stribling, Lena L. Roseberry, of **Point Pleasant.**

Mrs. Geo. W. Gist and Miss Maggie Hayman, **Letart.**

Mrs. W. L. Lawson and Miss May Jackson, **New Haven.**

Mrs. M. M. Brown, Mrs. D. E. Newton, **Hartford.**

Mrs. Joseph H. Windon, **Maggie.**

Mrs. V. A. Lewis, Mrs. W. E. Ruttencutter, Mrs. L. E. Bletner, Misses Maud and Annie Lewis, **Mason.**

Mesdames John McCoach, Edmond Sehon, Columbus Sehon, Taylor Vinson, Wm. R. Thompson, Mary Lesage, Margaret Lynn Harvey. C. R. Thompson and James A. Hughes, **Huntington.**

Mrs. Kate Sterrett, Mrs. Wm. H. Vaught, Mrs. John Thornberg, **Five Mile**.

Mrs. M. Ella Hutchinson, **Henderson.**

Miss Lizzie Smith, **McCausland.**

Miss Francis M. Maupin, **Arbuckle.**

Mrs. Charles E. McCulloch, **Five Mile.**

Miss Rhoda Long, Mrs. Monroe Poffenbarger, **South Side.**

Mrs. C. A. Green, **Otis.**

Mrs. James Henderson, **Five Mile.**

Dr. A. G. Martin, F. M. Middleton, **Winfield.**

Dr. C. McGill, **Red House.**

Robert Brown, O. F. Stribling, **Apple Grove.**

John H. S. Spencer, **Graham Station.**

F. C. Hute, John C. Levzey, L. Quickie, Thos. L. Finney, **Pliny.**

Frank Dunn, **South Side.**

George L. Sebrell, E. B. Nease, **Arbuckle.**

Will Armstrong, **Gallipolis.**

Dr. Blake, R. E. Blake, Henry McCoy, J. E. Frazier, **Buffalo.**

Robt. Somerville, **Maggie.**

W. W. Cornwall, **Glenwood**.

Earl Henry, **Clifton.**

A. G. W. Brinker, A. C. Cross, Thos. Z. Blessing, **Letart.**

Speakers Committee

Col. H. R. Howard, Capt. W. H. Howand, Wm. E. Hayman, Judge George Poffenbarger, Robt. L. Hutchinson, Hun. J. S. Spencer, Benjamin Franklin, Sr., Enos B. Thomas, Dr. E. J. Mossman, Carlisle L. Whaley, Rev. J. H. Gibbons, Rev. Pullin, Rev. R. P. Bell, O. A. Roush, Geo. McClintock, Capt. Rush H. Burnside, Benjamin H. Blagg.

Music Committee

E, B. Sisler, J. H. Norton. B. F. Gibbs, A. C. Van Gilder, Charles K. Blackwood, Lew Mc- Millen, Rankin Wiley, John G. Aten, Wm. Steenbergen, Dr. John Fadley, Mesdames Mary Margaret Bryan, J. M.

H. Beale, Carlisle L. Whaley, Eliza Waggoner, Charles Filson, Nannie E. Hale, Kossuth T. McKinstry, Misses Josephine Beale, Gertrude Howard, and Margaret Malone, Mrs. W. C. Whaley.

Program Committee

Lewis C. Somerville, Judge George Poffenbarger, Col. Hiram R. Howard, Howard L. Robey, Robt. L. Hutchinson, Charles Buxton, Judge John W. English.

Transportation Committee

Wm. C. Jordan, L. C. Kuhn, Moulton Houk, F. Gerald Musgrave, B. H Blagg, Wallace A. Barnett, John McCulloch Dr. Hugh A. Barbee, Wm. W. Bryan, Ed. C. Berridge, Capt. E. A. Burnside, Fred Smith, Capt. E, E. Varian, Capt. John Thornberg, Gus Fry, Jos. L. Ruth, Elmer Nutter, E. B. Martin, Capt. Gordan C. Greene, J. W Hooper.

School Children

Prof. H. E. Cooper of Point Pleasant and the teachers of Mason County.

Advisory Committee

Messrs. John W. Steenbergen, Beale; Wm. J. Keister, **Ashton;** Clinton Poffenbarger, Mason Long, **Beech Hill;** James W. Long, Hon. Jabez Beard, **South Side**; E. F. Bletner, W. E. Ruttencutter, **Mason;** Charles Juhling, Hon. J. M. Hensley, J. M. Chapman, D. E. Newton, Capt. M. M. Brown, **Hartford**; Judge W. W. Jackson, Geo. N. Capehart, W. L. Lawson, C. T. Bumgarner, **New Haven;** Geo. W. Gist, Dan Sayre, Wm. Klingensmith, **Letart**; Philip Click, Willow Tree, Judge Byrd Stone, W. P. Smith, Fred Sullivan, Wm. Jividen, Charles F. Thomas, **Leon**; Judge W. H. Vaught, Robert P. Morris, Henry Fry, **Henderson**; James Henderson, Rankin Hill, **Henderson**; Hon. Jas. L. Knight, Messrs. Asa Musgrave, James W. Windon, Jos. H. Windon, H. J. Norton, Judge B. J. Redmond, Dr. A. R. Girard, Hon. Geo. Parsons, **Pleasant Flats**; Capt. L. S. Parsons, John R. Couch, Hearne. W. H. Sayre, Chas. W. Hogsett, Wm. H. Rowsey, C. A. Green, of **Hannan District**, Shepherd W. Moore, **Elwell**; Geo. W. Pullin, C. G. P. Musgrave, **Debby;** Geo. J. Meadough, James W. Kindey, W. H. Clarke, J. W. Bryan, Ash Hughes, W. H. Zumbro, **Point Pleasant;** John McCausland, Jr., Jno. R.

Couch, B. K Bell, **Hearne**, R. W. Bateman, S. A. McNiel, Mercers Bottom, Judge J. L. Thome, **Wyoma**. Col. Jerome T. Bowyer, **Winfield;** B. J. Lerner, **Hartford**; John J. Dower, **Letart**; Jas. T. Edwards, Clifton; H. C. Turner, **Mason**; David Caldwell, **Gallipolis Ferry;** Judge A. M. Pugh, Col. John L. Vance, **Columbus, Ohio**; Gen'l. John McCausland, **McCausland**; James M. Nye, **Marietta, Ohio**; Mrs. Samaria, H. Palmer; **Athens, Ohio**; Miss Margaret Lynn Price, **Lewisburg**, Mrs. Miram Donnally, Mrs. E. W. Wilson, **Charleston**; Mrs. Sanders Johnston, Dr. Adeline E. Portman, **Washington, D. C** ; Mrs. Anna S. Greene, **Culpeper**, **Virginia**; Miss Mary C. Nye, **Marietta, Ohio**; Mrs. Sophia Dale, **Belpre, Ohio**; Mrs. M. C. Scott, **Pomeroy, Ohio.**

The State Gazette of August 15th, gives the following:

"On Monday August 2nd, 1909, at 11 a. m. the steam whistle on Captain Charles Homer Varian's pump-boat, lying in the mouth of Kanawha River, sounded a glad cry that was lustily joined in by the many steamboats lying in harbor. Our people came out in great crowds to learn the cause, and the oncoming tide of people were directed to Tu-Endie-Wei Park, where had just been set the apex stone that completed the stone work of the splendid Balfour granite monument, commemorating The First Battle of the Revolution, fought at Point Pleasant, October 10th, 1774.

It was an occasion that for many years has been devoutly wished for, and there were many upon the grounds prior to the blowing of the whistles, who for years had watched every step of the preparation for the monument building Among them were Mrs. J. D. McCulloch, who was a member of the Ladies Monument Association, that put by the first contribution, which with its accumulations, represented $2,000 invested in the Monument; Mr. C. C. Bowyer of the Monument Commission, who have so faithfully labored in the cause entrusted to them by the State; and Mrs. Poffenbarger whose interest has never lagged, and it was her little son, Perry Simpson-Poffenbarger, who suggested and induced Capt. Varian to start the whistles.

The monument has been erected so speedily that our people can scarcely believe it is so nearly completed. This is accounted for by the fact that the stones were cut and numbered and ready for placing, and needed little cutting when they came upon the grounds. The Van-Amringe Granite Company of Boston, are the contractors, with Mr. J. E. Amedon of Merchants Depot, of Vermont, as the superintendent of construction here. Captain Charles Fredrick Hess was the contractor, not only for the splendid cement walks and walls, but for the cement work of the Monument, and the great under-footing was laid prior to June 7th, when the first car load of granite reached here.

On June 9th, the corner stone was laid. There were no ceremonies attending it and no deposits made save that of a small coin of the issue 1909, the year of the Monument construction. However, as is the custom in the erection of such structures, a box was deposited in this monument. It was found that in the center tube in the top section immediately under the great cap stone that binds the building, there was room to admit a box three inches in diameter and twelve inches long. Filson Brothers were called upon to construct a copper box of these dimensions and make it air tight. In it were deposited an Industrial Edition of The State Gazette of the issue, of February 2nd, 1905, upon which was written the following inscription:

"Deposited, Monday, August 2d, 1909, the date of the setting of the cap stone of the Point Pleasant Battle Monument, by Nathan Simpson Poffenbarger and Perry Simpson Poffenbarger, sons, and Natalie Simpson Bryan, niece of Geo. and Livia Nye Simpson-Poffenbarger. " A copy of the diary written by Margaret Lynn Lewis, wife of John Lewis the emigrant and a founder of the city of Staunton, Virginia, was placed in the tube upon which was the following inscription:

"Deposited, August 2nd, 1909, the date of the setting of the capstone of the Point Pleasant Battle Monument, by Sallie Lewis McCulloch, (Mrs. J. D. McCulloch) Great- Great Granddaughter of Margaret Lynn Lewis and Great-Granddaughter of Col. Charles Lewis. Sallie Lewis McCulloch (Mrs. P. H. Steenbergen), Great-Great-Granddaughter of Col. Chas. Lewis."

An Indian arrow head taken from the ground when the excavation was made, was put in the box and with it a slip of paper bearing the following:

"This Indian arrow head is deposited by C. P. Hess, contractor for the cement work of this monument. It was found when the excavation was made."

The most important deposit made however, was a copy of "The Battle of Point Pleasant," bearing the following inscription: *Deposited, Monday, August 2d, 1909, the date of the setting of the cap stone of the Point Pleasant Battle Monument.*

The illustrations and last pages are omitted on account of the inability of the printer to finish the volume by the date of the completion of the monument. Livia Nye Simpson-Poffenbarger, the Author.

This was the most valuable because, though not quite completed, it carried the most complete roster of the participants of the battle ever as yet published, that of 1080 men who participated at Point Pleasant and were entitled to share in the honors of this victory.

When the last stone bad been set in place, Mr. Amedon presented Mrs. Poffenbarger the two remaining blocks of granite from which will be made souvenirs of the monument.

The statue which is to be placed on a base in the front of the monument has not reached here, nor have the eight bronze plates in bas relief, two of which bearing the coat of arms of the United States and of West Virginia, and six of which bear the inscription of the killed and wounded and the officers commanding the army, but they have been shipped and will be here to be put in place by Mr. Amedon upon his return from St. Louis less than three weeks hence. Upon his return, the monument will be pointed up, the statue and plates set and the monument veiled ready for the ceremonial attendant upon the unveiling of October 9th, 1909.

The End

Virgil Lewis's Book

HISTORY OF THE BATTLE OF POINT PLEASANT

FOUGHT BETWEEN WHITE MEN AND INDIANS

AT THE

MOUTH OF THE GREAT KANAWHA RIVER
(Now Point Pleasant, West Virginia)

MONDAY, OCTOBER 10TH, 1774.

By
Virgil A. Lewis

Roll back my soul to the times of my Fathers.
There comes a voice that awakes my soul!
It is the voice of days that are gone.
They roll before me with all their deeds.

Ossian

Originally Published in 1909

A PREFATORY NOTE

I was born within a few miles of the battle-field of Point Pleasant, the chief event of Lord Dunmore's War, and reared largely among the descendants of the men who participated in that struggle. It was therefore but natural that even in my early years there was awakened an interest in the history not only of the battle itself, but of all that related to the participants therein—to all that concerned the gallantry and achievements of the men of 1774. In my research I have sought to collect material from trust-worthy sources, because I have desired to give to this work the interest which every reader must have in a work treating of history. For this reason the only material used has been drawn from original sources, documents, and writings which were contemporaneous with the occurrence of the events described. Much error has been incorporated into the later writings regarding Dunmore's War. This is the result of a carelessness on the part of those, who without making research and investigation necessary to arrive at truth, seized rumors, traditions, and vague recollections, as sufficient authority upon which to base an assertion, and who substituted their own inferences for authenticated facts. These errors of statement have sometimes been repeated by considerate writers whose distrust was not excited; and this has increased the difficulties of pains-taking historians. But now, the publication of Thwaites and Kellogg's "Documentary History of Dunmore's War;" the "Revolution on the Upper Ohio," by the same authors; the printing by Virginia of the Journals of the House of Burgesses; Ford's reprint of the Journals of the Continental Congress and other sources of recent appearance, added to that which was previously available, has almost given to Dunmore's War a literature of its own. It is therefore, to be hoped that, henceforth, writers who heretofore, indulged in what may be termed the gossip of history, may no longer accept myths, legends and traditions as authority, and that they will thus cease to perpetuate the errors of statements long current, regarding Lord Dunmore's War and its chief event—the Battle of Point Pleasant.

V. A. L.

Charleston, West Virginia,
September 1, 1909.

HISTORY OF THE BATTLE OF POINT PLEASANT

CHAPTER I

THE VIRGINIA FRONTIER IN 1774
THE INDIAN NATIONS OF THE OHIO WILDERNESS

"An opinion had long prevailed that these mountains presented an everlasting barrier to the ambition of the Whites. Their great height, their prodigious extent, their rugged and horrid appearance suggested to the imagination unfeigned images of terror. The wolf, the bear, the panther, and the Indian, were the tenants of these forlorn and Inaccessible precipices."—Burk's *"History of Virginia,"* Vol. II, p. 331.

"Our immediate predecessors in the occupancy of Ohio where the Shawnees, Miamis, Delawares and Ottawas of the Algonquin linguistic stock and the Wyandots and Mingoes of the Iroquois linguistic family."—*"Ohio Archaeological and Historical Society Publications."*—Vol. VI., p. 75.

White Settlers West of the Blue Ridge

For a number of years after the founding of Jamestown the white settlements were confined to the banks of the James River. In time they extended over the Tide-Water Region; and thence into the Piedmont Region even to the Base of the Blue Ridge. Explorers made known the region beyond and civilized men crossed this great mountain barrier, and found homes in the beautiful Shenandoah Valley. The first to do this were Adam Miller and Morgan Morgan who came in 1726. The next year a number of Germans from Pennsylvania, in quest of fertile lands, crossed the Potomac at what is now known as the "Old Pack-Horse Ford," and a mile above it on its southern bank, founded a little village which they called New Mecklenburg—now Shepherdstown. In 1732, Joist Hite brought sixteen families from York, Pennsylvania, all of whom settled in the Shenandoah Valley. Speedily other white men found homes along the Upper Potomac, and in the South Branch Valley. In 1731, John Lewis, John Mackey, and others came to the Upper Shenandoah Valley. In 1736 Governor Gooch issued a patent for 118,000 acres of land including the settlement of John Lewis, to William Beverley, John Robinson and others. All surrendered their interests to Beverley, and the survey came to be known as "Beverly Manor." Within it, in 1748, the town of Staunton was established by law, and received its name in honor of Lady Gooch, wife of the Governor, whose maiden name was Staunton. This was the first home of Cavalier civilization west of the Blue Ridge. In 173G, Benjamin Borden, of New Jersey, visited the Upper Shenandoah Valley; and so pleased with the region was he, that he applied to and received from Governor Gooch a grant for 500,000 acres, chiefly in what is now Rockbridge County, Virginia. Borden went to Europe the next year, and returned with a hundred families— Irish, Scotch-Irish—from the north of Ireland all of whom settled on his lands. As early as 1732 two cabins were standing at the "Old Shawnee Springs" in the Lower Shenandoah Valley. In 1743 James Wood had laid out twenty-six lots, and the House of Burgesses that year established the town of Winchester—another center of Cavalier civilization. In 1745 Thomas, Sixth Lord Fairfax, whose Land Patent embraced the whole of the Lower Shenandoah Valley and extended westward to the South Branch of the Potomac, came to Virginia and having employed young George Washington to survey these lands, in quantities to suit purchasers, established his home at "Greenway Court" thirteen miles southeast of Winchester, and did all he could to induce immigration to his lands. Thus did civilized men find homes west of the Blue Ridge. Hither came and here met the devoted Huguenot, the pious Cavalier of Virginia, the strict Catholic of Maryland, the steady Quaker of Pennsylvania, the Baptists and Presbyterians from New Jersey, the sternly religious Puritans from New England and the Lutherans and Moravians from the banks of the Rhine. For a while these distinct elements maintained their individuality, but a long series of Indian wars, forced them into a united whole. From these settlements in the valleys of the Shenandoah, others rapidly extended westward to the valleys and highlands of the Allegheny mountains; thence westward they advanced along the trans-Allegheny Rivers, to the Tygart's Valley River, to the West Fork River and its tributaries; thence down the Monongahela to Fort Pitt, and to the Ohio at Wheeling, Moundsville, mouth of Fishing Creek, and Letart Falls; around the upper waters of the Little Kanawha, and to the Valley of the Greenbrier River; the upper waters of New River; and thence to and down the valleys of the Clinch and Holston Rivers. Such was the Virginia Frontier west of the Blue Ridge in 1774, where, as is believed, forty thousand white people—men, women and children—were residing in cabin homes between Fort Pitt and the source of the Tennessee River.

County Organization West of the Blue Ridge

In 1634 the Colony of Virginia was divided in eight counties or shires similar to those of England. Henceforth Virginia ever tried to keep civil government abreast of her most adventurous pioneers, and her House of Burgesses—the legislative body of the Colony—continued to pass acts creating new counties, until in 1734, thirty-three of these were checkered on her map, all east of the Blue Ridge.

From 1734 to 1738, all the territory of Virginia west of that mountain barrier was deemed to be in Orange County created in the former year. In the latter, an Act was passed creating the counties of Augusta and Frederick—both west of the Blue Ridge—to include all "the uttermost parts of Virginia," even to the Mississippi. It was stated in this Act that "great numbers of people had settled themselves of late upon the waters of the Shenandoah, Opequon, and South Branch of the Potomac, and the branches thereof, on the northwest side of the Blue Ridge." These two counties were divided by a line drawn from the head spring of Hedgman's River at the Blue Ridge to the source of the North Branch of the Potomac, Frederick County being to northward and Augusta to the southward thereof.

In 1753 it was shown to the House of Burgesses that Frederick County was "a very long and large extent, and therefore inconvenient to the inhabitants thereof," and it was enacted that all that part of said County, westward of the Great North Mountain and Warm Spring Mountain should henceforth be a distinct County to be called and known by the name of Hampshire County.

In 1769, a petition numerously signed by the inhabitants of the southern part of Augusta County, set forth to the Burgesses "that many inconveniences attended the inhabitants of the County of Augusta, by reason of the great extent thereof," and an Act was passed that year dividing Augusta by a line beginning at the Blue Ridge and running thence north fifty-five degrees west as far as the courts of the two counties should extend it. If extended to the confines of Virginia, it would have crossed Greenbrier River about five miles below the present town of Marlinton in Pocahontas County, and would have reached the Ohio River at or near where Bellville in the present County of Wood, in West Virginia, now stands. All that portion of Augusta north of this line retained the name of Augusta; and all that part south thereof, received the name of Botetourt County. A section of the Act creating this County provided that "because the people situated on the waters of the Mississippi, in the said County of Botetourt, will be very remote from the County-seat, they shall be exempt from the payment of taxes for the purpose of building a court-house and prison for the County."

In a preamble to an Act of the Burgesses passed in 1772, it was explained that the settlers on the waters of the Holston and New Rivers in the County of Botetourt "labor under great inconveniencies by reason of the extent of the said County." It was therefore enacted that Botetourt be divided by the Great Kanawha and New Rivers, and that all that part southwest of said streams should be called and known as Fincastle County

The same year it was made to appear to the Burgesses that many of the inhabitants of Frederick County suffered great inconvenience because of the extent of this County, and by an Act passed—1772—it was divided into three parts, the central portion retaining the name of Frederick; the southern part receiving the name of Dunmore County; and the northern part, that of Berkeley County.

About this time all the northern part of Augusta County west of Hampshire to the Monongahela and Upper Ohio Valleys, even beyond Fort Pitt—a region having at that time an undefined boundary—came to be known as the "District of West Augusta." It was the home of many as brave men as ever dared the perils of a wilderness.

Such was the County organization of Virginia west of the Blue Ridge in 1774—Augusta, Botetourt and Fincastle to the west and southwest—and Frederick, Dunmore, Berkeley and Hampshire to the northeast, all together with the "District of West Augusta," embracing the present states of West Virginia, and Kentucky, and all with undefined boundaries, Virginia's portion of the old Northwest Territory beyond the Ohio. At this time the fertile Shenandoah Valley had been largely brought under cultivation and thousands of domestic cattle ranged the forest lands adjoining the plantations. A like condition existed in the adjacent river valleys to the westward.

A SAVAGE EMPIRE

The Virginia Frontiersmen in 1774 were dwelling upon the borderland of a savage empire, the boundary of which they had been forcing back for many years. By the treaty of Albany in 1720 the Blue Ridge was agreed upon as the boundary line between the possessions of white and red men. In 1744, by that of Lancaster, this was made an imaginary line extending from the Potomac through the sites of the present cities of Martinsburg, Winchester and Staunton, in the Shenandoah Valley. At the treaty of Fort Stanwix— now Rome, New York,—between the English representative, Sir William Johnson and the Six Nations— Cayugas, Onondagas, Onedias, Senecas, Mohawks, and Tuscaroras—the Ohio was made the boundary, the title to all the region east of that river being transferred to the King of England. From it the tribes that once dwelt therein had previously removed. The Kanawhas had gone from the upper tributaries of the river which bears their name, to join their kinsmen, the Iroquois in New York; the Shawnees had abandoned the Indian Old Fields of the valley of the South Branch of the Potomac; the Delawares were gone from the valley of the Monongahela; the Cherokees who claimed all the region between the Great Kanawha and Big Sandy Rivers, had never occupied it. The Indian Nations, who were to be history makers in their wars with the Virginians, were dwellers in the Ohio Wilderness. These were as follows: — Miamis, Ottawas, Shawnees, Delawares, Wyandots and Mingoes.

The Miamis were a powerful nation whose habitat was in the region drained by the great Miami and Maumee Rivers. Their ancient name was "Twightwee," and they claimed to be the original proprietors of the lands they occupied—that they had always had them. They were the only Indians that ever waged successful war with the Six Nations. This ended in 1702 by a council between the two belligerent powers.

They were a warlike people, and were much of the time in broils with their neighbors. In 1763, they removed from Piqua, their chief town, the site of which is now in Miami County, Ohio, to the Miami of the Lakes.

The Shawnees were the most remarkable of all the people inhabiting the region east of the Mississippi. Thirty-one of them were present at the treaty with William Penn, at Shackamaxon in 1682. Soon thereafter, they fell under the rule of the Six Nations, and, henceforth, for more than half a century they existed in branches in various regions. Some of them occupied the Lower Shenandoah Valley, where they had a town at "Shawnee Springs" now Winchester, Virginia; at one time the hunting grounds of the principal part of them were in Kentucky; thence they removed to the valleys of the Cumberland and Tennessee Rivers, but were forced by the Cherokees to abandon this region; and four hundred of them, in 1678, found a home on the Mobile River, in New Spain; where, in 1745 they had four hundred and fifty warriors. Four hundred more, leaving the Mississippi Valley, settled on the

Congaree River in South Carolina. Seventy families later, removed from here to the valley of the Susquehanna in Pennsylvania; others followed, and in 1732 there were seven hundred and fifty Shawnee warriors on that river. But now there was to be a gathering of all the Shawnee people. Their future home was to be on the Scioto, where, on the Pickaway Plains, the "Wilderness Garden" of the valley of that river, their principal towns were located. Here, prior to 1760, the nation was completely reunited. It was composed of four tribes or branches—the *Piqua,* men born in ashes; the *Kiskapoke,* men of war; the *Mequacheke,* the fat men; and the *Chilicothe,* dwellers in a permanent home. They could put into the field a thousand warriors. Because of their past wanderings they have been called the "Bedouins of the American Wilderness;" and because of their bravery and heroism in defending their wilderness home against the advance of white invaders they won the proud title of "Spartans of their Race".

"Of all the Indians the Shawnees were the most bloody and terrible, (they) holding all other men, Indians as well as Whites in contempt as warriors in comparison with themselves. This opinion made them more restless and fierce than any other savages; and they boasted that they had killed ten times as many white people, as had any other nation. They were a well formed, active and ingenious people,—were assuming and imperious in the presence of others not of their own nation, and were sometimes very cruel".*

* Captain John Stuart's "Memoirs of the Indian Wars and Other Occurrences," p. 40

The Delaware Nation consisted of five tribal organizations. They like the Shawnees were one of the parties to the treaty with William Penn in 1682. They once occupied New Jersey and both sides of the Delaware River from which they derived their English name. From here they were driven by the Six Nations, and took refuge in the valley of the Susquehanna, then in that of the Monongahela, and finally, about 1760, in the Ohio Wilderness, where they established themselves in the valleys of the Muskingum and Tuscarawas Rivers and their tributaries. Here, in 1770, they had their densest population, though they were really in possession of the eastern half of the present State of Ohio. They had now reached their highest degree of greatness, and could put in the field six hundred and fifty warriors. In history, tradition and fiction, the Delawares have been accorded a high rank among the Indians of North America.

The Wyandot Nation had its chief towns in the valley of the Sandusky River, in what is now Wyandot County; but they were spread out over the whole region from Lake Erie to the Ohio River, with villages along the Hockhocking and other adjacent streams. By the French they were called Hurons, and sometimes Guyandots. They were of the Iroquois linguistic stock. It was a common saying along the border that a *"Wyandot will not be taken alive"*.

The tribe of Mingoes of the Ohio Wilderness was a small organization of the Senecas, one of the Six Nations of New York. When first known to the Whites they occupied the Mingo Bottom and all the region round about the present city of Steubenville in eastern Ohio; but later gave place to the Delawares, and removed to the upper waters of the Scioto, where they built their towns on the lands on which Columbus, the capital city of Ohio now stands.

These Nations of the Ohio Wilderness denied the right of the Six Nations of New York, to convey to the English a title to the hunting grounds south of the Ohio; and they prepared to defend them against their White invaders. They had commingled to some extent from the beginning of their sojourn in Ohio; and this increased as their animosities toward each other were supplanted by a common fear of the enemy of their race. They gradually grew stronger in sympathy, and more compact in union as the settlements encroached upon their forest domain.

The Shawnees and Wyandots realizing that in unity there is strength, formed an alliance, and in the autumn of 1770, Sir William Johnson, the British envoy to the Six Nations, learned of a Congress to be held by the Indians of the Ohio Wilderness, at the Pickaway Plains—the Shawnee capital—and of this he hastened to write the Earl of Hillsborough, saying that he had taken measures to be informed, at as early a date as possible, of the proceedings and issues of the Congress.

To this end he sent Thomas King, an Indian chieftain with an English name; and An-a-was-ke, next in authority; with Nick-a-roonda-se, and several young men. Johnson awaited their return for months; then learned that after the Congress completed its work and adjourned, the Catawbas had escorted his ambassadors to Charleston, South Carolina, where Thomas King sickened and died. The others sailed for Philadelphia, but An-a-was-ke died on ship-board; the others reached their destination, and thence proceeded to Sir William Johnson's home where Nick-a-roon-da-se, the principal survivor, detailed to him the result of the embassy. He said that: "Upon Thomas King's arrival at Scioto, he assembled all the nations and first addressed the Shawnees whom he upbraided for returning so far down the Ohio and for confederating with other people unmindful of their engagements...The Shawnees answered that the Six Nations had long seemed to neglect them and to disregard the promises they formerly made, of giving them the lands between the Ohio and the Lakes; that thus distressed they went on board their canoes, determined to go whithersoever fortune should drive them, but were stopped many years ago at Scioto by the Six Nations who took them by the hands and fixed them there, charging them to live in peace with the English...that they afterward sent belts to strengthen their union with the Six Nations by A-gas-tar-ax, the Seneca chief, and that they never received any answer thereto. The Shawnees and the representatives of other nations present then showed some emblematical belts representing themselves and the Illinois Indians In alliance with ten other confederate Nations.

Thus did these western nations, so long the allies and dependents of the Six Nations, now—in that Congress on the banks of the Scioto, in the autumn of 1771,—unite—Shawnees, Delawares, Wyandots, Mingoes, Miamis, Ottawas, Illinois, and others—in a great Northwestern Confederacy, the most powerful that ever menaced the frontiers or confronted English civilization in America. At its head was placed the famous Shawnee chieftain, Keigh-tugh-qua, signifying the cornstalk, or chief support of his people, and who was therefore known to the Virginians as the Cornstalk Indian. Thus it was that in the spring of 1774, White men were pressing down from the Alleghenies to the Ohio, and Red men had organized a great Confederacy for the defense of their Country beyond that river. Each awaited the sound of the tocsin of war.

CHAPTER II

LORD DUNMORE'S WAR—ITS CAUSES

FIRST PLAN OF CAMPAIGN
THE OHIO RIVER TO BE THE LINE OF DEFENSIVE
OPERATIONS
SECOND PLAN FOR PROSECUTION OF THE WAR
EXPEDITION OF MAJOR ANGUS MCDONALD INTO THE
OHIO WILDERNESS INSTRUCTIONS TO GENERAL ANDREW
LEWIS TO ERECT A FORT AT
THE MOUTH OF THE GREAT KANAWHA RIVER

"I would find great pleasure in narrating the campaigns under Dunmore and Lewis, but that would require a volume."—Brantz Mayer's *"Logan and Captain Michael Cresap,"* p. 58.

"Dunmore's War was a most important event. No work with which I am acquainted does the subject justice. It was truly a great event both in respect to the parties engaged and the consequences growing out of it. And it has been passed over too slightly by historians." Drake's *"History and Biography of the Indians of North America,"* Book V. p. 48.

"It is much to be regretted that a complete history of this campaign has never been given to the public. Several writers have noticed it incidentally, or given a meager outline; but no one, it is believed, has entered into these circumstantial details which alone give interest to such a work."*Southern Literary Messenger"* Vol. XIV., No. 1, p. 18, (1848).

In the year 1774, John Murray, Earl of Dunmore was the Governor of the Colony of Virginia; hence Dunmore's War was a designation applied to a series of bloody deeds between the Virginians and the warriors of the Indian confederacy of the Ohio Wilderness, that year. It stands out conspicuously midway between two great divisions of American History—the Colonial and the Revolutionary Periods—but apparently without connection with either. It was the last American war in which American troops waged battle under the flag of England; that is, under the command of a Royal Governor. Its results, as we shall see, wielded a mighty influence upon subsequent history; and there was scarcely a man who was prominent in Western annals in the next forty years who was not in some way connected with it.

John Murray, Fourth Earl of Dunmore, was born in 1732, and was descended in the female line from the Royal House of Stuart. His ancestors were related to most of the crowned heads of Europe, (see Sidney Lee's" *Dictionary of Biography*" Vol. XXXIX., p. 388) the founder of his family being Charles Murray, Master of Cavalry in the reign of Queen Mary; and who was elevated to the peerage of Scotland, August 16, 1684, as the First Lord Dunmore. He died in 1710, and was succeeded by his son John, who inherited his estate and titles and who, as the Second Earl of Dunmore, became a Representative Peer in 1713, and later a General Officer in the army. He died in April, 1732, and was succeeded in the peerage by his brother William, who became the Third Earl of Dunmore. He wedded Catherine, his cousin, a daughter of Sir William Murray who afterward became Lord Neirne; and they had Issue John Murray Fourth Earl of Dunmore, our subject, (see Burk's *Peerage of England*," p. 629 K He received a classical education and was raised to the peerage on the death of his father in 1756. On the 21st day of February 1759, he was united in marriage with Lady Charlotte Stuart, the seventh child of Alexander, Sixth Earl of Galloway, a niece of Admiral Sir George Keith, of the Royal Navy, and a cousin of Lieutenant Richard Fitzgerald of the Second Life Guards, who fell at Waterloo. In 1761, he took his seat as a representative peer of Scotland in the House of Lords of the Parliament of England where for nine years, he was associated with the foremost men of Great Britain and was himself a prominent member of that body, (see "Journals of the House of Lords, "Vols. XXX., XXXI., XXXII.) In 1770 he was appointed Governor of New York, but in 1771, became Lieutenant and Governor-General of the Colony of Virginia; and soon thereafter arrived at Williamsburg, the Capital of that colony. His Lordship brought with him Captain William Foy, who had served with distinction at the battle of Minden, and subsequently as Lieutenant-Governor of New Hampshire under John Wentworth, to be Secretary of the Colony. The arrival of his family was celebrated with an illumination of the city of Williamsburg and the people with acclamations welcomed them to Virginia. When the House of Burgesses met the following May, the capital presented a scene of much gayety, and a Court-Herald published a code of etiquette for the regulation of society of the vice regal court, (see Brock's "Virginia and the Virginians," Vol. I., p. 64) In 1773, Dunmore visited Pittsburg for the purpose of acquiring information regarding the territorial dispute between Virginia and Pennsylvania. In 1774, he commanded the Virginia army of invasion into the Indian country. When the Revolution came, he, like all the colonial Governors in America, adhered to the Royal cause. In 1786, he was appointed Governor of Bermuda Islands, and died at Ramsgate, England, in 1809.

A remote cause of the war was the general antagonism of the Red and White races now being brought continually nearer to each other on the boundary between barbarism and civilization along which a tide of emigration broke through the Alleghenies and flowed down in a continuous stream to the Ohio Valley. The immediate causes were the hostilities on the border in the early spring of the year 1774.

Scarcely had the storms of winter subsided when there was an army of surveyors and land-jobbers on the Ohio. In January of this year, William Preston, Surveyor-general, of Fincastle County, which then included all the territory south of the Ohio below the mouth of the Great Kanawha, gave notice to officers and soldiers who claimed land under his Majesty's proclamation of the 7th of October 1763, and who had obtained warrants for the same from the Earl of Dunmore, to meet his deputy surveyors at the mouth of the Great Kanawha River, on the ensuing 14th of April, that their lands might be located.

When the surveyors—John Floyd and Hancock Taylor—reached that place, they found forty-three men already there. From here a number of them removed twenty miles down the Ohio to the mouth of the Little Guyandotte. Ebenezer Zane, the founder of Wheeling, had a party of surveyors at the mouth of Big Sandy River. George Rogers Clark was with a party numbering ninety at the mouth of the Little Kanawha; and Michael Cresap with another party was at Long Beach, now in Tyler County, West Virginia. The Indians beheld their fate in the occupation, by white men, of their hunting grounds south of the Ohio. They resolved to defend them and hostilities began as early as the first of April that year. Thomas Green, Lawrence Darnell, and William Nash were prospecting for land near the mouth of Lawrence Creek, now in Mason County, Kentucky, when they were taken prisoners by a band of Shawnees who held a council over them for three days and then sent them off, telling them, that, henceforth all Virginians found on the Ohio, would be killed. A little later a party of surveyors in Kentucky, nearly opposite the mouth of the Scioto, killed several Shawnee warriors and took thirty horse-loads of skins from them.

An engagement with the Indians occurred near the mouth of the Little Kanawha, and the surveyors there joined Cresap's men and all proceeded up the Ohio to Wheeling. Dr. John Connolly at Fort Dunmore, now Pittsburg,* who was Royal Commandant of the "District of West Augusta," addressed a letter to Cresap at Wheeling, apprising him that messengers returned from the

Indian nations, stated that a war was inevitable; that the Indians would strike as soon as the season permitted. He urged upon the people of Wheeling to fortify themselves. Cresap received this letter April 21st. A meeting was held on the 26th. Connolly's letter was read, and White men that day voiced a declaration of war against the Indians. Soon it was reported that two Indians and some traders were coming down the river in a canoe and a party from Wheeling ascended the river and killed the Indians. The next day, April 27th, two canoes in which were several Indians, were discovered descending the Ohio, but keeping under cover of Wheeling Island. They were pursued Cresap and party to the mouth of Pipe Creek, about fifteen miles below Wheeling, where they were overtaken and a battle ensued in which three Indians were killed and scalped and three whites were wounded, one of whom died shortly after.

* When Lord Dunmore was at Pittsburg in 1773, old Fort Pitt, which had been dismantled after the French and Indian war in 1763, was falling into decay; but because of the territorial dispute between Virginia and Pennsylvania, and the probability of an Indian war, Dunmore after advising with Dr. John Connolly, thought best to repair the fortress; this was done and the name changed to Fort Dunmore.

On the West Virginia side of the Ohio, opposite the mouth of Yellow Creek, in what is now Grant Magisterial District, Hancock County, West Virginia, lived a man named Joshua Baker, who kept a house of entertainment and sold whiskey. On the lower fork of Yellow Creek on the Ohio side, was an Indian encampment in which were a number of relatives of Logan, the celebrated Mingo chieftain; and on April 30th, when a number of these were at the house of Baker, a party of Whites from Short Creek, twelve miles above Wheeling, at whose head was Daniel Greathouse, fell upon them and massacred ten in number. This meant all the horrors of an Indian war along the whole frontier. To enter into details would be to prepare a volume.

On the 6th of May, Valentine Crawford, then at Jacob's Creek now in Westmoreland County, Pennsylvania, writing Colonel George Washington of the massacre of Logan's people said: "*It has almost ruined all the settlements west of the Monongahela. There were more than one thousand people crossed that river going Eastward in a single day.*"

Two days later, Colonel William Crawford, brother of Valentine, wrote Colonel Washington saying: "*Our inhabitants are much alarmed, many hundred having gone Eastward over the Allegheny Mountains, and the whole country is vacated as far as the Monongahela."* That was in the whole region between that river and the Ohio.

The House of Burgesses Authorizes Governor Dunmore to Prosecute the War against the Indians

There was terror along the whole western frontier. Indian atrocities were committed almost daily. Messengers bore tidings of these to Governor Dunmore at Williamsburg, the old Colonial Capital of Virginia. On the 12th of May, Governor Dunmore communicated to the House of Burgesses information which he had received the preceding day concerning the horrid scenes being enacted on the border. May 13th, that body gave consideration to this as follows:

"It gives us pain, my Lord, to find that the Indians have made fresh encroachments and disturbances on our Frontiers; we have only to request that your Excellency -will be pleased to exert those powers with which you are fully vested by the Act of Assembly, for making provision against invasions and insurrections, which we have no doubt, will be found sufficient to repel the hostile and perfidious attempts of those savage and barbarous Enemies."

In compliance with this action of the House of Burgesses, Lord Dunmore resolved, first, to make the banks of the Ohio the seat of war, or line of defense; or, secondly to invade the Ohio Wilderness, the objective point being the Shawnee Capital on the Pickaway Plains, in the valley of the Scioto River. The military system then in use in the Colony was that embodied in the code prescribed by King George III., at the close of the French and Indian war. It provided that in each County there should be a chief military officer, known as the County-Lieutenant, who should enroll the militia and have general supervision thereof. Below him in rank was a Colonel, then a Lieutenant-Colonel, and lastly a Major. A regiment consisted of five hundred men, or ten companies, of fifty men each, the Company officers being a Captain, Lieutenant, Ensign, and several Sergeants. The Lieutenant and all above him in the County, were known as "Field Officers;" those in the rank below him as "Subalterns." Dunmore determined to give personal direction to the defensive warfare according to this plan. Leaving the Gubernatorial Mansion, July 10th, he crossed the Blue Ridge and established his headquarters at "Greenway Court," the home of Lord Fairfax, in the Lower Shenandoah Valley. On the 5th day of July, Andrew

Lewis,*County-Lieutenant of Botetourt County, wrote Governor Dunmore regarding existing conditions in the Greenbrier Valley and New River region. This letter was delivered to him two days after he had gone from Williamsburg on his journey over the Blue Ridge. While stopping at "Rosegill," the home of Ralph Wormsley, one of the Governor's councilors, residing in Middlesex County, he made reply under date of July 12th, to the letter of Lewis. In this he said:—

"I am sorry to find there is so great a probability of your being engaged in a war with the Indians. Wait no longer for them to attack you but raise all the men you think willing and able to go down immediately to the mouth of the Great Kanhaway, and there build a Fort and if you think you have force enough that are willing to follow you, proceed directly to their towns and if possible, destroy their towns and magazines; and distress them in every way that is possible. And if you can keep a communication open between you [and] Wheeling Fort (Fort Fincastle) and Fort Dunmore, (at Pittsburg), I am well persuaded [you] will prevent them [the Indians] from crossing the Ohio any more, and consequently from giving any further uneasiness to the inhabitants on that river. I am now on my way up to the Blue Ridge from whence there is already marched a large body of men."

** The first extended account of the Lewis family in Virginia was published in 1829, in the *Fincastle* (Va.) *Mirror,* and thence copied into *The Staunton Spectator*. It was written by Hugh Paul Taylor, an employee of the old James River and Kanawha Canal Company, who was fond of dwelling on the old Gaelic myths and legends of the British Isles in the third century. From old *Lochlin,* the ancient name of Scandinavia, or of the Peninsula of Jutland, he derived his *Loch Lynn,* which he made the birthplace of Margaret Lynn who became the wife of John Lewis, the emigrant ancestor of the family in Virginia. From the time that Taylor's account was published, the history of the family has contained many contradictions; and he has been followed by Withers, Howe, and others, who enlarged upon these.

There has been but one member of the family who has written extensively of it. This was George Rockingham Gilmer, a Governor of Georgia, whose mother was a daughter of Thomas Lewis, a niece of General Lewis, and a grand-daughter of John Lewis, the emigrant ancestor. She sat at his elbow while he was writing, and he must have obtained his information regarding the family very largely from her. He says that John Lewis was a native of the County of Dublin, in Ireland; his grand-father, or other more remote ancestor, having removed from Wales to that County during the civil wars in the time of Charles the First: that the Lewellyns of Wales were the kinspeople of the Lewises; that the red hair and irascible temper which still continues to distinguish the family, indicate Welch rather than French, Scotch, or English origin.

Continuing, he says that some writers have stated that his wife was of Scotch descent, but circumstances induce him to the opinion that the Lynns emigrated with the Lewises from Wales to Ireland. John Lewis was the first settler on the site of the present city of Staunton, in the Upper Shenandoah Valley, coming thence from Ireland in 1731. At the time of his settlement he had three sons—Thomas. Andrew and William—and two daughters—and to him after his arrival in Virginia, was added his youngest son, Charles, who fell in the Battle of Point Pleasant.

Andrew, who commanded at that battle was born in Ireland, in 1720, and wedded Elizabeth Givens of Augusta County, Virginia, and settled at the base of Bent Mountain on the upper Roanoke River, in what became Botetourt County; was long engaged in the Indian wars; served as a Brigadier-General in the Revolution; died, leaving issue, in 1781, and was buried on his estate, "Dropmore", near the present town of Salem, now in Roanoke County, Virginia. There a splendid monument has been erected to his memory. He needs not romance, fiction, nor legend to tell of his exploits. His services in the Border Wars, and in the Revolution, are preserved in the annals of his country. General Lewis was a leading actor in all the events in which he took part; yet fame has trumpeted to the world his exploits with far feebler tone, than the deeds of others of far less importance.

By "the large body of men already marched," Dunmore referred to the expedition of Major Angus McDonald to whom he had, before leaving Williamsburg, issued orders similar to those given Lewis, except that he was to erect a fort at the mouth of Wheeling Creek on site of the present city of Wheeling. This he hastened to do and with four hundred men collected in the Hampshire hills and Berkeley and Frederick counties, proceeded to Wheeling, where he began the erection of Fort Fincastle (afterward Fort Henry) and was thus engaged until relieved by Captain William Crawford who came from Fort Dunmore (at Pittsburg) with two hundred men, and prosecuted the work to completion; while McDonald with four hundred men— eight companies—prepared for an invasion of the Indian country. Among his Captains were Michael Cresap Sr., Michael Cresap Jr., Hancock Lee, Daniel Morgan, Daniel Cresap, Teabaugh and Hoagland".

Leaving Wheeling July 25th, on what was known as the Wakatomica campaign, the army descended the Ohio to the mouth of Fish Creek, now in Marshall County, West Virginia. From here the march into the Ohio Wilderness began; Wakatomica, the Shawnee town on the Muskingum River, distant ninety miles away, being the objective point. Jonathan Zane, Thomas Nicholson and Tady Kelly acted as guides. When within six miles of Wakatomica, the advance was met by a party of forty or fifty Indians, and a skirmish ensued, in which the Whites had two killed and nine wounded; while of the Indian loss was one killed and several wounded. When the town was reached it was found to be evacuated, the Indians lying in ambuscade on the opposite side of the river, believing as they did, that McDonald's men would cross at that place. In this they were disappointed, and sued for peace. They were required to send over five chiefs as hostages; then the army crossed over, only to be told that a treaty could not be made without the presence of the chiefs of the other tribes. These were sent for but did not come; meantime it was discovered that the Indians were removing their old people, women and children and effects to other towns. McDonald having heard of this treachery, laid Wakatomica in ashes; destroyed five hundred bushels of old corn; cut down seventy-five acres of growing corn, and then returned to Wheeling, having with him three chiefs who were sent as hostages to Williamsburg. Immediately thereafter, bands of Indians invaded the frontier settlements, spreading terror in all directions. The settlers fled to forts and block-houses but many were either killed or carried into a captivity worse than death.

When Major McDonald and his Valley men returned to the Shenandoah Valley about the 12th of August, they met Governor Dunmore and reported to him the failure of the expedition. His Lordship now abandoned his first plan of campaign, that of making the Ohio River the line of defensive operations—and hastened to put into operation the second—that of the invasion of the Ohio Wilderness. On the 14th of August, he addressed a letter from Frederick County, Virginia, to William Legge, Earl of Dartmouth, English Secretary of State for the American Colonies, in which he said:—

"The Shawnees, Mingoes and some Delawares have fallen on our frontier; killed, scalped, and most cruelly murdered a great many men, women and children. I hope in eight or ten days to march with a body of men over the Allegheny Mountains, and then down the Ohio to the mouth of the Scioto, and if I can possibly fall upon their towns undiscovered, I think I shall be able to put an end to this most cruel war."

Immediately the din of preparation was heard in the Lower Shenandoah Valley. Tents dotted the oak-shaded woodlands around "Greenway Court." James Parsons, Edward Snickers and others traversed the regions round and about for supplies; and the names of a thousand men were enrolled on the muster-rolls, among them those who had been with McDonald in the

Wakatomica campaign. Two regiments were formed, a first, the "Frederick County Regiment" Colonel William Crawford,* commanding; and a second, the "Berkeley County Regiment;" at the head of which was Colonel Adam Stephen;** Lord Dunmore was Commander-in-Chief, and the march to the West began. The Berkeley County Regiment left the site of the present city of Winchester on August 27th. Dunmore, with the Frederick County Regiment followed Braddock's Road, opened seventeen years before, from Winchester, and arrived at the mouth of the South Branch of the Potomac on the 30th of August. Thence onward by way of old Fort Cumberland—now Cumberland City, Maryland—thence over the road constructed for this purpose, by Abraham Hite, Thomas Rutherford and James Wood through the mountains from the Virginia Frontier, to the mouth of Eel-stone Creek on the Monongahela, where the regiments were separated, the Frederick County men going by way of Fort Dunmore; while the Berkeley men with the beef cattle, crossed the country to Wheeling. At Pittsburg, his Lordship was joined by the "West Augusta Battalion" of two hundred men, under the command of Major John Connolly. Valentine Crawford, writing Colonel George Washington from Fort Fincastle, (Wheeling) under date of October 1, 1774, said:—

"I have just time to give you a line or two by Lord Dunmore's Express, to let you know how we go on in this quarter with the Indian war. His Lordship arrived here yesterday (September 30th) with about twelve hundred men—seven hundred of whom came by water with his Lordship—and five hundred came under my brother—traveling by land, with the bullocks. His Lordship has sent him with five hundred men— fifty pack-horses and two hundred bullocks to meet Colonel Lewis at the mouth of Hockhocking River below the mouth of the Little Kanawha. His Lordship is to go by water with the rest of the troops in a few days."

* William Crawford was born about 1732, in what is now Berkeley County, where in 1749, he became acquainted with young George Washington while the latter was engaged in surveying lands for Lord Fairfax. As an ensign in a Virginia company he was at Braddock's defeat in 1755; the next year was made a Lieutenant, and in 1758 was a Captain in the expedition of General Forbes against Fort Du Quesne. In 1765, he built a cabin at Stuart's Crossing on the Yohogany River, now in Fayette County, Pennsylvania, but then believed to be in Virginia. Here he often entertained George Washington and in 1773 had Lord Dunmore for his guest; his Lordship knew him "to be prudent, active and resolute," hence he was placed at the head of five hundred men in the war of 1774. In 1778 he became Colonel of the Thirteenth Virginia Infantry, known as the "West Augusta Regiment" and was stationed at Pittsburg, the head-quarters of the Western Military Department. In 1782, he commanded the expedition against the

Sandusky Indians; was defeated; taken prisoner and burned at the stake, in what is now Wyandotte County, Ohio. The spot of ground on which he perished is now immortal, consecrated as it is, by the blood and martyrdom of this illustrious hero.

** Adam Stephen who commanded the Berkeley men in Dunmore's War was a native of Pennsylvania, born about 1818, and came to the site of the present city of Martinsburg, West Virginia, about 1738. He enlisted a company for the first Virginia Regiment, in the French and Indian war, which after the death of Joshua Fry, was commanded by Colonel George Washington, with himself as Lieutenant Colonel and Andrew Lewis as Major. He was in the engagement at Great Meadows; assisted in building Fort Necessity; and was later in command of Fort Cumberland. He was at Braddock's defeat at the fatal field of Monongahela July 9, 1755 and was with General Forbes at the capture of Fort Du Quesne. At the beginning of the Revolution he became Colonel of a Virginia Regiment; was commissioned a Major-General in 1777. He was in the battles of Trenton, Princeton, and Brandywine, but was dismissed from the service on the charge of intoxication at the battle of Germantown—done so his friends said— to create a place for General Lafayette. He returned to his estate—that on which Martinsburg now stands —and in 1788, was one of the Delegates from Berkeley County to the Virginian Federal Convention which ratified the National Constitution. Thereafter he was long active in civil offices and died in Martinsburg, in 1791, and was buried at that place.

In a little time the whole army was at what is now Harris' Ferry in Harris Magisterial District, Wood County, West Virginia, and thirteen miles below the city of Parkersburg. Here all crossed the Ohio, swimming the cattle and horses, and on the triangular point of land at the mouth of Hockhocking River on the site of the present town of Hockingport, Ohio, built a stockade fort, which received the name of Fort Gower, in honor of Earl Gower, the personal friend of Dunmore in the British House of Lords. Dunmore's force had been increased by the addition of one hundred men at Wheeling; and at the crossing of the Ohio, he had with him thirteen hundred men; one hundred beeves; two hundred pack-horses; and two hundred and fifty thousand pounds of flour.

CHAPTER III

GATHERING OF THE SOUTHERN DIVISION OR THE LEFT WING AT "CAMP UNION" ON THE BIG LEVELS OF GREENBRIER

The mustering of an army, by Lord Dunmore, in the northern counties—Frederick, Dunmore, Hampshire and Berkeley—west of the Blue Ridge, and its march to the Ohio, was but half of his second plan of campaign—that of the invasion of the Indian Country. This plan embraced the organization of an army of three thousand men, the Northern Division or Eight Wing being commanded by himself; while a Southern Division or Left Wing was to be organized in the Southern counties—Augusta, Botetourt, and Fincastle—west of the Blue Ridge, which should march by another route—the two divisions to be united at some point on the Ohio; whence the march of the entire army into the Ohio Wilderness should begin.

Andrew Lewis was the eldest and most experienced soldier in the Southern counties, and to him, Lord Dunmore issued orders from his head-quarters at "Greenway Court," in Frederick County, under date of July 24th, saying:—

"I desire you to raise a respectable Boddy of men and join me either at the mouth of the grate Kanaway or Whailen (Wheeling) as is most convenient for you.* Forward this letter to Colonel William Preston with the greatest Dispatch as I want his assistance, as well as that of your Brother, Charles Lewis. I need not inform you how necessary dispatch is. **

* The reader will observe that Dunmore here named two points on the Ohio for the uniting of the two divisions, but left it to General Lewis to decide which of these it should be—Wheeling or the mouth of the Great Kanawha.

** "Documentary History of Dunmore's War." p. 98. Original in the library of the State Historical Society of Wisconsin.

At this time Andrew Lewis,* was County-Lieutenant of Botetourt County, his home being at "Dropmore," at the base of Bent Mountain near the present town of Salem, now in Roanoke County; and William Fleming** the Colonel of the County, resided at "Belmont" then in Botetourt, but now in Montgomery County; and William Preston was County-Lieutenant and Surveyor-General of Fincastle County, his home being at "Smithfield," now Blacksburg, in Montgomery County; and William Christian*** Colonel of the County, lived on "Dunkard's

Bottom" on the west side of New River, now in Pulaski County. Charles Lewis was County-Lieutenant of Augusta County, his home being near the present village of Williamsville, on Cowpasture River, then in Augusta, but now in Bath County.

* There was no promotion for Andrew Lewis. In the military establishment of the Colony, he retained the title of Colonel, but because he discharged the duties of a Brigadier General in this war, and held that rank in the Revolutionary war, he is always spoken of as General Lewis, and therefore thus designated in this work.

** Colonel William Fleming was born at Jedburg, Scotland, February 18, 1729, and was the son of the sixth Lord Sterling, Earl of Wigton. He received a thorough education; was graduated In medicine from the University of Edinburgh; and entered the British navy as Assistant Surgeon. A fellow-countryman—-Robert Dinwiddie—was Governor of the Colony of Virginia in 1755, and he resolved to come hither. This he did, and the same year received a Commission as Ensign, in Washington's Regiment, in which he served until the close of the French and Indian war. In 1762, he served as Lieutenant under Major Andrew Lewis at Fort Chiswell, and the same year became a Captain in the Berkeley—Hampshire Regiment, commanded by Colonel Adam Stephen. In 1774, he was residing at his home—"Belmont," in Botetourt County, and commanded the regiment, mustered there, at the Battle of Point Pleasant. He was a member of the First senate of the Commonwealth of Virginia; in 1780, he became a member of the Council of State, and in June of that year, he was the Acting Governor of the Commonwealth. Colonel Fleming died at "Belmont" August 1795, and carried to his grave, in his body, a bullet received at the Battle of Point Pleasant, twenty-one years before.

*** Colonel William Christian was a representative of a family which long resided on the Isle of Man. Gilbert Christian wedded Margaret Richardson in Ireland, and their children, one of whom was Israel, came to Virginia, and settled on Christian's Creek, In Augusta County, in 1733. Here William, the subject, was born in 1743. He was a member of the House of Burgesses from Fincastle County in 1774, and was Colonel of his County at the time of Dunmore's war. In 1775 he was a member of the Virginia Convention that assembled March 20th, and same year he became Lieutenant-Colonel of the First Virginia Regiment of which Patrick Henry was Colonel. In 1776, he became Colonel of the first battalion of Virginia and commander of an expedition against the Cherokee Indians. In 1780, he commanded another expedition against that nation; and was the next year, appointed by General Green, head of a Commission to conclude a treaty with them. In 1785, he removed to Kentucky and settled near Louisville. The year following, he with others, pursued a party of Indians across the Ohio, where he was shot and killed on the site of Jeffersonville, Indiana.

Promptly on receipt of these orders from Dunmore, General Lewis sent copies thereof to all the military officers of the Southern Counties; and at the same time summoned them to attend a council of war at his home, on the 12th of August. In this call he said:—

"Don't faile to come; and let us do something. I would, as matters stand, run great risk rather than a miscarriage should happen." At this council, plans were completed for enlisting the troops; and it was determined that all should rendezvous at "Camp Union" so designated because the troops were to be united

there, on the Savannah or Big Levels about seven miles from White Sulphur Springs, on the site of the present town of Lewisburg, the seat of Justice of Greenbrier County, West Virginia. All were to be there in readiness to march to the Ohio on the 30th of August. Immediately the din of preparation was heard throughout the Southern counties. Colonel Charles Lewis established his headquarters at Staunton; Colonel William Christian fixed his at the "New River Ford," later known as Ingles' Ferry; Colonel William Fleming made his at his home at "Belmont." General Lewis and Colonel William Christian moved here, there, and everywhere, encouraging enlistments, and looking after supplies. Recruiting stations were established at Warm Springs, now Bath County; at other points in the valley of the Cowpasture and Bullpasture Rivers; at Staunton and other points on the upper tributaries of the Shenandoah River; at Tinkling Springs and elsewhere in Southern Augusta; at Smithfield, "Belmont," the "New River Ford" and elsewhere in Botetourt; and at "Royal Oak," "Castle Woods," "Seven Mile Ford," on Holston River, at Wolf Hills, (now Abingdon); at "King's Meadows" on the site of the present city of Bristol, Tennessee-Virginia, and other places in Fincastle.

One company did not wait for another, but as speedily as organized, repaired to Camp Union, the place of general rendezvous. Captain John Stuart's company of Greenbrier Valley men arrived August 1st—the first at Camp Union. Then came Captain John Dickinson's company from the valley of the Cowpasture and Jackson's Rivers; Captains Alexander McClennahan and George Mathews arrived with their companies from Staunton; the company of Captain Andrew Lockridge came from Bullpasture River, now in Highland County; Captain John Lewis (son of Thomas) and Captain Benjamin Harrison reported with their companies from that part of Augusta, now included in Rockingham County; Captains George Moffatt and Samuel McDowell came with their companies from Southern Augusta— that part now included in Rockbridge County. The Fincastle Battalion was recruited mainly in the valleys of the Holston, Clinch, Watauga, and Powell's Rivers. Captain Evan Shelby brought with him fifty-two of the first settlers from the valley of Watauga, chiefly from what is now Sullivan and Carter counties, Tennessee; the companies of Captains William Russell, William Campbell, William Herbert, and John Floyd were from the valleys of the Clinch and Holston River settlements; and Captains Anthony Bledsoe and Joseph Crockett came from along the southern banks of the upper New River. These companies assembled at the "New River Ford," latter "Ingles' Ferry," and thence proceeded down that river and through Rich Creek Gap, now "Symms' Gap," in Peters' Mountain; thence across the present County of Monroe, West Virginia to Camp Union. Colonel John Field, (acting Captain) brought a company of Culpeper County Minute Men; Captain Thomas Slaughter came with a company from Dunmore, (now Shenandoah County;) and Captain Thomas Buford arrived with a company of Riflemen from Bedford County. Later still, eighty unorganized men came from Augusta County; and a like number from Culpeper; and Captain James Harrod brought out of the Kentucky wilderness the founders of Harrodsburg, the oldest town in that State.

Colonel Charles Lewis executed his will at Staunton, August 10th, and then hastened away to Camp Union. Colonel Fleming arrived there on the 29th of August; General Andrew Lewis came on the 1st of September; and Colonel William Christian, on the 6th of that month. Colonel William Preston did not accompany the army because of sickness in his family.

The complete organization of the army as perfected at Camp Union may be shown as follows:—

SOUTHERN DIVISION OR LEFT WING OF LORD DUNMORE'S ARMY

General Andrew Lewis, Commanding

THE AUGUSTA COUNTY REGIMENT

Colonel Charles Lewis, Commanding

CAPTAINS OF COMPANIES

Captain John Dickinson.	Captain Samuel McDowell.
Captain George Moffatt.	Captain Alexander McClennahan.
Captain George Mathews.	Captain Andrew Lockridge.
Captain John Skidmore.	Captain Samuel Wilson.
Captain John Lewis.	Captain Benjamin Harrison.
Captain William Nalle.	

THE BOTETOURT COUNTY REGIMENT

Colonel William Fleming, Commanding (450 men)

CAPTAINS OF COMPANIES

Captain Philip Love.

Captain John Lewis.

Captain John Stuart.

Captain James Ward.

Captain Mathew Arbuckle.

Captain John Murray.

Captain Robert McClennahan.

Captain Henry Pauling.

THE FINCASTLE COUNTY BATTALLION

Colonel William Christian, Commanding (350 men)

CAPTAINS OF COMPANIES

Captain William Russell.

Captain Joseph Crockett.

Captain William Campbell.

Captain Anthony Bledsoe.

Captain Evan Shelby.

Captain William Herbert.

Captain John Floyd.

INDEPENDENT COMPANIES.

The Culpeper Minute Men, Colonel John Field, commanding (40 men); The Dunmore County Volunteers, Captain Thomas Slaughter, commanding, (40 men); the Bedford County Riflemen, Captain Thomas Buford, commanding. (44 men); the Kentucky Pioneers, Captain James Harrod, commanding. (27 men.)

The Culpeper Minute Men were attached to the Augusta Regiment; the Bedford Riflemen to the Botetourt Regiment; and the Dunmore Volunteers, and the Kentucky Pioneers to the Fincastle Battalion.

Colonel William Fleming and Captains Thomas Buford and Robert **McClennahan**, all regularly educated physicians, composed the Medical Board of the army. Rev. Terry was

Chaplain of the army. Major Thomas Posey was chief Commissary and Quarter Master-General; Sampson Mathews was Quarter-Master of the Augusta Regiment with John Lyle as his assistant; Thomas Ingles was Quarter-Master of the Botetourt Regiment; and Anthony Bledsoe was Commissary of the Fincastle Battalion. James Hughes was Pack-horse Master; William McClure chief Driver of Cattle; John Warwick was chief Butcher; Captain Mathew Arbuckle was chief Guide; Frederick Burley was chief Indian Spy; and John Coalter, carpenter. The lead used, came from the mines at Fort Chiswell, on the Upper New River, then the seat of Justice of Fincastle County; and the powder was largely manufactured near the Natural Bridge, now in Rockbridge County. The cattle were from the southern counties west of the Blue Ridge, and the flour was ground on water-mills in the Shenandoah Valley.

This army at Camp Union was the most remarkable body of men that had ever assembled on the American frontier. Of the men comprising it, some had been with Washington at the surrender of Fort Necessity; some with Braddock at the fatal field of Monongahela; others with Forbes at the capture of Fort Du Quesne; and still others with Bouquet in the Ohio Wilderness; and all, or nearly all, had been engaged all their lives in the Border wars. Hence the men collected at Camp Union were not only schooled in both the English and Colonial military systems, but were familiar with the methods of Indian warfare as well. Every man knew his duty and the importance of the undertaking in which he was engaged. "It may be doubted if a braver or physically finer set of men will ever get together on this continent.

This army was not uniformed as such; a few of the officers on Colonial establishment, wore the regular military uniform, but far the greater number wore the individual costume of the Border. They were clad in the hunting-shirt with leather leggings; breeches of domestic make; and caps made from the skins of wild animals or knit from wool. Each carried the long flint-lock rifle, or English musket, with bullet-pouches and quaintly carved powder-horns; with tomahawk and butcher knife. They had been the Border Rangers of past years, but now an offensive warfare was theirs. It was an army composed of fighters impatient for the fray. It was an army of civilized men, encamped on the borderland of a Savage Empire. There on the "Levels" around Camp Union were heard the voices of men, the neighing of horses, the lowing of cattle, the rattle of the drums, and the sharp whistle of the fife— sounds all so strange in the solitude of the Allegheny wilderness.

CHAPTER IV

THE WESTWARD MARCH OF GENERAL ANDREW LEWIS' ARMY FROM CAMP UNION TO THE OHIO RIVER
THE ARMY LEAVING CAMP UNION
THE ADVANCE THROUGH THE MOUNTAINS TO THE GREAT KANAWHA RIVER THENCE DOWN THAT RIVER TO
CAMP POINT PLEASANT ON THE OHIO RIVER

As usual some were behind and the army was not ready to move from Camp Union the first of September, as provided by the council of war, held at the home of General Lewis on the 12th of the preceding August. On Tuesday, the 30th of August, Lord Dunmore, then at the mouth of the South Branch of the Potomac on his westward march to the Ohio, wrote General Lewis, expressing his Lordship's warmest wishes, and that he (General Lewis) would with all his troops, join him at the mouth of the Little Kanawha River— now Parkersburg,* West Virginia. Lewis received this letter on Sunday, September 5th, ensuing, and made reply by saying that it was then too late to alter the route to the Ohio, and he must, needs to proceed to the mouth of the Great Kanawha.

* It will be observed that Lord Dunmore desired General Lewis to meet him at the mouth of the Little Kanawha Instead of the Great Kanawha. After conversing with Major McDonald and others familiar with the geography of the Ohio Valley, he had learned that the route to the Pickaway Plains by way of the Valley of the Hockhocking River was much shorter than to descend the Ohio to the mouth of the Great Kanawha and then go hence.—V. A. L.

Advance of the Augusta Regiment

On Tuesday, September 6th, there was a busy scene at Camp Union. The cattle were being corralled, the pack-horses laden; then the drums and fifes were heard and the Augusta Regiment, together with Colonel Stuart's company of the Botetourt Regiment, fell into line and with its drove of cattle and cavalcade of pack-horses, passed over the high hill west of Camp Union and disappeared in the wilderness. We know but little of its march through the Alleghenies, one hundred and three miles to the mouth of the Elk River, on the Great Kanawha—now Charleston the capital of West Virginia. Colonel William Christian writing Colonel William Preston the next day says:

"*Colonel Charles Lewis marched yesterday with, about 600 Augusta men. His business is to proceed as far as the mouth of Elk, then to make canoes to take down the flour. He took with him 108 beeves and 500 pack-horses carrying 54,000 pounds of flour.*"

This left a shortage of beef at Camp Union but Sampson Mathews, the Quarter-Master of the Augusta Regiment was expected to furnish an immediate supply. His contract was to furnish 160,000 pounds of flour, of which 80,000 had been delivered; of this 54,000 had gone forward with the Augusta Regiment. Caleb Atwater, an early historian of the State of Ohio, when speaking of this march said:—

"*His route lay wholly through a trackless forest. All his baggage, his provisions, and even his ammunition, had to be transported on pack-horses, that were clambering about among the tall cliffs, or winding their way through dangerous defiles, ascending or descending the lofty summits of the Alleghenies. The country at this time, in its aspect is one of the most romantic and wild in the whole Union. Its natural features are majestic and grand. Among these lofty summits and deep ravines, nature operates on a scale of grandeur, simplicity and sublimity, scarcely ever equaled in any other region, and never surpassed in the world. During nineteen entire days, this gallant band pressed forward descending from the heights of the Alleghany Mountains, to the mouth of the Kenhawa, a distance of one hundred and sixty miles.*"*

* "Atwater's History of the State of Ohio". Second Edition, p. 112.

The second body of troops to leave Camp Union was the Culpeper Minute men—forty in number—under Colonel John Field, (then serving as captain) who brought orders from Lord Dunmore, to General Lewis to admit him and the Culpeper men to service in the Southern Division. Field followed in the wake of the Augusta Regiment, gone thirty hours before, but the smaller body moved the more rapidly, and came up with the advance on the third day.**

*Letter of Colonel Christian to Colonel Preston, dated "Camp Union," September 7th, 1774; printed in "Documentary History of Dunmore's war." p. 185.

Advance of the Botetourt Regiment

Captain Philip Love, writing Colonel William Preston on September 12th, says:—"*The Botetourt troops marches in a few hours for the mouth of Elk, our next post from this.*"

Colonel William Christian writing Colonel William Preston says:

"*General Lewis has just marched with Colonel Fleming and the Botetourt troops, (men from his own County) with an addition of the companies of Captains Shelby and Russell, from Fincastle, and Buford's Bedford County Riflemen.*"

We do not know how many pack-horses or beeves went forward with Colonel Fleming's Regiment. It took with it 18,000 pounds of flour from Camp Union, leaving 8,000 pounds at that place. Major Christian was left in command with the remainder of the Fincastle troops, the Dunmore Volunteers, and a few men from each of the counties of Augusta and Culpeper. Several persons were absent collecting supplies. Already 72,000 pounds of flour had gone forward and Christian was expecting 130 horse-loads to arrive the next day. He had information that there were 96 horse-loads at the Warm spring, now in Bath County; and that there were from 30,000 to 40,000 pounds to be brought up from beyond these springs.

JOURNAL AND ORDERLY BOOK OF COLONEL FLEMING

Fortunately the Journal and Orderly Book* kept by Colonel William Fleming has been preserved, and from these we learn of the westward march of the Botetourt Regiment, and the Fincastle companies and Buford's Riflemen which accompanied it.

* The original is in the library of the State Historical Society of Wisconsin. It is printed in the "Documentary History of Dunmore's War," pp. 313-360.

From it we make extracts and insert material relating to the region through which the march was performed—that from Camp Union, to "Camp Point Pleasant"—a distance of one hundred and sixty miles

September 11th, Sunday—The last day for the Botetourt Regiment at Camp Union. Parole Greenbrier. There was a stirring scene at that place. The second Regiment with companies attached thereto were to move for the West. Six days had elapsed since the Augusta Regiment departed from Camp Union. Posey and Ingles were* *having the packhorses laden and the Quarter-Master was arranging for the transportation of tools and ammunition.*

* The *parole* was a watchword or password issued by the commanding Officer to officers of the guard. It differed from the *countersign,* which was a word given to all guards. It was usually at that time, a geographical term but sometimes the name of an individual.

September 12th, Monday—Divine service at 12 o'clock M. Marched from Camp Union; crossed Muddy Creek Mountain, and encamped at "Camp Pleasants," seven miles west of Camp Union; Parole Frederick. First Camp: Now near Asbury Post Office in Blue Sulphur Magisterial District, Greenbrier County, West Virginia.

September 13th, Tuesday—Resumed the March; passed "Hamilton's Plantation" and "Jackson's Clearing," and having marched eleven miles, encamped on a branch of Muddy Creek— "a bad place for both food and good water;" Parole George. Second camp: Now near Elton Post Office in Green Sulphur Magisterial District, Summers County.

September 14th, Wednesday—Marched up a branch one and one half miles and then passed over to Meadow Creek, a tributary of Gauley River; over Walker's Creek, a tributary of New River, where the army encamped; Parole Quebec. Third Camp: Now near Backus Post Office, in Quinnimont Magisterial District, Fayette County.

September 15th, Thursday—Left the third camp and marched up Buffalo Spring Lick, and fell in on the road made by the advance, under Colonel Charles Lewis, which was followed for a mile and a half. Then another mile and a half to the fourth encampment on Buffalo Fork, a western affluent of Meadow River. (Manuscript torn.) Fourth Camp: Now near Crickmer Post Office still in Quinnimont Magisterial District, Fayette County.

September 16th, Friday—March resumed. Firing of guns forbidden. Here on this day they were joined by Captain Robert McClennahan's and Captain Henry Pauling's companies, which were left behind to bring up some beef cattle which were lost. Parole Washington. Fifth camp: Now in the vicinity of Maplewood Post Office, Sewell Mountain Magisterial District, Fayette County.

September 17th, Saturday—Left the fifth encampment at an early hour, and took up the line of march westward. The march was over "Chestnut Hills;" crossed Great and Little Laurel Creeks, the first of which empties into the New River near Quinnimont, at what is known as the "Warrior's Ford," and passed Mann's Hunting Camp on a stream now known as

Mann's Creek, an eastern branch of New River. Parole Byrd. Sixth camp: Now near Winona Post Office, in Nuttall Magisterial District, Fayette County.

September 18th, Sunday—Started early in the morning and marched twelve miles over broken ridges covered with a chestnut forest and late at night encamped on Laurel Run. Parole Corbin. Seventh camp: Now near Mountain Cove Post Office, on Shade Creek, a tributary of Mill Creek, in Mountain Cove Magisterial District, Fayette County.

September 19th, Monday—The line of march was taken up. It was a day of alternate showers and sunshine; early in the day the present site of Ansted, in Fayette County, was reached and then began the ascent of Gauley mountain by a different path from that of Lewis' Advance Column, over the crest of which the columns passed, and thence down to the head of Rich Creek, a southern tributary of Gauley River. But six miles were made and an encampment fixed at the head of Rich Creek. Parole Page. Eighth camp: Still in Mountain Cove Magisterial District, Fayette County.

September 20th, Tuesday—There was an inspection of arms by the Captains, and then the march began and continued down Rich Creek for five miles, crossing it many times until the Gauley River was reached. This was "about one hundred yards wide, a stony ugly fording." This river was crossed by two fords within one and a half miles of Rich Creek, and encamped on Bell Creek, having marched eleven miles. Parole Johnson. Ninth camp: Now on Bell Creek in Falls Magisterial District, Fayette County.

September 21st. Wednesday—*The army proceeded up Lick (Bell) Creek five miles, passed the divide, and over on the head of Kelly's Creek, "thick with laurel for two miles" then the western tops became lower, the valley to widen, the tulip, maple, pawpaw, with leatherwood, and pea vine, and buffalo grass made their appearance, then appeared the sweet gum; and then the Great Kanawha River, two hundred yards wide, made its appearance. It was the site of the settlement of Walter Kelly, who was killed by the Indians two years before. Thence the march continued down to an encampment opposite the mouth of Cabin Creek. Parole Kanhaway. Tenth camp: Now opposite the mouth of Cabin Creek, in Cabin Creek Magisterial District, Kanawha County.

* "Leaving home In August, they (the men of the Southern Division), joined the army of western Virginia at Camp Union, on the Great levels of Greenbrier. From that place, now called Lewisburg, to the mouth of the Great Kanawha, the distance Is about one hundred and sixty miles. At that time there was not even a trace over the rugged mountains; but the young woodsmen who formed the advance party moved expeditiously with their pack-horses and droves of cattle

through the home of the wolf, the deer, and the panther. After a fortnight's struggle, they left behind them the last rocky masses of the hill-tops; and, passing between the gigantic growth of primeval forests, in which at that season the golden hue of the linden, the sugar tree, and the hickory contrasted with the glistening green of the laurel, the crimson of the sumac, and the shadows of the somber hemlock, they descended to the widening valley of Elk River."—Bancroft's "History of the United States," Vol. IV., p. 86.

September 22d, Thursday—March continued down the north side of the river. Arrived at the mouth of Elk River, the present site of Charleston, the capital of West Virginia, where it joined the Augusta Regiment. Eleventh camp. Parole Charlestown. Distance by computation from Camp Union, one hundred and eight miles. The actual distance was one hundred and three miles. Both regiments engaged in building a store-house and making canoes for transporting supplies down the Great Kanawha.

September 23rd, Friday—Details of men made to work on the canoes and the scouts reported early for instructions. All the tools in camp were put in working order. Parole Dunkirk.

September 24th, Saturday—Pack-horses were sent back to Camp Union for flour. The men detailed for this purpose were busy with the canoes. A court martial consisting of Colonel Fleming, President, and five Captains, sat to try Timothy Fitzpatrick for stealing a gun. He was acquitted and joined Captain McDowell's company. The provisions and ammunition were deposited in a magazine, built for the purpose. Three scouts were sent up Elk River toward Pocatalico; three across the Kanawha to Coal River; and some down the Kanawha on the north side. Divine services were held at twelve o'clock. Parole Bedford.

September 25th, Sunday—James Mooney, one of the scouts sent over Kanawha to Coal River returned and reported that four miles below the mouth of Elk, they had discovered the tracks of three horses, one shod, and two moccasin tracks that had passed them in the night going down the river. All attended divine services and had a good discourse. Scouts sent to the mouth of the Kanawha, launched their canoes at the mouth of Elk, and began the voyage down the river. Parole Winchester.

September 26th, Monday—Men at work were exempted from guard duty. Orders prohibiting the miscellaneous firing of guns were read at the head of each company immediately after the beating of Reveille. Parole Cumberland.

September 27th, Tuesday—At a review of the Botetourt Regiment Including the Fincastle and Culpeper men attached thereto, there were 523 men in line, and together with the Augusta Regiment, 1000 answered roll-call, that meaning exclusive of the sick and those on service or command in this vicinity. Parole Duke.

September 28th, Wednesday—Scouts from Coal River returned and reported that they had discovered where fifteen Indians had encamped. Captain Arbuckle with his scouts, was ordered out after them, but failed to come up with them. The confusion in camp resulting from the sale of liquors by the sutlers, made it necessary to prohibit the sale otherwise than on the orders of the Captains; and no more than the present stock was to be brought into Camp. Parole Prince.

September 29th, Thursday—James Fowler returned. He was one of the scouts which left on the 25th for the mouth of the Great Kanawha. He reported that when they were within fifteen miles of the mouth of the river, they saw two fires on its banks; that on their making a noise these were covered up; that on his return up the river in the canoe he saw five Indians with three horses going down the river. Parole Westmoreland.

September 30th, Friday—Drums beat at day break; the fleet of canoes —27 in number—which had been constructed, were taken one and a half miles up Elk River, where It was a hundred yards wide and where there was a "fording." The cattle and pack-horses were driven over, and there the army crossed the river and encamped on the level plain below the mouth of the Elk. It was "still dead running water." Parole King. Twelfth camp: Now on the present site of West Charleston, in Charleston Magisterial District, Kanawha County.

The March or Lewis' Army
From the Mouth of Elk River
To the Mouth of the Great Kanawha

October 1st, Saturday—Because of incessant rain the army remained in camp throughout the day and ensuing night. Parole Pitt. Same camp as on September 30th.

October 2d, Sunday—Early in the morning the army formed for line of march down the north side of the Great Kanawha River; Captain Lewis of the Botetourt Line led the advance. That line was the left column, while the Augusta Line was the right; both flanks were covered by one hundred men each. In the center were the beef cattle and packhorses. The orders to march were given, and the army made twelve miles that day. Parole Burk. Thirteenth camp: now in Union Magisterial District, opposite the mouth of Coal River—now St. Albans, Kanawha County.

October 3rd, Monday—The march was continued, and in the afternoon Pocatalico River crossed and an encampment affected one mile below the mouth of that stream, the distance from the last camp being eight miles. Parole Dinwiddie. Fourteenth camp: Now in Pocatalico Magisterial District, Putnam County.

October 4th, Tuesday—Onward marched the army through the wilderness and through the narrows at Red House Shoals "where large masses of rock the height of which exceeded the base, stood partly much in line;" they saw the "Fallen Timber" where the hills were swept "bare as a field," and encamped two miles below the mouth of Hurricane Creek. Parole Fauquier. Fifteenth camp: now near Midway Post Office, in Union Magisterial District, Putnam County.

October 5th, Wednesday—The march was resumed early in the morning; Buffalo Creek was crossed; the site of the present town of Buffalo passed; Eighteen-Mile Creek forded; the site of Leon passed and an encampment made two miles below the mouth of Thirteen-Mile Creek, the distance from the last encampment being twelve miles. Parole Charlestown. Sixteenth camp: Encampment on the Yauger farm, Cologne Magisterial District, Mason County.

October 6th, Thursday—Again the march continued; early in the morning Ten-mile Creek was crossed; Upper and Lower Debby Creeks passed; then Eight-mile and Three-mile Creeks forded and late in the afternoon the army crossed Crooked Creek and encamped on the upper triangular point of land at the confluence of the Great Kanawha and Ohio Rivers, having marched eleven miles. It was a magnificent scene. The dense forest clothed in its autumnal tints; and the rivers at low-water, with the Ohio resembling a lake and the Great Kanawha an estuary, the whole landscape presenting an enchanting scene. An army of weary men appreciated it, and bestowed upon it the name of Camp Point Pleasant. Parole York. "Encamped in the forks of the river" says Major Ingles, "in safe possession of a fine Encampment, we thought ourselves a terror to all the Indian tribes on the Ohio."

The accuracy with which Colonel Fleming estimated distances is surprising. These he gives for each day's march down the Great Kanawha, from the mouth of Elk, to the Ohio, equals fifty-seven and three-fourth miles; and the actual distance between these two points by railroad measurements is fifty-seven miles.

The fourth detachment to leave Camp Union was the company of Captain William Herbert, of the Fincastle Battalion, which took up the line of march therefrom on Friday, September 23rd. When it came up with the regiments in advance does not appear; but this was doubtless at the mouth of Elk River about the first of October.

Departure of the Fincastle Battalion From Camp Union

Colonel Christian left Camp Union for the west, Tuesday, September 27th, having with him the companies of Captains William Campbell, Joseph Crockett, George Moffatt and John Floyd, of the Fincastle Battalion; Captain Thomas Slaughter with the Dunmore Volunteers; Captain James Harrod with the Kentucky Pioneers; about eighty unorganized Minute Men from Culpeper County, who arrived too late to march with Colonel Field; and a like number who came from Augusta County, after the regiment therefrom, had marched from Camp Union. He estimated the total number at about 400 men.

We know little of the march of Christian through the mountains, save that it was made in shorter time that that of either of the divisions gone before. He arrived at the mouth of Elk River—now Charleston—on the 6th of October, eight days after leaving Camp Union, the distance being one hundred and three miles. October 7th, General Lewis at the mouth of the Great Kanawha, received letters from Christian stating that he was at the mouth of Elk "with 220 men, with 350 beeves; 24,000 lbs. of flour, and a supply of gunpowder." Sergeant Obediah Trent, of Captain Pauling's company, with a party of canoe-men, was sent up the Kanawha to bring down supplies.* On the 8th, Christian having detailed Captain Slaughter with the Dunmore Volunteers, to remain at the mouth of Elk, he, with the remainder, crossed that river and began the march down the north side of the Great Kanawha. The night was spent in the vicinity of what is now the West Virginia Colored Institute, in Union Magisterial District, Kanawha County. On the 9th, when Christian was near what is now Red House Shoals, on the Great Kanawha, he was met by scouts with a letter to him from General Lewis, requesting him to leave fifty beeves at Elk for those who should be there from time to time. This Christian could not do for he was then too far on his march.** The march was therefore continued and that evening an encampment was made near where the town of Buffalo, in Buffalo Magisterial District, Putnam County, now stands.

* "Documentary History of Dunmore's War," p. 340. Original in the library of the State Historical Society of Wisconsin.

** "Documentary History of Dunmore's War," p. 267.

The Detachment Left at Camp Union

Colonel Christian left Captain Anthony Bledsoe of the Fincastle Battalion in command at Camp Union. The troops with him were those of his own company, and the sick of the entire army who had been unable to leave with their respective commands. He was to receive and forward the supplies collected when the pack-horses were returned from the mouth of Elk. A number of these returned September 30th, but in such a jaded condition that they must rest before going to Warm Springs for their loads of flour. There was at that place 150 horse-loads, and an equal number at Staunton.* Under date of Saturday, October 15th, he again wrote Colonel Preston from Camp Union saying:—

"I propose starting from this place tomorrow with about two hundred horses and eighty cattle and hope to reach the mouth of New River (Great Kanawha) in 12 days, if the weather is good."**

Because of stirring news from the front he never marched on the expedition.

    * "Documentary History of Dunmore's War," p. 223. Original In the library of the State Historical Society of Wisconsin.

    ** "Documentary History of Dunmore's War," p. 261. Original In the library of the State Historical Society of Wisconsin.

CHAPTER V
THE BATTLE OF POINT PLEASANT

THE CHIEF EVENT OF THE LAST COLONIAL WAR IN AMERICA

The Battle of Point Pleasant was fought exactly three months from the day that Lord Dunmore left the gubernatorial mansion at Williamsburg; and in that brief time an army numbering more than twenty-seven hundred men had been organized in two divisions, each composed almost exclusively of frontiersmen west of the Blue Ridge and placed in the Ohio Valley. On Sunday, the ninth of October, the Northern Division or right wing, comprising the Berkeley and the Frederick County Regiments, and the West Augusta Battalion, the whole numbering thirteen hundred men, and commanded by Lord Dunmore in person, lay at Fort Gower, on the northwest bank of the Ohio, at the mouth of the Hockhocking River, now in Athens County, Ohio. The Southern Division or left wing, composed of the Augusta and the Botetourt Regiments; and the companies of Shelby, Russell, and Herbert, of the Fincastle Battalion; together with Buford's Bedford County Riflemen, the whole commanded by General Andrew Lewis, lay at Camp Point Pleasant, at the mouth of the Great Kanawha River. Colonel Christian with the companies of Campbell, Crockett and Floyd, of the Fincastle Battalion, and Harrod's Kentucky Pioneers, together with a number of unorganized men from the counties of Augusta and Culpeper, lay on the north or right bank of the Great Kanawha River, distant about twenty-five miles from its mouth. Captain Thomas Slaughter with the Dunmore Volunteers was at the mouth of Elk River—on the site of the Capital city of West Virginia—and Captain Anthony Bledsoe, with his company of Fincastle troops was still at Camp Union, on the Big Levels of Greenbrier. Christian's men were the only ones that moved that day; this was due to his desire to come up with General Lewis before he would cross the Ohio. At Camp Point Pleasant a communication had been received from Lord Dunmore stating that he should move directly across the country from Fort Gower to the Pickaway Plains, and requesting Lewis to join him at the latter place. Preparations were made to resume the march for this purpose. Then, says Major Ingles: "After hearing a good sermon preached by the Rev. Mr. Terry, (we) went to repose." That evening General Lewis' scouts reported to him that there was so no enemy within fifteen miles of the camp. But fleet-footed

Indian warriors from the peaks of the Alleghenies and the highlands along the Great Kanawha, had watched the progress of the Southern Division all the way from Camp Union to Camp Point Pleasant, and bore tidings of its advance to the Shawnee capital on the Pickaway Plains, where the assembled sachems and chiefs had, in their bark council-house in the valley of the Scioto, resolved upon war against the English Border. Their message went forth to summon the warriors to arms; this was speedily obeyed and hundreds of them gathered, ready for the fray. It was the plan of Cornstalk to defeat the two wings of the army before they could be united and if Lewis could be beaten and his army destroyed at the mouth of the Great Kanawha, the men composing the Northern Division under Dunmore could be shot down in the narrow defiles of the valley of the Hockhocking River. All day long that Sunday—October ninth— with silent tread, they approached the Ohio, and late in the evening, halted in the dense forest in the valley of Campaign Creek near the site of the present village of Addison, in Gallia County, Ohio, and distant about three miles above the mouth of the Great Kanawha. Soon after dark the warriors began crossing the Ohio on rafts, seventy-nine of these having been prepared previously. To ferry so many over this wide stream on these clumsy transports, must have required a considerable time. But before morning they were all on the southern bank on the site of "Old Shawane Town" a former home of the Shawnees, near the mouth of Old Town Creek and distant about three miles from Camp Point Pleasant; and were ready to proceed to action. Their route lay down through the bottom lands on the east bank of the Ohio. Here was a heavy growth of timber with foliage so dense, as in many places to intercept, in a great measure, the light of the moon and the stars. Beneath lay many trunks of fallen trees strewed in different directions and in various stages of decay. The whole surface of the ground was covered with a luxuriant growth of weeds interspersed with close-set thickets of spice-wood and other undergrowth. A journey through this in the night must have been tedious, tiresome, dark and dreary. The Indians, however, entered upon it promptly and pursued it until break of day. When, about a mile distant from the camp of the sleeping Virginians, one of those unforeseen incidents occurred which so often totally defeat or greatly mar the best concerted military plans. This was the discovery by the Virginians of the advancing Indian line, a most fortunate occurrence for, by it, the whole army was saved from destruction; because it was the design of the Indians to have attacked them at break of day, and to force all whom they could not kill, into the two rivers. Had that vast barbarian column swept down in the darkness of the morning upon Lewis' army of sleeping Virginians, it would have been doomed not only to defeat but to total destruction.

The Beginning Of The Battle

In the gray dawn of the morning twilight, Monday, October 10th, two young men went up along the east bank of the Ohio in quest of deer.* When in the narrowest portion of land between Crooked Creek and the Ohio River, they were discovered by the Indians, who were advancing in solid phalanx toward the camp of the Virginians. They fired) upon the hunters, one of whom they killed, and the other ran into camp and gave the alarm. Instantly the drums beat to arms, and the backwoodsmen rolled out of their blankets, started from the ground, looked to their flints and priming, and were ready on the moment.

* Captain John Stuart says: Two young men were sent out early to hunt for deer, and when up the river (Ohio) two or three miles, they fell on the camp of Indians who fired on them. One was killed; the other escaped and got Into camp Just before sunrise. He stopped before my tent, and I discovered a number of men collecting around him as I lay In my bed; I jumped up and approached him to know what was the cause of alarm ; when I heard him declare that he had seen about five acres of land covered with Indians as thick as they could stand one besides the other."—"Stuart's *Memoirs of the Indian Wars and Other Occurrences."* p. 46.

"These were Joseph Hughy, of Shelby's company, and James Mooney, of Russell's. The former was killed by a white renegade, Tavenor Ross, while the latter brought the news to camp."—Note by Reuben G. Thwaites, in *Documentary History of Dunmore's War."* p. 272.

Haywood, the Historian of Tennessee, says that those who discovered the Indians were James Robertson, and Valentine Sevier, sergeants in Captain Evan Shelby's company. He adds: "It fell to the lot of men from East Tennessee to make an unexpected discovery of the enemy and by that means save from destruction the whole army of Provincials, for it was the design of the enemy to have attacked them at day-dawn and then to have forced all they could not kill, into the two rivers."—*"Civil and Political History of Tennessee."* p. 58.

Isaac Shelby's Account of the Battle

The following description of the battle was written on the field, October 16th—six days thereafter—by Isaac Shelby,* a Lieutenant in Captain Evan Shelby's company, which he commanded after his father assumed the chief command. It was addressed while on the field to an uncle, John Shelby, on the Watauga River, "for the satisfaction of the people" in that region:—

"On Monday morning, about half an hour before sun-rise, two of Captain Russell's Company discovered a large party of

Indians about a mile from Camp, one of which men was shot down by the Indians, the other made his escape and brought the intelligence. In two or three minutes after, two of Captain Shelby's came in and confirmed the account. General Andrew Lewis being informed thereof, immediately ordered out Colonel Charles Lewis to take the command of one hundred and fifty of the Augusta Troops, and with him went Captain Dickinson, Captain Harrison, Captain Wilson, Captain John Lewis, of Augusta, and Captain Lockridge, which made the first Division. Colonel Fleming was also ordered to take the command of one hundred and fifty more of the Botetourt, Bedford, and Fincastle Troops, viz: Captain Thomas Buford, from Bedford, Captain Love, of Botetourt, Captain Shelby and Captain Russell, of Fincastle, which made the second Division. Colonel Charles Lewis's Division marched to the right some distance from the Ohio; and Colonel Fleming, with his Division, on the bank of the Ohio, to the left. Colonel Charles Lewis's Division had not marched quite half a mile from Camp, when, about sun-rise, an attack was made on the front of his Division, in a most vigorous manner, by united tribes of Indians, Shawnees, Delawares, Mingoes, Tawas, (Ottawas) and of several other Nations, in number not less than eight hundred, and by many thought to be a thousand. In this heavy attack, Colonel Charles Lewis received a wound, which in a few hours caused his death,* and several of his men fell on the spot. In fact, the Augusta Division was forced to give way to the heavy fire of the enemy. In about a second of a minute after the attack on Colonel Lewis's Division, the enemy engaged the front of Colonel Fleming's Division, on the Ohio, and in a short time the Colonel received two balls through his left arm, and one through his breast and after animating the officers and soldiers in a most calm manner, to the pursuit of victory, retired to the Camp.** This loss from the field was sensibly felt by the officers in particular; but the Augusta Troops being shortly reinforced from the Camp by Colonel Field, with his Company, together with Captain McDowell, Captain Matthews, and Captain Stuart, from Augusta, Captain John Lewis, Captain Pauling, Captain Arbuckle, and Captain McClennahan, from Botetourt, the enemy, nolonger able to maintain their ground, was forced to give way till they were in a line with the troops, which Colonel Fleming had left in action on the bank of the Ohio.

*Lieutenant Isaac Shelby, son of Captain Evan Shelby, and whose account of the battle, is regarded by historians as the best of all that was written on the field, was born near North Mountain, Maryland, December 11, 1750. He received a common English education, and with his father's family removed to King's Meadows, now Bristol, Tennessee, in 1771. The year after the

Battle of Point Pleasant, he was engaged in surveying in Kentucky; then became prominent in the Indian wars; then served in the Virginia State Line in the Revolution; in 1792, when Kentucky was admitted into the Union, he was almost unanimously elected first Governor of that State. He was again elected Governor in 1812; commanded Kentucky troops under General Harrison in the second war with England; and in 1817, was tendered the post of Secretary of War, a position which he declined. He died near Stanford, Kentucky, July 18, 1826, fifty-two years after the Battle of Point Pleasant, a victory he and his father did so much to win.

** Several statements have been made regarding the death of Colonel Charles Lewis. The following are from eye-witnesses. Captain John Stuart says: "Just as the sun was rising, a heavy fire soon commenced, and Colonel Lewis was mortally wounded, but walked into camp and died a few minutes afterward, observing to Colonel Charles Simms with his last words that he had sent one of the enemy to eternity before him."—Stuart's *Memoirs of the Indian Wars and Other Occurrences."* p. 46.

"Colonel Lewis was shot in clear ground, as he had not yet taken a tree, while speaking to his men to come on. He turned and handed his gun to a man and walked to camp, telling the men as he passed along, "I am wounded, but go you on and be brave."—*Documentary History of Dunmore's War,"* p. 265.

Three members of the Augusta Regiment—Joseph Mayse, Andrew Reed, and James Ellison—all in the column led out by Colonel Lewis,—told Samuel Kercheval the historian of the Shenandoah Valley that: "Colonel Charles Lewis, who had arrayed himself in a gorgeous scarlet waistcoat, (that of the British uniform) against the advice of his friends, thus rendering himself a conspicuous mark for the Indians, was mortally wounded early in the action; yet was able to walk back, after receiving the wound, into his own tent, where he expired. He was met on his way by the Commander-in-Chief, his brother, General Andrew Lewis, who remarked to him: "I expected something fatal would befall you," to which the wounded officer calmly replied, "It is the fate of war," and died.—Kercheval's "History of the Valley," pp. 101, 102.

*** "Colonel Fleming was shot with three balls; two in the left arm and one in the left breast, while speaking to his division in a piece of clear ground; with great coolness and deliberation, he stepped slowly back and told them not to mind him but to go up and light."—*Documentary History of Dunmore's War."* p. 265.

"Fleming was a heroic officer; after two balls had passed through his arm, he continued on the field, and exercised his command with the greatest coolness and presence of mind. His voice was continually heard, "Don't lose an inch of ground; advance; outflank the enemy; keep between them and the river." This was his last command; there came a shot which passed through his lungs and he fell, but insisted still to be permitted to remain upon the field. As he was borne from the field a portion of the lung protruded from the wound, and he pressed it back with his own hand "—Drake's *"History and Biography of the Indians of North America."* Book V., p. 43.

In this precipitate retreat, Colonel Field was killed.* During this time, which was till after twelve o'clock, the action continued extremely hot. The close underwood, many steep banks and logs, greatly favored their retreat; and the bravest of their men made the best use of them whilst others were throwing their dead into the Ohio, and carrying off their wounded. After twelve, the action in a small degree abated, but continued, except at short intervals, sharp enough till after one o'clock. Their long retreat gave them a most advantageous spot of ground, from whence it appeared to the officers so difficult to dislodge them, that it was thought most advisable to stand, as the line was then formed, which was about a mile and a quarter in length, and had sustained till then a constant and equal weight of the action, from wing to wing. It was till about half an hour of sunset they continued firing on us scattering shots, which we returned to their disadvantage. At length night coming on, they found a safe retreat. They had not the satisfaction of carrying off any of our men's scalps, save one or two stragglers, whom they killed before the engagement. Many of their dead they scalped, rather than we should have them; but our troops scalped upwards of twenty of their men that were first killed. It is beyond doubt their loss in number, far exceeds ours, which is considerate.**

* "Colonel Field was killed behind a great tree, (who) was looking for an Indian who was talking to amuse him, whilst some others were above him on his right hand among some logs, who shot him dead."—"Documentary History of Dunmore's War." p. 265.

** Shelby's Letter is printed substantially in the "American Archives" Fourth Series, Vol. I., p. 1016; and completely in the "Documentary History of Dunmore's War." p. 269, etc.

COLONEL WILLIAM FLEMING'S ACCOUNT OF THE BATTLE

Colonel William Fleming's Orderly Book has the following account of the battle:—

Monday, October the 10th, 1774

"This morning before sunrise two men came running into Camp and gave information that a considerable body of Indians were encamped about two miles up the Ohio a small distance from it, who made a very formidable appearance. This important intelligence was very quickly confirmed by two or three more. The drums by order immediately beat to Arms and 150 men were ordered to be paraded out of each line and march against the enemy in two columns. The right column headed by Colonel Charles Lewis with Captains Dickinson, Harrison and Skidmore. The left column commanded by Colonel Fleming with Captains Shelby, Russell, Love and Buford. Thus disposed they marched pretty briskly about one hundred and fifty or two hundred yards apart up the river about half a mile when on a sudden the enemy lurking behind bushes and trees gave the Augusta line a heavy fire which was briskly followed by a second and third and returned again by our men with much bravery and courage. This attack was attended with the death of some of our bravest officers and men also with the deaths of a great number of the enemy. Nor were the enemy less tardy in their attack upon the left Column; for immediately after the fire upon the right line succeeded a heavy one on the left and a return from us with spirit and resolution. As the disposition in which the men were first placed would never promise success against an Indian enemy, the men were forced to quit their ranks and fly to trees in doing this the enemy made a small advance and forced our men of both lines to retreat the distance of perhaps one or two hundred yards under heavy fires attended with dismal yells and screams from the enemy. About this time we were succored with a detachment from the Camp commanded by Captains Mathews, McDowell, and others of the Augusta line and some time afterwards by all the Captains of each line except Captain McClennahan of Augusta who was upon guard and Captain Lewis of Botetourt, who was ordered to form a line round the Camp for its defense. With the re-enforcement from the camp our men found their strength much increased and making a fierce onset, forced the enemy from their stations and caused them to retreat by degrees about a mile, giving them many brisk fires and hitting many of the leading men as was imagined. We at last with difficulty dislodged them from a fine long ridge leading from a small slash near the river towards the hills and being discontinued by a small wet bottom again rose and was continued to the hills half a mile or more from the river. This advantageous post being gained about one o'clock, all the efforts of the enemy to regain it proved fruitless. Though they would summon all the force they could raise and make many pushes to break the line; the advantage of the place and the steadiness of the men defied their most furious essays. About three or four o'clock, the enemy growing quite dispirited and all attempts of their warriors to rally them proving vain, they carried off their dead and wounded, giving us now and then a shot to prevent a pursuit; so that about an hour by sun we were in full possession of the field of Battle. Victory having now declared in our favour, we had orders to return in slow pace to our Camp carefully searching for the dead and wounded and to bring them in, as also the scalps of the enemy. The day being by this time far advanced with (out) any written orders, double guards were ordered to be mounted. That night the Parole was "Victory."*

* Fleming's "Orderly-Book," printed in "Documentary History of Dunmore's War," pp. 313, 360.

CAPTAIN JOHN STUART'S ACCOUNT

Captain John Stuart,* of the Botetourt Regiment, who participated in the battle, says:—

"General Lewis immediately ordered out a detachment of Augusta troops, under his brother, Colonel Charles Lewis, and another detachment of the Botetourt troops, under Colonel William Fleming. These were composed of the companies commanded by the oldest captains; and the junior captains were ordered to stay in camp to aid the others as occasion would require. The detachments marched out in two lines, and met the Indians in the same order of march, about four hundred yards from our camp, and in sight of the guard. The Indians made the first fire and killed both the scouts in front of the two lines.

* John Stuart, one of the most remarkable men whose name is connected with frontier history, was born in Augusta County, Virginia, in 1749. He came over the mountains in 1769 to find a home when only nineteen years of age and settled in the "Rich Lands" of what became Greenbrier County, West Virginia. He commanded a company in the Botetourt County Regiment, and was one of the most prominent actors in the Battle of Point Pleasant. From thence he accompanied the army to the Pickaway Plains in the Scioto Valley, and was present when the two divisions of the army were united. He witnessed the murder of Cornstalk at Point Pleasant in 1777. He led the relief from Lewisburg, that saved Fort Donnally, ten miles from that place, when besieged by the Indians in 1778. He rose to the rank of Colonel in the Military establishment of Virginia, and was engaged in the Indian wars until their close in 1795. In 1788, he was one of the Delegates from Greenbrier County to the Virginia Federal Convention which ratified the National Constitution, for which he voted. He was a man of culture and refinement and for that day possessed an excellent education. He was a member of "The American Philosophical Society," and of other learned bodies. He was clerk of the County court of Greenbrier County from 1780, to 1807—a period of twenty-seven years. His wife was Agatha, the widow of John Frogge, who was killed in the Battle of Point Pleasant. He died August 23, 1823, fifty years after the battle, and because of his writings regarding that and other events, may be designated as the "Historian of Dunmore's War."

Just as the sun was rising, a very heavy fire soon commenced, and Colonel Lewis was mortally wounded. During his life it was his lot to have frequent skirmishes with the Indians, in which he was always successful; had gained much applause for his intrepidity, and was greatly beloved by his troops. Colonel Fleming was also wounded; and our men had given way some distance before they were reinforced by the other companies issuing in succession from the camp. The Indians in turn had to retreat, until they formed a line behind logs and trees, across from the bank of the Ohio to the bank of the Kanawha, and kept up their fire 'till sundown."

General Lewis now knew that if the battle was not ended before darkness settled down upon the field, it would be a night of massacre, or the morrow a day of great doubt, and he resolved to throw a body of men into the rear of the Indian army. He therefore sent three of the most renowned companies on the field to execute this movement. They were those of Captains George Mathews, John Stuart, and Evan Shelby, the latter now commanded by his son, Lieutenant Isaac Shelby, the father having become the chief field officer after the fall of Colonels Lewis, Fleming and Field. They were called from the front to the point where the two rivers meet, and then proceeded under cover of the bank of the Great Kanawha for three quarters of a mile to the mouth of Crooked Creek; and thence along the bed of its tortuous course, to their destination; there they ascended the high bluff bank about where Tenth Street, in the town of Point Pleasant now is, and poured a destructive fire upon the Indian rear; and they believing that this was the long expected re-enforcement, under Colonel Christian, gave way, falling back toward the place from which they came that morning.

General Lewis took another precaution against a disastrous defeat. At three o'clock in the afternoon, he sent messengers up the Great Kanawha River to inform Colonel Christian that he was hotly engaged and to request him to hasten to his assistance. They met that officer about twelve miles from the battlefield, near the site of the present town of Leon, in Cologne Magisterial District, in Mason County—His march was quickened, but it was eleven o'clock that night when his troops came upon the field, and the battle had been fought and won. All was quiet save the groans of the wounded, for "only the dead could rest in such a night as that."

On the field the Indians left twenty-three guns; eighty blankets; twenty-seven tomahawks, with match-coats, skins, shot-pouches, powder-horns and war-clubs, which were sold for about £100:00:0.

VIRGINIANS KILLED IN THE BATTLE.

Careful estimates, made from the most authentic documentary evidence extant, place the number killed at eighty-one. The following is a list of names of persons known to have been among the slain, together with the organization to which each belonged:

FIELD OFFICERS.

Colonel Charles Lewis, commanding the Augusta County Regiment, Colonel John Field of the Culpeper County Company, Captain John Murray of the Botetourt County Regiment, Captain Robert McClennahan of the Botetourt County Regiment, Captain Samuel Wilson of the Augusta County Regiment, Captain Charles Ward of the Augusta County Regiment.

SUBALTERN OFFICERS.

Lieutenant Hugh Allen of Captain George Mathews' Company of the Augusta County Regiment, Lieutenant Jonathan Cundiff of Captain Thomas Buford's Company of Bedford County Riflemen, Ensign Mathew Bracken of Captain Robert McClennahan's Company of the Botetourt County Regiment, Ensign Samuel Baker of Captain Henry Pauling's Company of the Botetourt County Regiment.

PRIVATES.

John Frogg, a sutler of the Augusta County Regiment.

Mark Williams, Roger Topp and Joseph Hughey, of Captain Evan Shelby's Company, of the Fincastle County Battalion.

James Mooney and ____Hickman, of Captain William Russell's Company, of the Fincastle County Battalion.

George Cameron, of Captain George Mathews' Company, of the Augusta County Regiment.

Samuel Croley, Organization to which he belonged not known.

To these add <u>sixty-four</u> others of whom either the name or organization to which they belonged or both are unknown.

The day after the battle, the bodies of the men slain therein, together with those who died of wounds that night, were buried in different places; the following officers—Colonel Charles Lewis, Colonel John Field, Captain John Murray, Captain Robert McClennahan, Captain Samuel Wilson, Lieutenant Hugh Allen, John Frogg and George Cameron—being laid to rest inside of the Magazine directly on the upper point of land, at the confluence of the rivers—now Tu-enda-wee Park. All were interred without the pomp of war, but that day the cheeks of many a hardy Virginia-West Virginia mountaineer were bedewed with tears.

VIRGINIANS WOUNDED IN THE BATTLE

Captain John Stuart, the historian, who was in the battle, says that one hundred and forty men were wounded; and this statement is verified by documentary evidence yet extant. Ensign James Newell, who kept a journal, himself wounded, says, under date of October 21st—eleven days after the battle: "At Point Pleasant was a stockade, built to secure the wounded men who are dying daily, and it is a most shocking sight to see their wounds." The following are names of persons known to have been among the wounded:

FIELD OFFICERS.

Colonel William Fleming, Commanding the Botetourt County Regiment. Captain John Dickinson, of the Augusta County Regiment. Captain John Skidmore, of the Augusta County Regiment. Captain Thomas Buford, of the Bedford County Riflemen.

SUBALTERNS.

Lieutenant David Laird, of the Augusta County Regiment. Lieutenant Samuel Vance, of Captain John Lewis' Company, of the Augusta County Regiment. Lieutenant Edward Goldman, of Captain Henry Pauling's Company, of the Botetourt County Regiment. Ensign James Newell, of Captain William Herbert's Company, of the Fincastle County Battalion.

PRIVATES.

John Stuart, Reece Price, Joseph Hughey, and John McCormack, of Captain Evan Shelby's Company, of the Fincastle County Battalion.

John Basdell and William Prince, of Captain William Russell's Company, of the Fincastle County Battalion.

Thomas Baker, of Captain William Campbell's Company, of the Fincastle County Battalion.

John McMullen, David Glascom, John Freeland, and William Morris, of Captain Mathew Arbuckle's Company, of the Botetourt County Regiment.

Thomas Huff and Thomas Carpenter, of Captain John Lewis' Company, of the Botetourt County Regiment.

James Alexander and William Franklin, of Captain Philip Love's Company, of the Botetourt County Regiment.

Stephen Arnold, of Captain John Murray's Company, of the Botetourt County Regiment.

Charles Kennison, William Clendennin, and Thomas Ferguson, of Captain John Stuart's Company, of the Botetourt County Regiment.

Henry Bowyer, of Captain James Robertson's Company, of the Fincastle County Battalion.

James Curry and Alexander Stuart, of Captain George Moffat's Company, of the Botetourt County Regiment.

Benjamin Blackburn, Joseph Mayse, Thomas Price and James Robinson, the organization to which they belonged being unknown.

To these add <u>one hundred and six</u> others of whom either names or organization to which they belonged or both are unknown.

The number of Indians killed and wounded* could never be known for they were continually carrying off their dead and throwing them into the river. A never-failing characteristic of the dying Red-man was a desire that his body might not fall into the hands of his pale-faced antagonist; and his comrades in battle were wont to bear his body from the field when he had fallen. His loss has been stated at two hundred and thirty-three.**

<small>* *Pu-kee-she-no* a Shawnee, whose name signified "I light from flying" was killed in the battle. He was the noblest warrior that perished there. His wife was a Cherokee woman whose name was *Mee-thee-ta-she*, which signified "a turtle laying her eggs in the sand." These were the parents of Tecumseh and his brothers *Ells-scat-a-wa* one who foretells; otherwise the Prophet, and *Kum-sha-ka*, signifying "A tiger that flies in the air." The mother is said to have transplanted the beautiful Cherokee rose from the banks of the Tennessee to those of the Scioto, whence it has spread far and wide. Their home was on the banks of that river, on the site of the present city of Chilicothe, and there the little son, Tecumseh, but six years of age, played while his father was killed at Point Pleasant."— Drake's *"Biography and History of the Indians of North America."* Book V., p. 123
** "American Archives," 4th Series Vol. I., p. 1018.</small>

The three men who served in the Augusta Regiment—Joseph Mayse, Andrew Reed, and James Ellison—from whom Samuel Kercheval, the historian, obtained his information regarding the Battle of Point Pleasant, informed him that some little time after the battle, Indian traders visited the garrison at that place, and stated that "the loss of the Indians in killed and wounded was not short of three hundred warriors.*

<small>* "History of the Shenandoah Valley," p. 102.</small>

Captain John Stuart said: *"The Indians were exceedingly active in concealing their dead that were killed. I saw a young man draw out three in the heat of the battle. The next morning twenty of the enemy were found slain upon the ground. Twelve were afterwards found all concealed in one place; and the Indians confessed that they had thrown a number into the river in time of battle; so that it is possible that the slain on both sides were about equal."**

<small>* "Memoirs of the Indian Wars and Other Occurrences," p. 46</small>

The dead bodies of the Indians who fell in the battle were never buried, but left to decay on the ground where they expired, or to be devoured by the birds and beasts of prey. The Mountain Eagle, lord of the feathered race, while from his lofty flight, with piercing eye, surveyed the varied scenes around and beneath, would not fail to descry the feast prepared for his use. Here he might whet his beak and feast and fatten. Over these, the gaunt wolf, grim tyrant of the forest, might prolong his midnight revelry and howl their funeral dirge; while far remote in the deepest gloom of the wilderness, whither they had fled for safety, the surviving warriors might bewail their fate or chant a requiem to their departed spirits.

There were widely published accounts of the Battle of Point Pleasant. The first of these was written by Captain Thomas Slaughter, commanding the Dunmore Volunteers. This he sent to his brother in Culpeper County, who received it November 2d, and the next day, sent it to William Rind and John Pinkney, the publishers of the *Virginia Gazette,* at Williamsburg, in which it was published, November 10, 1774. The *Pennsylvania Gazette* had a full account the following week. The *Royal American Magazine* of Boston, Massachusetts, contained details of the battle in its November No. pp. 438, 439. The first account received in Europe, went across the ocean in the good ship "Harriott," Captain Lee. She touched at Falmouth, England, where the New York mails were landed, and the *London Daily Advertiser,* in January 1775, had a lengthy article on the battle the same week the Belfast, (Ireland) *News Letter* published it; and that month (January) the *Scots Magazine,* published in Edinburg, Scotland, had a full account thereof. Contempory with this, *The Gentlemen's Magazine* and *Historical Chronicle,* Vol. XLV., January No. pp. 42, 43, of London, contained full details, including lists of killed and wounded. French and German newspapers on the Continent, likewise, published extended articles descriptive of the battle. Thus it was, that, notwithstanding there were then no telegraph lines, no ocean cables, nor steamships, yet because of its importance, details of the great battle, were published practically all over the civilized world.

CHAPTER VI
THE VIRGINIAN ARMY IN THE OHIO WILDERNESS
TREATY OF CAMP CHARLOTTE
RETURN OF THE ARMY
THE SUPPLEMENTAL TREATY AT PITTSBURG

The Indians, defeated at Point Pleasant, fled from the field at sundown and crossed the Ohio on the same rafts which brought them over the preceding night. Thence they trod the long, wearisome journey through the lonely wilderness to their towns on the Pickaway Plains. There Cornstalk called a council of his nation to consult on what was to be done. He upbraided the other chiefs for their folly in not permitting him to make peace before the battle. "What" said he, "Will you do now? The Big Knife (the Virginians) is coming on us, and we shall all be killed. Now you must fight or we are undone." But no one made answer. He then said, "let us kill all our women and children and go and fight till we die." But none would answer. At length he rose and struck his tomahawk in the post in the center of the council house; "I'll go," said he and "make peace;" and the warriors all grunted "ough, ough, ough," and runners were instantly dispatched to the Governor's army to solicit peace and the interposition of the Governor in their behalf.*

* This was related by Cornstalk to a council of officers at Point Pleasant, November 10, 1777, less than an hour before his death—Stuart's *"Memoirs of the Indian War and Other Occurrences."* p. 62.

On the morning of the 12th of October—the second day after the battle—General Lewis, sent James Fowler, James McAnore, and Samuel Huff to Dunmore with a full account of the battle. But this he did not receive, for having sent a messenger to General Lewis with a request to meet him at the Pickaway Plains, he left a garrison of one hundred men at Fort Gower, and with twelve hundred, without a knowledge of the battle, took up the line of march October 11th, up the Hockhocking Valley which he followed by way of the present town of Athens, Ohio, and thence to where the town of Logan, in that State, now stands; from here he crossed the highland between the valleys of the Hockhocking and the Scioto Rivers, and proceeded towards his destination—the Pickaway Plains.

Before arriving in the vicinity of the Indian towns, and when fifteen miles distant therefrom, he was met by Mathew Elliott, a white man, bearing a flag of truce, and accompanied by several Indian chiefs who requested the assistance of an interpreter through whom they could communicate with Lord Dunmore. Captain John Gibson, commanding a company in the "West Augusta Battalion" was designated for this purpose. It was thus learned that Cornstalk and other chiefs, desired to treat for peace, and requested that Dunmore halt his army until terms could be agreed upon. Captain Gibson was sent forward to speak with them,* but the army marched onward and on Monday, October 17th, on a spot, now in the southwest quarter of Section Twelve, of Range twenty-one, in Pickaway Township, Pickaway County, Ohio, fixed his encampment, to which he gave the name of "Camp Charlotte," in honor of his wife, the Lady Dunmore, whose given name was Charlotte.

*See affidavit of Captain John Gibson, in Jefferson's "Notes on Virginia. Appendix, p. 16.

The next day preliminary arrangements were made. Dunmore was the presiding officer; Major John Connelly, Secretary; Captain John Gibson, and Thomas Nicholson, interpreters; and Major Thompson was chief officer of the day. On the 19th, Lord Dunmore admitted the chieftains to a conference. It was a great day away out in that western wilderness. White and Red men met to consummate a treaty of peace, after a march of two thousand four hundred men from the heart of Virginia to the center of the then known American wilderness. As the head official of that army and as the presiding officer of that convention, there sat a royal Colonial Governor, a Lord, a Peer of Great Britain, who had sat for ten years in the House of Lords, and had now walked on foot,* from the Shenandoah Valley to the banks of the Scioto. There too, was Colonel Adam Stephen, Colonel William Crawford, Major Angus McDonald, Captain George Rogers Clark, Captain John Gibson, Captain Daniel Morgan, Captain James Parsons, and many others who were to be future history makers. And there was Cornstalk, the foremost warrior of his race, who, in tones that rang out over the Pickaway Plains, electrified his hearers, and told of the wrongs which his people had suffered, detailed their woes, and afterward quietly submitted to the terms offered, and entered into a treaty which, three years later, at Point Pleasant, he sacrificed his life to maintain. The next day Lord Dunmore submitted to the Convention what he called "the Terms of Our Reconciliation." These afterward known as the terms of the treaty of Camp Charlotte** and to which the Indians agreed, were as follows:

I. To give up, without reserve all the prisoners ever taken by them in war with the white people; and to never again wage war against the frontier of Virginia.
II. To give up all Negroes taken by them from white people since the last war; and to pay for all property destroyed by them in that time. III. To surrender all horses and other valuable effects which they had taken from the white people since the last war.
IV. To no more in the future hunt on or visit the south side of the Ohio River, except for the purpose of trading with the white people.
V. To no more molest boats of white people, while descending or ascending the Ohio River.
VI. To agree to such regulations for trade with the white people as should hereafter be dictated by the King's instruction.
VII. To deliver up hostages as a guarantee for the faithful compliance with the terms of the treaty; to be kept by the Whites until convinced of the sincerity on the part of the Indians to adhere to all these articles.
VIII. To have from the Governor a guarantee that no white people should be permitted to hunt on the northern or Indian side of the Ohio River.
IX. To meet at Pittsburg the next spring and enter into a supplemental treaty by which the terms of the treaty of "Camp Charlotte" should be ratified and fully confirmed.

In consideration of an agreement with these covenants, Lord Dunmore gave them every promise of protection and good treatment on the part of the Virginians.

* "American Archives." Fourth Series, Vol. II., pp. 310. 312.
** For data relating to the terms of the treaty of "Camp Charlotte" see Bancroft's "History of the United States." Vol. IV., p. 88; "Documentary History of Dunmore's War", pp. 304, 386; "Journal of the Continental Congress," Vol. II., pp. 174, 175, 183, 251; Journal of the "House of Burgesses" of Virginia, Session beginning June 1. 1775; Thwaites and Kellogg's "Revolution on the Upper Ohio" pp. 25-127; and Windsor's "Narrative and Critical History of America" Vol. VI., p. 114.

Advance of General Lewis' Army To The Pickaway Plains

On the 11th of October, General Lewis received orders issued on the day of battle by the, Earl of Dunmore to cross the Ohio with his army, and proceed to the Pickaway Plains, there to meet the right wing marching from Port Gower. But Lewis could not obey this command. The dead were to be buried, and this was done on the 11th of October; Colonel Christian must send a company to bring in the cattle which he had left on the Great Kanawha, and this he did on the 12th; the store-house and breastworks must be provided for the supplies and the protection of the wounded, and this work was progressing on the 13th. Because of the loss of officers in the battle, there must be re-organization in the army, and this took place on the 14th, when Lieutenant William McKee succeeded to the command of Captain John Murray's company; Lieutenant Givens to that of Captain Samuel Wilson; and Lieutenant William McCoy to that of Captain Robert McClennahan. Additional supplies must be received, and these arrived on the evening of the 14th, being brought from the mouth of Elk River by Captain Thomas Slaughter, with his Dunmore Volunteers. The horses which were stampeded on the day of the battle, had to be collected, and on the 15th, three men were detailed from each company, and under the command of three Sergeants were sent out for this purpose—one to go four miles up the Ohio; another up the Great Kanawha to the "first narrows" (mouth of Three-mile Creek) and the third "to take the ridges" between the two rivers. On the 16th, the horses were gathered in, and sixty selected to carry flour; then two were assigned to each company to carry "tents and bundles." Colonel Fleming, though desperately wounded, was appointed commander of the post. Officers left were Captains Dickinson, (wounded) Lockridge, Herbert and Slaughter; and Lieutenants Draper and Vance and Ensign Smith. The garrison was composed of men detailed from the various organizations, who were formed into companies; by Captains Lockridge, Herbert and Slaughter. It consisted of four lieutenants, four ensigns, fifteen sergeants, one drummer one fifer, and two hundred and fifty privates, making a total of two hundred and seventy-eight men. At length all was in readiness, and on the evening of the 17th of October, General Lewis crossed the Ohio with one thousand, one hundred and fifty men, with ten days rations, Sixty-one pack-horses, and one hundred and eighteen beeves, and encamped on the site of the present town of Kanauga, in Gallia County, Ohio. The next morning fifteen additional beeves were taken over; and then the march along the Ohio, and thence up the valley of Champaign Creek, still in Gallia County, was continued for six miles when an encampment was made for the night. Onward marched the army until the 22nd, when it arrived on the banks of Kinnickinnick Creek, now in the northeastern portion of Ross County, Ohio, distant fifteen miles from Camp Charlotte. Here he, (Lewis,) received the first information of the treaty. It was conveyed to him by the hands of Whitefish, an Indian chief, in the form of a communication from Lord Dunmore. From here Lewis's army proceeded to Congo Creek, distant four and one half miles from Camp Charlotte, where it arrived on the 23rd, and went into camp on what is now the southeast quarter of Section Thirty, in Pickaway Township, Pickaway County, Ohio,* The following statements, the first by General Lewis, the second by Captain John Stuart, the historian, both of whom were present, explain in a most interesting manner, the meeting of General Lewis and his Lordship, on this occasion:

*"October 29th, Saturday:—General Lewis returned to Camp Point Pleasant from the Northwest of the Ohio, and explained to the wounded Colonel Fleming how he met Lord Dunmore at the Pickaway Plains. He stated that when near the Indian towns, an express came from Lord Dunmore with the information that he had very nearly concluded a peace, and for General Lewis to halt his troops. The place being inconvenient to encamp, he marched on in quest of a more suitable spot. Another messenger arrived saying that the Shawnees had agreed to the terms of Lord Dunmore; that peace was in a manner concluded; and an invitation was extended to General Lewis and other officers of the southern wing to visit his camp. Lewis proposed to march the southern wing to his Lordship's camp, but the guide mistook the path and followed one leading between the Indian towns and the Governor's camp. This put the Indians into a fright, they believing that General Lewis would attack their towns, and they left his Lordship and ran off. Lord Dunmore, then, accompanied by Colonel John Gibson, and White-fish, an Indian, rode over to Lewis' camp. Dunmore then asked Lewis if he proposed to march to the Indian towns. Colonel Lewis assured him that he had no thought of attacking the towns after receiving his Lordship's orders."***

* "History of Franklin and Pickaway counties" (Ohio) p. 265.
**Fleming's Orderly Book in "Documentary History of Dunmore's War." p. 356.

Captain John Stuart the historian, who was present, thus tells of the visit of Lord Dunmore to General Lewis's camp:

"When the Governor reached General Lewis's camp, his Lordship requested that officer to introduce him to his officers; and we were accordingly ranged in rank and had the honor of

an introduction to the Governor and Commander-in-Chief, who politely thanked us for services rendered on so momentous occasion, and assured us of his high esteem and respect for our conduct."

Captain Stuart speaking of this meeting says further:

"On the Governor's consulting General Lewis, it was deemed necessary that a garrison should be established at the mouth of the Great Kanawha to intercept and prevent the Indians from crossing the Ohio to our side; also to prevent any whites from crossing over to the side of the Indians; and by such means to preserve a future peace according to the conditions of the treaty thus being made by the Governor with the Indians."*

* "Memoirs of the Indian Wars and Other Occurrences," p. 57, 58.

Governor Dunmore having informed General Lewis that the Shawnees had agreed to all his terms and that the presence of the left wing of the army could be of no service, *"but rather a hindrance to the peace being concluded,"* now ordered him to return, and on the next day, his army began to retrace its steps back to the Ohio. Thus ended the connection of the Southern Division with the Treaty of Camp Charlotte.

The Treaty in Progress

Dunmore now urged promptness on the part of the chieftains, saying that if the war was to be ended by a treaty, he was anxious to proceed with it at once, otherwise, he would be forced to resume hostilities. Logan, the Mingo chief returned at this juncture from an incursion into the settlements in the valleys of the Holston and Clinch Rivers. Lord Dunmore dispatched two interpreters to invite him to attend the treaty. To this he replied by saying:—*"I am a warrior, not a councilor, and shall not come."* His people, the Mingoes, whose towns were on site of the present city of Columbus, the capital of Ohio, were much displeased with the terms of peace dictated by Dunmore and resolved to slip away from the treaty. When his Lordship learned this he determined to prevent it and placed the matter in the hands of Colonel William Crawford, who writing Colonel George Washington under date of November 14, 1774, says:—

"Lord Dunmore ordered myself with two hundred and forty men to set out in the night. We were to march to a town about forty miles distant from our camp, up the Scioto, where we

understood the whole of the Mingoes were to rendezvous upon the following day, in order to pursue their journey. This intelligence came by John Montour, son of Captain Montour, whom you formerly knew.

Because of the number of Indians in our camp we marched out of it under pretense of going to Hockhocking for more provisions. Few knew of our setting off anyhow, and none knew where we were going.

Our march was performed with as much speed as possible. We arrived at a town called the Salt-Lick Town the ensuing night, and at daybreak we got around it with one-half our force, and the remainder were sent to a small village half a mile distant. Unfortunately one of our men was discovered by an Indian who lay out from town some distance by a log which the man was creeping up to. This obliged the man to kill the Indian. This happened before daylight which did us much damage, as the chief part of the Indians made their escape in the dark; but we got fourteen prisoners, and killed six of the enemy, wounding several more. We got all their baggage and horses, ten of their guns, and 200 (two) hundred white prisoners. The plunder sold for four hundred pounds sterling, besides what was returned to a Mohawk that was there. The whole of the Mingoes were ready to start, and were to have set out the morning we attacked them."*

* The "Washington-Crawford Letters." p. 55.

This was the only fighting done by the right wing of the army during the war. At length the treaty closed with the understanding that, for "the sake of greater solemnity," a supplemental one should be held at Pittsburg the next spring. The Shawnees delivered as hostages, as a guarantee for good behavior, and a compliance with the terms of the treaty, five of their chiefs, of whom Chenusaw, "The Judge" Cutenwa and Newau, were three, and they were taken to Williamsburg, the capital of Virginia. Dunmore likewise conveyed twelve warriors of the Mingoes, to be detained at Pittsburg.

The Return of the Army

The southern Division under General Lewis left the Pickaway Plains on the 25th of October; two days later, several men returned to Point Pleasant and brought the first intelligence of the treaty. On the 28th, numbers of the troops arrived at the same place; and the next day General Lewis with the rear guard came in. Here the left wing practically disbanded. Colonel Christian writing Colonel Preston under date of November 8th says: *"I dare say the Army is now scattered from Elk—now Charleston, West Virginia—to Camp Union;" perhaps from Point Pleasant to the Warm Springs, all In little companies. Many of the Fincastle men crossed the Ohio at Point Pleasant and intended to steer for Clinch River. Others by Kelly's—that is to the mouth of Kelly's Creek, on the Great Kanawha, twenty miles above the mouth of Elk."*

* "Documentary History of Dunmore's War," p. 306.

Dunmore's division left Camp Charlotte about the last day of October, and was back at Fort Gower, on the 5th day of November. He detailed a garrison of twenty-five men for Fort Fincastle, at Wheeling, and one hundred to remain at Fort Dunmore; then he hastened homeward by way of the latter place and arrived at Williamsburg on the 4th of December. From Fort Gower many of the men returned to their homes by way of the Little Kanawha Valley, and the site of the present town of Clarksburg, West Virginia. At the Conference of Dunmore and Lewis at the Pickaway Plains, when it was decided to erect a fort at the mouth of the Great Kanawha, it was agreed that Captain William Russell's Company of the Fincastle Battalion should be detailed for this work. Accordingly, Russell accompanied Dunmore's Northern Division back to Fort Gower, whence he descended the Ohio to Point Pleasant, where he found that nothing had been done on the Fort since General Lewis crossed the Ohio; and the supply of flour was sufficient for only eight days. General Lewis had left a letter for him saying that his Commissary's report showed that he had left one hundred and sixty beeves in the woods at that place, and Russell hoped that his company might get eighty or a hundred of them.* Here Russell constructed a small palisaded rectangular fort about eighty yards long with block-houses at two of its corners, and bestowed upon it the name of "Fort Blair."*

* "Documentary History of Dunmore's War," p. 308

Captain Russell was still at Fort Blair in June 1775. Writing Colonel Fleming at that time, he said:—

"I am this morning preparing to start oft the cattle up Big Sandy, and expect (the) command will leave here this Wednesday or Thursday at (the) furtherest; and I shall Decamp myself with a convoy with the other stores next Monday; and

expect to overtake the stock at Big Painted Lick about sixty miles up Big Sandy."

At the same time that year, Dunmore discharged the garrisons at Fort Fincastle and Fort Dunmore; and the last men in service in Dunmore's war, returned to their homes.

The Supplemental Treaty at Pittsburg, 1775

By reference to the ninth article in the terms of the treaty of Camp Charlotte, it was agreed on the part of both parties thereto, that a supplemental convention, or treaty, should be held at Pittsburg, the ensuing spring for the purpose of ratifying and confirming the treaty of Camp Charlotte, and for the further decision of some minute details connected therewith, but which could not receive attention at the hurried meeting on the Pickaway Plains. Lord Dunmore promised that he would, by messenger, inform the chiefs of the several nations when it would be most convenient for him to meet them at Pittsburg, there to complete the work left unfinished at Camp Charlotte.

The House of Burgesses assembled at Williamsburg, June 1, 1775. Five days thereafter, Governor Dunmore sent to it a written message, saying that he was transmitting therewith a paper containing the "Substance of the peace agreed to between me and the Indians which has not been formally ratified; that having been deferred to a meeting intended to be held at Fort Dunmore this spring, when all the Ohio Indians, for the greater solemnity, were to be present, but which I have not been able to find time to proceed to."*

The title of this Document was:—

"SUBSTANCE OF THE PEACE AGREED TO BETWEEN THE EARL OF DUNMORE, GOVERNOR OF VIRGINIA, ON THE PART OF THAT COLONY; AND THE CORNSTALK ON THE PART OF THE SHAWNEE INDIANS.

*Intended to be ratified at a general meeting of the Ohio Indians, at Fort Dunmore"**

* "Revolution on the Upper Ohio." pp. 13, 14

This was laid on the table the same day, "to be perused by the members of the House." There it remained until Friday, June 20th, when it was taken up, considered, and a bill passed, entitled *"An Act for appointing Commissioners to ratify and confirm the late treaty of peace with the Ohio Indians."* With this, the Council of State—a Senate under the Colonial form of government— refused to concur. A Committee of Conference considered the subject; and reported that an address should be presented to the Governor requesting that his "Excellency would appoint persons to ratify the treaty with the Indians; and recommended to the House to vote a sum of money not exceeding two thousand pounds, for that business."*

* See Journal of the House of Burgesses, Session beginning Thursday, June 1, 1775.

But the next day, June 24th—the last of the session—the members of the house had intelligence from the west to the effect that there was dissatisfaction on the part of the Indians, because of the failure to make provision for the treaty supplementing that of Camp Charlotte. There was hesitation no longer. That body at once took action as follows:—

(Whereas) *"Certain Information having been received of the great discontent of the Ohio Indians, by reason of the delay of the Ratification of the late treaty of peace concluded upon by his Excellency the Governor, on the part of this Colony and the Cornstalk (at Camp Charlotte) on the part of the said Indians, and that the inhabitants on our frontier are under just apprehension of a renewal of an Indian war, and no steps having been pursued by his Lordship for carrying on the said treaty, or delivering up the Indian Hostages, agreeable to the terms of said treaty:—*

(Therefore) Resolved, That the said treaty be immediately entered upon; and that George Washington, Thomas Walker, James Wood, Andrew Lewis, John Walker, and Adam Stephen, Esquires, or any three or more of them, be, and they are hereby constituted and appointed, Commissioners, on the part and behalf of this colony, to meet the chiefs or head men of the said Ohio Indians, as soon as the same can be done, at such place as they shall find most proper, to ratify and confirm the said treaty, on the part of this colony, and to demand and receive of the said Indians the ratification and full performance of the said treaty on their parts; and that Robert Carter Nicholas, Esquire, Treasurer, or the Treasurer for the time being, shall, and (he) is hereby directed and required to pay all such expenses and charges, out of the public money in his hands, as may be incurred on account of such treaty, provided the same do not exceed the sum of two thousand pounds, for which the said Commissioners shall account to the next General Assembly."

Ordered, that Mr. Mercer do carry this Resolution to the Council and desire their concurrence.

A message from the Council by Mr. Blair:

Mr. Speaker,

"The Council has agreed to the Resolve for appointing Commissioners to ratify the treaty of peace with the Ohio Indians; and for defraying the expense thereof."*

* See Journal of the House of Burgesses, Saturday, June 24th, session beginning Thursday, June 1, 1775.

The Commissioners named above, held a meeting the same evening and appointed Captain James Wood, one of their number, to proceed to the Ohio and invite the Indians to a treaty at Pittsburg, on the 12th of September, ensuing. He left Williamsburg, the day after his appointment; spent three days at his home at Winchester in the Shenandoah Valley, and arrived at Pittsburg on the 9th of July. There he met many chiefs of various nations, to all of whom he explained the object of his visit. July 19th, he left Pittsburg and visited the Delawares, Mingoes, Wyandots, Shawnees, and other nations, all of whom he requested to send their chiefs to attend the treaty. He returned to Pittsburg August 11th, having been in the Ohio Wilderness for thirty-four days. His mission was eminently successful. The next day he departed for Winchester, where he arrived on the 17th, ensuing, and from there transmitted his report to the Commissioners, in whose service he had been employed. Now all awaited the coming of the Convention.

Meantime, the people of the "District of West Augusta," appointed a Committee of Safety. It prepared and forwarded a petition to the Continental Congress, and that body on July 12th, decided that there was "too much reason to apprehend that the British Government would spare no pains to excite the several nations of Indians to take up arms against these Colonies;" and that "it becomes us to be very active and vigilant in exerting every prudent means to strengthen and confirm their friendly disposition toward these Colonies." That day three Indian Departments were therefore created—The Southern, Central, and Northern—and it was provided that five Commissioners be appointed for the first, and three each for the second and third. On the next day, Benjamin Franklin, James Wilson, and Patrick Henry were unanimously appointed Commissioners for the Central Department, which included all of the Indian nations which had been parties to the treaty of Camp Charlotte. September 14th, ensuing, Lewis Morris, then at Pittsburg, was appointed in place of Benjamin Franklin, who was unable to attend the convention at that place; and the next day, Dr. Thomas

Walker, who was one of the Virginia Commissioners, was appointed by the Continental Congress in place of Patrick Henry, who declined to serve. The appointment of these Commissioners by Congress carried therewith, an appropriation of $6,666.63, from the Continental Treasury, for their expenses and the purchase of presents for the Indians.*

* See Journal of the Continental Congress. (Ford's Edition) Vol. II., pp. 174, 175, 183, 251.

Because of the tardiness of the Indian chiefs to arrive at Pittsburg, the treaty convention did not convene on September 12th, but, on that date Commissioners of the Continental Congress, as well as those of Virginia, were present. They organized by electing Dr. Thomas Walker, chairman of the Joint Commission, he being a member of both. On the 15th many Indians had arrived and the treaty convention was duly opened, and continued in session until October 19th— a period of thirty-four days—in all of which Thomas Nicholson and his associate interpreters were busy almost day and night. Many chieftains were present—The White Mingo for the Mingoes; Cornstalk, Nimwha, Wryneck, Silver Heels, Blue Jacket, and fifteen other chiefs for the Shawnees; White Eyes, Custaloga, and Captain Pipe, for the Delawares; the Half King for the Wyandots; Flying Crow and Kyashuta for the Six Nations; Shaganaba for the Ottawas; and many other orators of the wilderness.. It was by far the largest deliberative congress of Indians that ever assembled in the valley of the Ohio. Every article in the preliminary treaty at Camp Charlotte the preceding autumn was fully discussed by both Whites and Indians. At length all were agreed to, confirmed and ratified, and when this convention adjourned, every Indian nation from the Upper Allegheny to the Falls of the Ohio, and from that river to Lake Erie—in short every one of the Confederated Nations of 1771—of those participating in the preliminary treaty of Camp Charlotte, and in the supplemental treaty at Pittsburg—entered into a pledge of peace and friendship, not only to Virginia, but to the New American Nation as well.

CHAPTER VII
THE INFLUENCE OF THE BATTLE OF POINT PLEASANT UPON THE SUBSEQUENT HISTORY OF THE UNITED STATES

In America at the time the Battle of Point Pleasant was fought and won, a few hundred soldiers decided questions of equal magnitude to those which, in Europe, would have called into action on the field, as many thousands. Thus in this country, issues of vital importance were changed by the results of battles in which apparently insignificant numbers were engaged. At the same time many thousands of men on battlefields in the old world were necessary to settle questions of far less import. This was due to the difference of the state of society and of population here and there. The numbers on the field at Point Pleasant, to those acquainted with European wars, and those of our own country in more recent times, must appear to be very inconsiderable; but such then were conditions as to society and population, that in the wilds of America, a few hundred Virginians could, and did decide issues of such mighty importance and far reaching effects, that historians in a century have not seen them in their full force and operation. Roosevelt has said:

"Certainly, in all the contests waged against the northwestern Indians during the last half of the eighteenth century there was no other where the whites inflicted so great a relative loss on their foes. Its results were most important. It kept the northwestern tribes quiet for the first three years of the Revolutionary struggle; and above all it rendered possible the settlement of Kentucky, and therefore the winning of the west. Had it not been for Lord Dunmore's War, it is more than likely that when the colonies achieved their freedom, they would have found their western boundary fixed at the Allegheny Mountains."

* "Winning of the West." Vol. I., p. 240.

The victory won at the Battle of Point Pleasant, made possible the preliminary treaty with the confederated Indian nations at Camp Charlotte, away out in the Ohio Wilderness. Speaking of it Bancroft says:—

"The results inured exclusively to the benefit of America. The Indians desired peace; the rancor of the white people changed to confidence. The royal Governor of Virginia and the Virginian army in the valley of the Scioto nullified the act of parliament which extended the province of Quebec* to the Ohio, and in the name of the King of Great Britain triumphantly maintained for Virginia the western and northwestern Jurisdiction which she claimed as her chartered right."**

* The "Quebec Act" was passed by the parliament of England June 22, 1774. By its provisions the bounds of the Province of Quebec were so enlarged as to comprise all the country northwest of the Ohio to the heads of Lake Superior and the Mississippi. Thus it was that Quebec was made to include all the present States of Ohio, Indiana, Illinois, Michigan, Wisconsin and a large part of Minnesota; and the treaty of Camp Charlotte was thus negotiated on the soil of Canada.

** "History of the United States," Vol. IV., p. 88.

    This treaty led to the supplemental one at Pittsburg, to which there were three parties— the allied Indian Nations, the Government of Virginia, and the Continental Congress. The results were most gratifying. All parties were greatly pleased. A substantial peace had been secured to the Western Border, which was not broken until the spring of 1778—quite three years after the treaty stipulations had been concluded. What did this mean in America? Simply this: There were no Indian wars in these years. The Border men were free from New York to Georgia, and General Gates was thus enabled to collect the American soldiery from the Penobscot to the Savannah, and with this, overthrow Burgoyne at Saratoga. This meant France to the aid of the Colonies; and that meant the Independence of the United States. Does anyone believe that if, in 1777, a vast barbarian army, an ally of England, had been carrying desolation and death along the whole frontier of civilization, that Gates could have mustered the men who achieved victory at Saratoga.

    Again, at the time of the Battle of Point Pleasant, no white man had found a permanent home within the present limits of the State of Kentucky. But the long continued peace with the Indians through treaty stipulations which were made possible by that battle opened the way for a large immigration to that State within the next three years. Will anyone say that if the Shawnees and their confederated nations had been carrying on a relentless warfare against the Virginians, that Kentucky could have been settled at that time? But what of these Kentucky settlements? Did they not form the basis of operations of General George Rogers Clark in his conquest of the Illinois County in 1777-8? And did not this conquest induce the General Assembly of Virginia, in the last mentioned year, to pass an Act creating Illinois County, an Act by which civil government was extended to the Mississippi River? In the treaty Convention of Paris in 1783, whereby the independence of the United States was being recognized, and the western boundary of the new Nation determined, the British representatives voted to place this at the crest of the Alleghenies, and the Spanish representative in that body voted with them. But the Americans stoutly asserted that, not only had they conquered the vast Illinois region, but that Virginia had established civil government therein. So the Mississippi River, and not the Alleghenies, became the western boundary of the United States. Verily, the men who fought the Battle of Point Pleasant were Empire Builders, and the victory achieved by them on that field changed the course of American history.

CHAPTER VIII

PAY OF THE SOLDIERS IN DUNMORE'S WAR
TOTAL EXPENSES OF THAT WAR
HOW THEY WERE PAID

No work with which the author is acquainted contains any reference to the compensation of the soldiers serving in Dunmore's War, or to a settlement of any of the expenses pertaining to it. When on May 14, 1774, the House of Burgesses authorized Governor Dunmore to prosecute the war against the western Indians, it made no provision whatever for meeting the expenses thereof.

In the circular letter of Colonel William Preston, addressed to the people of Fincastle County, July 20, 1774, he urged enlistments for the war; and as an inducement, he said: "The House of Burgesses will, without doubt, enable his Lordship to reward every volunteer in a handsome manner."*

* "Documentary History of Dunmore's War." p. 92.

Lord Dunmore writing General Lewis from Winchester, July 24th, used the following language:—

"The expense of the numerous scouting parties in the different counties forming an extensive frontier, will soon exceed the expenses of an expedition against the towns which will be more effectual, and we may as well depend on the House of Burgesses providing for the expedition as for a greater expense of action on the defensive. At any rate we know the old law is still in force, (and) as far as it goes, we are sure of being reimbursed."

* "Documentary History of Dunmore's War." p. 98.

It was with this assurance of compensation for service that the men of the border enlisted and filled the ranks of both divisions of the army in Dunmore's war. The first session of the House of Burgesses held after its close convened at Williamsburg, Thursday, June 1, 1775. In his written message to this body, that day, Governor Dunmore said:— *"I must recommend to you to fall upon some means for paying the officers and private men employed in repelling the late invasion and incursions of the Indians, as I make no doubt you will think their services on that occasion deserving of your attention."*

On the third day of the session, the House by resolution requested his Lordship to communicate to it:

"The best information he has had respecting the number of the militia lately drawn into actual service in the defense of this Colony, by his Excellency's command, and the probable expense attending the same; and that his Lordship will inform the House, what militia his Excellency has ordered on duty since the conclusion of the late Indian Expedition and for what purposes."*

* "Journal of the House of Burgesses," Session beginning June 1, 1775

June 5th, the Governor made extended reply to this request. In it he said:—

"I can only from recollection (not having been furnished with exact returns.) acquaint you that the body of militia which Colonel Andrew Lewis conducted, and that which I marched in person amounted, together to about three thousand men, officers included. But I refer you to the Lieutenants of the counties from whence the militia were drawn for that service; to the commanding officers of the different Corps, and to the Captains under them for the returns and lists of whose respective companies you will obtain the information in regard to number, and from that of expense which you require, in the best and most particular manner."

With respect to what militia have been ordered on duty since the conclusion of the Indian Expedition, it was thought requisite to continue a body of one hundred men at a temporary Fort (Fort Blair) near the mouth of the Great Kanhaway, as well for taking care of the men who had been wounded in the action between Colonel Andrew Lewis' Division and the Indians, as for securing that part of the back country from the attempts of straggling parties of Indians, who might not be apprised of the peace concluded, or others of the tribes which had joined in it."

"It was likewise necessary to keep up a small body of men at Fort Dunmore (Pittsburg) in like manner for the security of the Country on that side, and also for guarding twelve Indian Prisoners belonging to the Mingo Tribe which had not surrendered or acceded to the peace concluded, only, with the Shawnese; and seventy-five men were employed at this place for these purposes."

"Twenty-five men were likewise left at Fort Fincastle (Wheeling) as a post of communication between the two others, and altogether for the further purpose of forming a chain on the back of the settlers to observe the Indians until we shall have good reason to believe nothing more was apprehended from them; which as soon as I received favorable accounts of, I *ordered the several Posts to be evacuated and the men to be discharged.*

The members of the House of Burgesses were greatly pleased with the interest manifested in his communications concerning the Indian Expedition—Dunmore's War—and that body the same day sent to him an address in which they said:—

"*We assure your Lordship that we will pursue the most speedy Measures for defraying the Expenses of the Military Expedition against the Indians. That proper Provision has not yet been made for those gallant officers and Soldiers, who so nobly exposed their Lives in defense of this country cannot be justly imputed to any delay or Neglect on our part, this being the first Opportunity your Lordship hath been pleased to afford us in paying a proper Attention to their signal Services and giving them their due Reward.*"

Acting in harmony with this declaration, the House on "Wednesday, June 19th, passed a Bill entitled "*An Act for appointing Commissioners to settle the Accounts of the Militia lately drawn out into actual Service and for making Provision to pay the Same.*" This was agreed to by the Council of State, two days later, and as a source of revenue, a provision was inserted *imposing a duty on imported slaves*. This Dunmore declared to be in violation of an Act passed in the tenth year of his Lordship's reign, and he vetoed it, saying that he very much "*regretted the miscarriage of the Bill I had so much at heart.*" He offered to send it to the King and request his favorable consideration thereof; but for reasons now to be explained this was not done.

The Revolution was at hand. On the 20th of April preceding, Dunmore removed the powder from the magazine at Williamsburg to a British vessel. Great excitement prevailed; the people took up arms under the leadership of Patrick Henry, and the Governor compromised the matter by paying for the powder. On the 6th of June, he, with his family, went on board the British man-of-war "Fowey" lying in James River. From there he kept in communication with the House of Burgesses. On the 24th of June, his civil administration in Virginia terminated, and the same day, that body adjourned, never to meet, as such, again. Before separating the members resolved to meet in convention, on the 17th day of July, ensuing, in Richmond. This they did, and the convention having organized, proceeded to appoint a general Committee of Safety, consisting of eleven members, which was henceforth the governing body in Virginia, until it became an independent State. The convention also adopted a number of

Ordinances which had the force of law. One of these was practically the Act which the House had passed the preceding month, and which Dunmore had vetoed, the title being "*An Ordinance for appointing Commissioners to settle the Accounts of the Militia lately drawn out into actual Service, and for making Provision to Pay the same.*"

In this Ordinance the action formerly taken by the Governor and House of Burgesses relative to the matter was revived; and it was decided that because the former had thought fit to refuse his assent to the Act passed by the latter, "*many of the inhabitants particularly on the frontiers of this colony, are left in the greatest distress, from which there is no prospect of their being relieved but by the intervention of this Convention.*" It was therefore ordained:

"*That Archibald Cary, William Cabell, Colonel William Fleming, John Winn, and John Nicholas be, and they are hereby appointed Commissioners for the counties of Fincastle, Botetourt, Culpeper, Pittsylvania, Halifax and Bedford, and that part of Augusta which lies to the eastward of the Allegheny Mountains; and Richard Lee, Francis Peyton Josias Clapham, Henry Lee, and Thomas Blackburn, for the other counties, and for that part of the County of Augusta which lies to the westward of the Allegheny Mountains, and for the provinces of Maryland and Pennsylvania,* to examine, state and settle the accounts of such, pay for provisions, arms, and ammunition, and other necessaries furnished the Militia of the counties for which they were appointed Commissioners, and all demands against the colony on account thereof, who shall be allowed £1:05:0 per day each. And the said Commissioners, or any three or more of them shall, and they are hereby empowered and required to meet for the purposes aforesaid at such times and places as they shall respectively think fit and convenient of which public notice shall be advertised at the Court-House of each respective County, at least one month before such meeting, and adjourn from time to time until they shall have settled all accounts relating to said Militia.*"

* It would appear from this that there were volunteers from both the Colonies of Maryland and Pennsylvania, in service in the Northern Division of the army, under Dunmore.—V. A. L.

These Commissioners were required to certify all accounts so examined, stated and settled, to the General Committee of Safety; then six or more members thereof were required to issue warrants on the Treasurer, who was required, on or before the first day of January, 1776, to pay such certified accounts.

For the raising of the money necessary to meet the payments of these bills the rates of taxation were increased, but because of the remote payment of these, Robert Carter Nicholas, Treasurer for the time being, was empowered to issue Treasury Notes for such sum as might be requisite to meet the purposes of the Ordinance, these to be signed by Henry King and John Pendleton.

The rate of compensation per day for the Officers and Privates engaged in the war was fixed as follows:

For the Commanding Officer	£1:	5s.	0d.
For the County Lieutenant	1:	00:	0.
For a Colonel		16:	0.
For a Lieutenant-Colonel		13:	0.
For a Major		12:	0.
For a Captain		10:	0.
For a Lieutenant		7:	6.
For an Ensign		7:	0.
For a Quarter-Master		6:	0.
For a Sergeant		2:	6.
For a Corporal		2:	0.
For a Drummer		2:	0.
For a Fifer		2:	0.
For a Scout		5:	0.
For a Private		1:	6.

Finally all the claims were adjusted. To follow this in detail, would prove interesting, but require far too much space. Suffice it to say that Lord Dunmore's War in 1774, cost Virginia, in her Colonial currency, the sum of £350,000:00:0.

Point Pleasant Battle Monument
Photo by Brian M. Powell

22 feet square at the base, 86 feet high

CHAPTER IX
HISTORY AND DISCRIPTION OF THE POINT PLEASANT BATTLE MONUMENT
The Battlefield Unmarked
Steps Leading to the Erection of a Battle Monument
Description of the Same

The day after the Battle of Point Pleasant, Colonel Christian's Fincastle men, who had arrived at eleven o'clock the preceding evening, collected the dead who were buried without the pomp of war. "*This day*," says Colonel Fleming, "*were buried the men who were slain yesterday and died last night, in different burying places, and the following officers and Gentlemen in the Magazine: To-wit, Colonel Charles Lewis, Colonel John Field, Captain John Murray, with his half brother, George Cameron, Captain Robert McClennahan, Captain Samuel Wilson, Lieutenant Hugh Allen and Mr. John Frogg.*"*

* "Documentary History of Dunmore's War." p. 345

It was a heap of slain, and here they lay for many years, on a neglected battle plain. Early travelers expressed regret because of this.

Stephen T. Mitchell, editor of *The Spirit of the Old Dominion*, was on the field at Point Pleasant in 1827—fifty-two years after the battle and at that time wrote as follows:

"*I have often passed the tombs of those who fell that fatal day; and, frequently, upon the mild summer's evening, have I strayed over the open common which was the battle ground. Fifty years have elapsed, and the remains of the gallant Lewis and his officers, are yet suffered to moulder within the unhallowed precincts of a stable yard. No index save vague rumor guides the curious traveler to their graves; no sculptured marble, no plain monument reminds the free born of Virginia that on this ground the gallantry of his fore-fathers led them to a bloody but glorious death.*"*

* See *Spirit of the Old Dominion*, Vol. I., No. 3, p. 155

Resolutions in the Virginia Assembly

On the 10th of March, 1849, Hon. James M. Ladle, a member of the Virginia House of Delegates from the Kanawha-Putnam Delegate District, submitted the following Preamble and Resolutions relative to a Battle Monument at Point Pleasant:

WHEREAS: It has been a time honored custom to perpetuate, in an enduring form, a people's gratitude to those who have signalized themselves by deeds of patriotic heroism: And whereas, it is meet and proper that the people of Virginia shall commemorate, in a suitable manner, the bravery of her sons who nobly fell at Point Pleasant in the defense of the soil -which has since become the home of a peaceful, nourishing and happy people:

1. Be it therefore resolved, by the General Assembly of Virginia, that a grateful tribute to the memory of her gallant citizens who fell on the tenth day of October, seventeen hundred and seventy-four, in the battle which was fought near the mouth of the Great Kanawha River, between the Virginia forces, under command of Gen. Andrew Lewis, and the confederated tribes of Shawnee, Delaware, Mingo and Cayuga Indians, a plain, substantial monument, with appropriate inscriptions, shall be erected at or near the scene of said battle.

2. Resolved, That Charles Clendennin and Thomas Lewis, of Mason County; John D. Lewis, of Kanawha County; Samuel H. Lewis, of Rockingham County; Rice D. Montague, of Montgomery County; Madison Pitser, of Roanoke County; Rufus Pitser, of Botetourt County; James A. Cochran, of Augusta County; Robert G. Ward, of Culpeper County; Milton Kirtley, of Madison County, and Thomas Creigh, of Greenbrier County, be, and they are hereby appointed collectors, to receive donations to aid in the execution of the purpose hereby declared.

3. Resolved, That George W. Summers, of Kanawha County; and Charles Clendennin and Peter H. Steenbergen, of Mason County, be, and they are hereby appointed commissioners to design said monument, and to direct what inscriptions shall be placed thereon; and also to contract for and superintend the erection of the same, and to take all necessary measures for the proper execution of the work. And the General Assembly hereby pledge the faith of the State that when a sum not less than $____ thousand dollars has been contributed by individuals for the construction of said monument, a sum not exceeding $____

*thousand dollars shall be appropriated by the General Assembly in the aid of the same."**

* See Pub. Doc. No. 82, session of the General Assembly of Virginia, 1848-49

On motion of Mr. Laidley, this was laid on the table and ordered printed. No further action was taken thereon.

Point Pleasant Monument Association Created

Years passed by with nothing done, but finally on the first day of April, 1860, the General Assembly passed an act to incorporate the *"Point Pleasant Monument Association."**

This provided that Mrs. John S. Lewis, Miss Ellen Steenbergen, and Miss Elizabeth Smith, all of Mason County, (now West Virginia) together with such others as might be associated with them, be made a body politic and corporate, with authority to purchase land and erect a monument on the battlefield of Point Pleasant. But action was soon stayed. The Civil War was at hand, and when that storm had passed away, a new Commonwealth—West Virginia—had arisen on the western slope of the Alleghenies, and in it lay the battlefield of Point Pleasant with its story of historic achievement.

* See acts of the General Assembly of Virginia 1859-60, p. 576

A Centennial Celebration

Saturday, October 10, 1874, was the Centennial Anniversary of the Battle at Point Pleasant, and the day was fittingly observed. Dr. Samuel G. Shaw was President of the Centennial Society under the auspices of which the exercises were held. Francis A. Guthrie, Attorney-at-Law was the chairman of the committee on arrangements. The morning was dark and gloomy, but soon the sun broke forth and ushered in a beautiful autumn day. A large procession was formed on Main Street and marched to the Mason County Fair Grounds. In the line were a company of Cadets from the West Virginia University; an artillery Company from Gallipolis, Ohio, and the Knights of Pythias, a splendid body of men, from that place. The music was furnished by the Drum Corps with the Cadets; the Cornstalk Brass Band of Point Pleasant, and a Brass Band from Ravenswood. On the Grand Stand at the Fair Grounds, were, among others, Dr. S. G. Shaw, Dr. Andrew E. Barbee, of Point Pleasant, together with Hon. George C. Sturgis of Morgantown; Dr. Thomas Creigh, of Greenbrier County; and Colonel Lewis Ruffner and Hon. Benjamin H. Smith, of Charleston, the latter the orator of the day.

Addresses were also made by Hon. Henry S. Walker, Dr. Creigh and Mr. Sturgis. Then Rev. William E. Hill offered the following preamble and resolution which was unanimously adopted:

WHEREAS: The Battle of Point Pleasant has hastened the material prosperity of this and other states by the sacrifice of noble blood:—

1. Therefore, be it Resolved, That a committee of three with power to engage others, be appointed to solicit contributions for the purpose of erecting a monument and purchasing the ground around about the spot where the remains of our heroes now repose:

2. That this committee be empowered to raise a subscription on the ground today; to write to the descendants of the brave men who were engaged in, or fell on the field at Point Pleasant; asking them to aid in this work by contribution; to ask the Legislature of Virginia, West Virginia, Kentucky, and Ohio to make appropriations to this work and to request also the Congress of the United States to make an appropriation to the same end.

Dr. Shaw, the president, then appointed as a soliciting committee, Rev. William E. Hill, Dr. William P. Neal, Dr. Charles T. B. Moore, and it raised by subscription about six hundred dollars that day.

In the evening the procession was re-formed and took up the line of march from the Fair Grounds to the town, where, at the head of Viand Street, the column received the hearse and casket containing the bones of some of the heroes who fell in the battle, they having been exhumed the preceding day. Here the cadets, with reversed arms and muffled drums, took their position as an escort and the column moved to the point of land where once stood old Fort Randolph, and where the remains were re-interred with military honors. During this time the church bells of the town were tolled and minute guns fired by the Artillery Company. The beautiful Burial Service of the Church was read; a benediction pronounced, and thus ended the first Centennial celebration of the Battle of Point Pleasant.*

* See the *Weekly Register*, printed at Point Pleasant, October 15, 1874.

First Appropriation for a Monument

The interest and patriotism aroused on that centennial day never entirely ceased. Application was made to the Legislature of the new State of West Virginia the next year, and that body appropriated the sum "of $3,500.00 to aid in the purchase of land

and the erection of a monument in commemoration of the Battle of Point Pleasant."

* See acts of West Virginia, 1875, pp. 29-30.

This money was drawn from the State Treasury, but before it was expended, the Legislature on the 6th of December, 1875, adopted Joint Resolution No. 24.* in which it was declared that:

"*The Battle of Point Pleasant was an event of deep and enduring interest, exhibiting in a remarkable degree the courage and patriotism of the early settlers of our country; that an event so distinguished in our history should be commemorated by a monument to be erected upon the spot where those gallant defenders sacrificed their lives, and where their sacred remains now lie buried.*"

* See acts of 1875, p. 245

Then it was stated that West Virginia had already made an appropriation from her treasury for this purpose and it was resolved that the Governor be requested to communicate with those of Virginia, Ohio, and Kentucky, and solicit aid from their states in the erection of the monument. In addition to this, the Senators and Representatives of these states were requested to co-operate with those from West Virginia in their efforts to secure aid from the National Government for this purpose. The persons who had drawn the money from the State Treasury now decided to await in anticipation of further appropriations, and invested the sum in hand at a good rate of interest.

Legislative Action In 1897

Thus matters continued for twenty-one years, in all of which no additional aid was received, and on the 26th of February, 1897, the State Legislature adopted House Joint Resolution No. 34,* in which it was set forth that:

The money which had been appropriated in 1875, to aid in the purchasing of land and erecting a monument at Point Pleasant, had never been expended for that purpose; and the Governor was authorized to appoint three trustees to carry into effect the act making that appropriation.

* See acts of West Virginia, 1897, p. 278.

In compliance therewith Governor George W. Atkinson appointed Judge John W. English, Dr. Andrew E. Barbee, and Judge Francis A. Guthrie, trustees. But these gentlemen found the money invested for a specified time, therefore not available, and they were unable to accomplish anything.

Legislative Action In 1901

Four more years passed away, and on February 7th, 1901, the Legislature adopted Resolution No. 12, which declared it to be the duty of the Legislature to carry into effect the object of the appropriation of 1875, for a monument at Point Pleasant and directing the Governor to appoint three trustees for this purpose.

The Trustees Appointed—Work Begun

In compliance with this resolution, Governor Albert B. White, did, on the 29th day of March, 1901, appoint as such trustees for the purpose aforesaid John P. Austin, of Redmond; Virgil A. Lewis, of Mason City; Charles C. Bowyer, of Point Pleasant, all of Mason County. As such they qualified April 18, 1901, and entered into a personal bond jointly in the penalty of $10,000.00 which was approved by the County Court of Mason County. May 25th ensuing, they affected an organization by electing Mr. Austin, President; Mr. Lewis, Secretary; and Mr. Bowyer, Treasurer. On the 13th of July, 1901, they received from the former trustees the sum of $8,788.33, this being the amount of the appropriation of 1875, together with accrued interest, the fund having more than doubled itself in the twenty-six years of its investment. Further, the trustees were informed that there were in the hands of Mr. Peter S. Lewis, Treasurer of the Ladies Monument Association the sum of $2,007.84, which amount had been contributed by individuals to aid in the erection of a monument. The land selected for this, is the square at the apex of the angle formed by the confluence of the two rivers—the Ohio and Great Kanawha—on which the Virginian army was encamped at the beginning of the battle, and where its honored dead who fell in the contest, were buried. This is high land and contains about two and one half acres. It had been laid out in lots, and from the owners, the trustees bought and paid for these, as follows:

To Thomas J. Darst, $550.00; to J. H. Stone, and others $3,000.00; to John D. McCulloch, $1,000.00; to Nancy A. Varian and others, $1,200.00; and to E. A. Comstock, $2,250.00—a total of $8,000.00.

For these properties deeds were properly executed, vesting title in the State of West Virginia, and were recorded in the office of the clerk of the County Court of Mason County. The Legislature in 1905, made an appropriation of $5,000.00 to aid in the erection of the monument.

Aid from Congress

Hon. Charles E. Hogg, of Mason County, while a member of the Fiftieth Congress introduced a bill carrying with it an appropriation to aid in the erection of a Battle Monument at Point Pleasant, but this failed of passage. Imbued with the idea, of the National character of the battle, the trustees, in February 1902, went to Washington, where the State's entire Delegation—Senators and Representatives—urged upon Congress an appropriation for the purpose desired. Annually for six years, the trustees kept the matter before that body and at length, in 1908, the sum of $10,000.00 was appropriated to be expended under the direction and approval of the Secretary of War, in aid of and for the erection of the monument. The trustees feeling that at last they had a sufficient sum with which to erect a suitable structure took steps to do this. In August, 1908, they proceeded to Washington where they had an interview with Hon. Luke B. Wright, Secretary of War. He requested a map of grounds showing elevation and other data, and evidence as to right of way thereto. Captain William H. Howard, a Civil Engineer of Point Pleasant, made the map, and Colonel Hiram E. Howard, mayor of the town, made official statement as to the streets leading to the site on which the monument was to be erected. On the 21st day of October, ensuing, the trustees had a second interview with Secretary Wright, who approved plans, they having been previously approved by Governor William M. O. Dawson. They then requested government supervision in the erection of the monument, and this was referred to Captain A. F. Alstaetter of the War Department, who was stationed at Wheeling. The Van Amringe Granite Company, of Boston, Massachusetts, which had erected many monuments at Gettysburg and on other fields, furnished plans and specifications, which were accepted, and a contract awarded it at a meeting at the office of Captain Alstaetter, in Wheeling, December 14th, 1908. These people employed Charles Frederick Hess, of Point Pleasant, to put in the concrete foundation at the center of *Tu-enda-wee Park** as designated by Captain William H. Howard. This he began on the 11th day of May, 1909, when ground was broken by Daniel Crump Wartenburg, an employee of Mr. Hess. The large mass of human bones—the remains of those who fell in battle—which were removed, from the excavation, were carefully placed in a box and re-interred by Captain Hess under the northeast corner of the monument, there ultimately to mingle with mother earth. James E. Amedon, of Manchester Depot, Vermont, arrived May 23rd, and assumed the supervision of construction. His stone or granite "setter" was John Kernehan, of Adams, Massachusetts; the "rigger," the man in charge of the derrick, being Herman Kappes, of Gettysburg, Pennsylvania. The first car load of granite arrived at Point Pleasant, June 1st, from the quarries of the Balfour Pink Granite Company, which is distant five miles from the town of Salisbury, North Carolina, it being shipped by the Southern Railroad, and the first block thereof was set in place on the 14 of the same month. At 11:30 P. M. Thursday, July 22nd, the upper part of the derrick, standing 105 feet above the surface was struck by lightning and badly damaged, but the monument, then but thirty feet high, was uninjured. The capstone was put in place at 11:10 a. m. Monday, August 22nd, 1909, when the structure was completed. It is twenty-two feet square at the base; eighty-six feet high; and contains one hundred and fifty-two granite blocks, the whole weighing one hundred and forty-three tons. The statue, facing the east, standing eight feet high, and weighing two tons, is cut of Westerly Granite, by the Smith Granite Company, of Westerly, Rhode Island. The bronze panels and bas-relief were cast by Albert Russell & Sons Company, of Newburyport, Massachusetts, the historical data thereon having been compiled by Virgil A. Lewis, in compliance with an order of the trustees. At last, one hundred and thirty-five years thereafter, the National Government and that of the State of West Virginia, acting jointly, have properly marked the spot on which was waged the most desperate as well as the most important battle ever fought between the White men and Indians in America.

* Tu-enda-wee Park—This is a name bestowed in 1901, upon the square on which the monument has been erected. In that year the writer was engaged in some research work relative to Indian geographical names in West Virginia. Among numerous other works he consulted the "Glossary of Indian Names," prepared by Colonel John Johnston, who was the Government Indian Agent at Upper Piqua, Ohio, for fifty years. In the list of Wyandot terms, he found that of *Tu-enda-wee*, signifying a "triangular point of land at the confluence of rivers," not a particular point at any particular place, but a kind of common noun, applicable to any one of a class or kind. He spoke of this at the time to members of the Charles Lewis Chapter of the Daughters of the American Revolution, at Point Pleasant. These suggested at once that it would be a good name for the battle park at that place; and it was due to their suggestion that it was thus named. That was but eight years ago, but in that time, it has been stated that it is a Shawnee term; that it signifies the mingling of waters; and it has been misspelled almost as many times as it has been used. The truth is that it is a Wyandot term; that it means a triangular point of land; and its proper spelling is *Tu-enda-wee*—pronounced as if spelled *Too-endy-wee.*

CHAPTER X
HISTORY VERSUS TRADITION
TRUTH VERSUS ERROR

As a boy residing near the battlefield of Point Pleasant, the author heard the oft repeated stories of how Captain Michael Cresap had, in cold blood, murdered the relatives of Logan, the Mingo chieftain; how Lord Dunmore had, in 1774, encouraged the Indians to wage war against the frontier for the purpose of distracting the attention of the Virginians from the complications between the Colonies and the Mother Country, then pending, and how he had delayed the march of the Northern Division of the army commanded by himself, that the Southern Division under General Lewis, might be destroyed at Point Pleasant; and that therefore, that battle was the first of the Revolution and how General Lewis, on meeting Lord Dunmore on the Pickaway Plains, had disobeyed the orders of the Governor, by continuing to advance after receiving orders to halt his army. Later, he read one or more of these statements in the writing of Joseph Doddridge, published in 1824; of Hugh Paul Taylor, in 1829; of Alexander Scott Withers, 1831; and of others who followed them, and assuming that these authors had followed unimpeachable authority for the statements they made, instead of vague traditions, he, himself, years ago, when writing of the Border Wars, believed and accepted their statements, as history. Since then he has had the opportunity of examining a great mass of contemporary documents relating to Dunmore's War, which have been collected and rendered available to all students who desire to consult original sources of information. A careful examination of these reveals incontrovertible proof of the innocence of Captain Cresap; of the honesty of purpose and faithfulness of Lord Dunmore to the interests of the people of "Virginia; and of the soldierly qualities of General Lewis, who did not disobey the orders of his superior officer, in front of an enemy on the Pickaway Plains.

Because Captain Michael Cresap was the most prominent man in the vicinity of Wheeling, at the time Logan's people were killed, it was but natural that this chieftain should suspect him of committing the barbarous act. Of this he had no proof, but in his speech delivered to Captain John Gibson at the treaty of Camp Charlotte, he preferred the charge against Cresap therein, as the perpetrator of the bloody deed. At the time, Captain Gibson assured him that Cresap was entirely innocent of it. Within the next few years affidavits testifying to this, were made by Ebenezer Zane, the founder of Wheeling; Charles Polk at whose house on Cross Creek, now in Brooke County, West Virginia, Daniel Greathouse assembled the men who perpetrated the horrid deed; by William Robinson, who was taken prisoner by Logan July 12, 1774, on the West Fork of the Monongahela River, about two miles from Clarksburg, now Harrison County, West Virginia; by Joshua Baker at whose house the Indians were killed; and by John Sappington who was one of the men with Greathouse; and all printed in the appendix to Jefferson's "Notes on Virginia." And further: The letter* written by General George Rogers Clark, June 17, 1798, to Doctor Samuel Brown, this being now among the "Jefferson Papers," in the Department of State at Washington. In it he stated that he was at Wheeling at the time Logan's people were killed; that he was personally acquainted with Captain Cresap; and that he was in no wise connected with the barbarous act; that he (Cresap) was violently opposed to it; that he left Wheeling to go to Redstone on the Monongahela River, two days before it was committed; and that it was the work of Daniel Greathouse and party. Yet in the face of all this evidence, some of the writers of the Border Wars have been for a hundred years repeating the story and connecting with it the name of Captain Michael Cresap, a brave soldier of the Revolution who lost his life in the struggle for American Independence. Certainly, no one who had made proper investigation of the subject would do this.

* Printed in English's "Conquest of the Northwest," Vol. II., p. 1029.

The Alleged Treachery of Lord Dunmore

Let us make a calm and unprejudiced enquiry, regarding this, and in doing so, use only competent witnesses and contemporary documents relating to Dunmore's War. We know of his part therein; so it will be needless to further consider that. He criticized the House of Burgesses for authorizing him to prosecute the war, and then adjourning without providing for its exigencies. He gave assurance to the messengers who bore to Williamsburg, tidings of the savage atrocities that he would not only supply the border men with ammunition, at his own risk; but, that he would furnish men for the defense of the frontier."*

* "The Washington-Crawford Letters," p. 90.

Under date of June 8th, 1774, Captain Valentine Crawford, of Frederick County, Virginia, then at Jacobs' Creek, on the Yohogany River, wrote Colonel George Washington regarding the distressed condition of the frontier and said: *"But it is a happy circumstance for us that Lord Dunmore is so warm in our favor."**

<small>* "The Washington-Crawford Letters," p. 90.</small>

Colonel William Preston in his Circular Letter of July 20, 1774, addressed to the Fincastle men, urging them to enlist for the defense of the frontier settlements, said:—*"The Earl of Dunmore is deeply engaged in it. The House of Burgesses will no doubt enable his Lordship to reward every Volunteer in a handsome manner."**

<small>* "Documentary History of Dunmore's War," p. 92</small>

From Winchester in Frederick County, Virginia, under date of Sunday, August 14th, Lord Dunmore then engaged in organizing the Northern Division of the Army, wrote William, Earl of Dartmouth, the British Secretary of State for the American Colonies, and said:—

"The Shawnees, Mingoes, and some of the Delawares, have fallen on our frontiers, and killed, scalped, and most cruelly murdered a great many of our men, women and children. I hope in eight or ten days to march with a body of men over the Allegheny mountains, and then down the Ohio, to the mouth of the Scioto, and if I can possibly fall upon these lower towns undiscovered, I think I shall be able to put an end to this cruel war."*

<small>* "Documentary History of Dunmore's War." p. 151</small>

If there were no other evidence extant, this letter should exonerate Dunmore from the charge of a betrayal of the Virginia people.

Let us continue this examination of contemporary documents relating to Dunmore's War, and thus learn of the estimation in which he was held by those who served under him, as well as other representative Virginians who were otherwise associated with him. The Northern Division of the Army, homeward bound from Camp Charlotte, halted at Fort Gower, at which place the officers assembled and gave expression to the following:

A Resolution by the Officers, Who Served Under Lord Dunmore, Adopted at Fort Gower, Mouth of Hockhocking River, November 5, 1774

"Resolved, That we entertain the greatest respect for his Excellency the Right Honourable Lord Dunmore, who commanded the expedition against the Shawanese; and who, we are confident underwent the great fatigue of this singular campaign from no other motive than the true interest of this country.

Signed by order and in behalf of the whole Corps,

Benjamin Ashby, Clerk."

Among these officers were Colonel William Crawford, and Colonel Adam Stephen, both General officers in the war for Independence; and Captain Daniel Morgan, afterward General Morgan, likewise of the Revolution; Captain George Rogers Clark, later the Conqueror of the Illinois Country; and many others afterward prominent in military life.

Lord Dunmore returned to Williamsburg, on Sunday, December 4th, having been absent one hundred and fifty days, and found that an interesting event had occurred in his family. Just twenty-four hours before his arrival, there was the birth of a daughter who received the name of Virginia, in honor of the Colony in which the father was the executive head. On the next day, December 5th he was the recipient of the following:

ADDRESS OF THE CITIZENS OF THE CITY OF WILLIAMSBURG, DECEMBER 5, 1774, TO JOHN, EARL OF DUNMORE

"To his Excellency the Eight Honourable John, Earl of Dunmore, his Majesty's Lieutenant and Governor-General of the Colony and Dominion of Virginia, and Vice Admiral of the Same,

My Lord:—We his Majesty's most dutiful and loyal subjects, the Mayor, Recorder, Aldermen, and Common Council, of the city of Williamsburg, in Common Hall assembled, beg leave to embrace the earliest opportunity of congratulating your Lordship on the conclusion of a dangerous and fatiguing service in which you have lately been engaged, and on your return to this City.

It is with pleasure we hear your Lordship has been able to defeat the designs of a cruel and insidious enemy and at the same time that your Lordship has escaped those dangers to which your person must have been frequently exposed.

Permit us also upon this occasion, to express our congratulations on the addition to your family by the birth of a daughter; and to assure you that we wish to your Lordship every degree of felicity, and that we shall contribute towards its attainment, as far as lies in our power during your residence among us.

THE REPLY OF LORD DUNMORE TO THE CITIZENS OF WILLIAMSBURG

To the above Address, his Excellency was pleased to return the following Answer:

"Gentlemen:—I am obliged to you for the Address. The fatigue and danger of the service which I undertook, out of commiseration for the deplorable state which, in particular, the back inhabitants were in, and to manifest my solicitude for the safety of the country in general, which his Majesty has committed to my care, has been amply rewarded by the satisfaction I feel in having been able to put an effectual stop to a bloody war.

I thank you for the notice you are pleased to take of the event which has happened in my family; and, I doubt not that, as I have hitherto experienced the marks of your civility, you will continue in the same friendly disposition toward me."

* "American Archives," Fourth Series, Vol. 1., pp. 1018-19.

William and Mary College at Williamsburg, founded in 1692, is the oldest institution of its kind south of the Potomac River. In it at this time two of Lord Dunmore's sons, George and Alexander, were students. How the President and Faculty of the College extended a welcome to the Governor on his return from the Indian Expedition is shown by the following:

ADDRESS OF THE PRESIDENT AND PROFESSORS OF WILLIAM AND MARY COLLEGE TO JOHN, EARL OF DUNMORE

To his Excellency, the Earl of DUNMORE, Governor of VIRGINIA.

May it please your Excellency: We his Majesty's dutiful and loyal subjects, the President and Professors of William and Mary College, moved by an impulse of unfeigned joy, cannot help congratulating your Excellency on such a series of agreeable events, as the success of your enterprise against the Indians, the addition to your family by the birth of a daughter, and your safe as *well as glorious return to the capital of this Dominion.*

May the great fatigues and dangers which you so readily and cheerfully underwent in the service of your Government, be ever crowned with victory! May you ever find the publick benefits thence arising attended with domestic blessings! And, may you always feel the enlivening pleasure of reading in the countenances around you, wherever you turn your eyes, such expressions of affection as can be derived only from applauding and grateful hearts!"

To which his Excellency was pleased to return the following answer:

THE REPLY OF LORD DUNMORE TO THE PRESIDENT AND FACULTY OF WILLIAM AND MARY COLLEGE

"Gentlemen:—I cannot but receive every instance of the attention of a learned and respectable body, such as yours, with a great degree of satisfaction; but the affectionate and very obliging terms in which you are pleased to express your good wishes towards me, on this occasion, demand my cordial thanks, and will ever be impressed on my mind."

Away down on the sea coast was the borough of Norfolk overlooking historic Hampton Roads. Intelligence of the return of the Governor from his western expedition speedily reached the old town, and its officials took the following action:—

ADDRESS OF THE MAYOR, RECORDER, ALDERMAN, AND COMMON COUNCIL OF THE BOROUGH OF NORFOLK, TO JOHN, EARL OF DUNMORE

To the Right Honourable JOHN", Earl of DUNMOEE, his Majesty's Lieutenant and Governor-General of the Colony and Dominion of Virginia, and Vice Admiral of the Same,

"My Lord:—We his Majesty's most dutiful and loyal subjects, the Mayor, Recorder, Aldermen, and Common Council of the Borough of Norfolk in Common Hall assembled, impressed with a deep and grateful sense of the important services rendered to this Colony by your Excellency's seasonable and vigorous exertion in the late expedition against a deceitful and treacherous enemy, conducted under your auspices to so fortunate an issue, beg leave, by this testimony of our general respect, to congratulate your Excellency on the Happy event, and on your safe arrival at the capital.

While we applaud your Lordship's moderation in giving peace to a merciless foe, we cannot but exult in the happiness of our fellow-subjects on the Frontiers, who, by your unremitted zeal and spirited conduct have acquired the blessings of ease, security, and domestick enjoyment. As we sincerely participate in every circumstance of your publick glory, neither can we be insensible of your private happiness in the birth of a daughter, and the recovery of Lady Dunmore, on which joyful occasion we beg leave also to add our most cordial congratulations; and we devoutly wish that, to the pleasing remembrance of having faithfully discharged your important trust of Government, you may have superadded the approbation of your Royal Master, the grateful returns of an happy people, and the honor of these distinctions reflected on a numerous and flourishing family."

THE REPLY OF LORD DUNMORE

"The Address of the Mayor, Recorder, Aldermen, and Common Council of the Borough of Norfolk, expressive of their duty and loyalty to the King, cannot but be extremely acceptable to me.

His Majesty, in his tender solicitude for the safety of his subjects, so lately exposed to the calamities of an Indian war, having signified his full approbation of the measures which I at first adopted for their relief, and as the issue of that event, the *only circumstance of it of which he could not yet be informed, will entirely remove the paternal anxiety which he suffered on the occasion, I already enjoy, and have good reason to expect the continuance of one part of that high recompense which the gentlemen of the Borough of Norfolk have so kindly wished me, and the applause which they are pleased to bestow upon me greatly contributes toward another part, which is my ardent ambition to merit.*

The notice which they take of my private concerns is obliging, as their approbation of my publick conduct is honorable to me, and both demand my most cordial thanks."

The Council of State of the Colony of Virginia occupied to the House of Burgesses, the relation of a Senate. It consisted of twelve members, who were the advisors of the Governor. They likewise extended greetings and a welcome home, from the Ohio Wilderness.

ADDRESS OF THE COUNCIL OF THE STATE OF VIRGINIA, TO JOHN, EARL OF DUNMORE

To the Right Honourable JOHN", Earl of DUNMOEE, his Majesty's Lieutenant and Governor-General of the Colony and Dominion of VIRGINIA, and Vice-Admiral of the Same:

"M Lord:—We, his Majesty's dutiful and loyal subjects, the Council of Virginia, with the most heartfelt joy and unfeigned pleasure, beg leave to offer our congratulations to your Lordship on your safe return, after the fatigues and dangers of a troublesome expedition.

Your Lordship's vigorous opposition to the incursions and ravages of an Indian enemy, hath effectually prevented the desolation of a growing back country, and the horrors of human carnage. The scene of war was remote from us; our properties and estates were not immediately exposed to the miseries consequent thereon; but though not equally interested, we sensibly participate in the blessings that are derived to our fellow-subjects in that quarter of the Colony, from the prospect of a permanent peace. The lenity you exercised towards the Indians, when they expected the cruelty of the victor, hath attached them to you from principle; and unless the intrigues of Traders, or the insidious arts of the enemies to this Government, should again foment differences, we flatter ourselves the present tranquility will not speedily be interrupted. You have taught them a lesson to which the savage breast was a stranger to—that clemency and mercy are not incompatible with power; and that havock and bloodshed are not the inseparable concomitants of success and victory.

Permit us, my Lord, to express our lively satisfaction at the addition to your family, by the birth of a daughter, and, to assure you it is greatly heightened by the promising hopes the your Lady's recovery will be unattended with danger. We should be wanting in respect to her Ladyship, to omit any opportunity of testifying our esteem for her; an esteem that her exemplary piety and true dignity of conduct will ever command."*

* "American Archives," Fourth Series, Vol. I., pp. 1019-20.

To which his Excellency was pleased to return the following answer:

THE REPLY OF LORD DUNMORE

"Gentlemen:—I am in the most sensible manner obliged to you for this Address. The motives which induced me to exert my efforts to relieve the back country from the calamity under which it lately laboured, would have been disappointed in one of their principal ends, if it had not met your approbation; and this very honourable testimony which you are now pleased to give me of it, conveys the highest gratification to me.

The cordiality of your expressions on the occasion of the addition to my family, and the distinguishing mark of the notice which you so kindly take of Lady Dunmore, attaches me to you by the strongest ties of gratitude and the warmest affection."

Resolution adopted by the Virginia Convention which assembled at Richmond, March 20, 1775

On the 20th day of March, 1775, one of the most important conventions, the proceedings of which are recorded in the annals of Virginia, assembled in the town of Richmond. On the fifth day of the session, this body adopted, among others, the following Resolution:—

"*Resolved Unanimously, That the most cordial thanks of the people of this Colony are a tribute justly due to our worthy Governour, Lord Dunmore, for his truly noble, wise, and spirited conduct on the late expedition against our Indian enemy; a conduct which at once evinces his Excellency's attention to the true interests of this Colony, and a zeal in the Executive Department which no dangers can divert or difficulties hinder* *from achieving the most important services to the people who have the happiness to live under his administration."**

* Journal of this Convention in "American Archives," Vol. II., pp. 165-170.

Among the members of that Convention who had served in Dunmore's War, were Colonel William Christian, of Fincastle; Captain James Mercer, of Hampshire County; Captain Samuel McDowell, of Augusta County; General Andrew Lewis and Lieutenant John Bowyer, of Botetourt County; General Adam Stephen and Colonel Robert Rutherford, of Berkeley County; and Captain John Neville and John Hardie, of the "District of West Augusta." Every one of these men voted for the above Resolution, for the Journal states that it was adopted *unanimously*. Does anyone think that if there had been the least suspicion of treachery on the part of Dunmore in that war that these men or any one of them, would have voted in favor of that resolution? There too, sat Colonel George Washington, a delegate from Fairfax County, the military genius of his time; he too voted for the resolution. Would he have done this, had he thought there had been dishonor on the part of Dunmore?

Of all the contemporary Documents which throw light on Dunmore's War none is of greater value than the following:

Colonel Christian's Fincastle men were heroes in that war, many of them were among the killed and wounded at Point Pleasant; and the survivors on that April day, 1775—the year following the war—assembled in convention, and voiced the public sentiment of that time regarding Lord Dunmore.

Address of Freeholders of Fincastle County (Virginia)
To Lord Dunmore, April 8, 1775

To his Excellency the Eight Honourable JOHN, Earl of DUNMOEE, His Majesty's Lieutenant and Governor-General of the Colony of Virginia:

"My Lord:—Notwithstanding the unhappy disputes that at present subsist between the Mother Country and the Colonies, in which we have given the publick our sentiments, yet justice and gratitude, as well as a sense of our duty, induce us collectively to return your Lordship our unfeigned thanks for the great services you have rendered the frontiers in general, and this County in particular, in the late expedition against our enemy Indians.

In our former wars with the savages, we long suffered every species of barbarity; many of our friends and fellow-subjects were inhumanly butchered and carried into captivity, more to be dreaded than death itself; our houses plundered and burned and our country laid waste by an enemy, against whom, from our dispersed situation, and their manner of carrying on war, it was impossible to make a proper defense on our frontiers. Your Lordship being convinced of this, proposed to attack the enemy in their own country, well judging that it would be the most effectual means to reduce them to reason, and be attended with little more expense to the community than a partial defense of such an extensive frontier. The proposal was cheerfully embraced, and the ardour of the Militia to engage in that very necessary service, could only be equalled by that of your Lordship in carrying it on. That the plan of an expedition should be laid when the season was far advanced, and near three thousand choice troops raised in a few Counties, and put under the command of many brave and experienced Officers; that those forces should be equipped and fully supplied with provisions, and march several hundred miles through mountains to meet the enemy; that so many Nations of warlike Indians should be reduced to sue for peace; that those Troops should return victorious to their homes by the last of November; and all this without any publick money in hand to defray any part of the expense, shows at first view the immediate utility of the undertaking, and must be a convincing proof that the Almighty, in a peculiar manner, blessed our Lordship's attempts to establish peace, and stop the further effusion of human blood; but that your Lordship should forego your ease, and every domestick felicity, and march at the head of a body of those Troops many hundred miles from the Seat of Government, cheerfully undergoing all the fatigues of the campaign, by exposing your person, and marching on foot with the officers and soldiers, commands our warmest returns of gratitude; and the rather, as we have no Instance of such condescension in your Lordship's predecessors on any similar occasion.

We should be wanting in point of gratitude, were we to omit returning our thanks on this occasion to the Officers and Soldiers who entered into the service with so much alacrity. The memory of such as fell nobly fighting for their Country ought to be very dear to it.

That your Lordship may enjoy every domestic blessing; that you may long govern the brave and free people of Virginia, and *that the present disturbances may be amicably settled, is the ardent wish of the inhabitants of Fincastle."**

THE REPLY OF LORD DUNMORE

*"I am very much obliged to the freeholders and inhabitants of the County of Fincastle for their Address, and am happy to find they think the service I undertook upon the occasion of the Indian disturbances merits their publick thanks. I assure them that they will ever find me equally ready to exert my best endeavours for every purpose which may tend to the security or promote the happiness of the people of VIRGINIA.**

* See "American Archives," Fourth Series, Vol. II., pp. 310.312.

Major Angus McDonald, who commanded the preliminary expedition, and afterwards served under Dunmore in the Northern Division, writing Captain William Harrod, in January, 1775, says: *"All the Country is well pleased with the Governor's Expedition."**

* See "Documentary History of Dunmore's War." p. 153.

What Historians Say

George Brancroft says, *"Virginia has left on record her judgment, that Dunmore's conduct in this campaign was truly noble, wise, and spirited."**

* See "History of the United States." Vol. IV., p. 88.

Theodore Roosevelt, speaking of the compliments paid Dunmore by the Virginians, adds, *"And he fully deserved their gratitude."**

* See "Winning of the West," Vol. I., p. 239.

Consul W. Butterfield says:—*"There can be no doubt of his Lordship's sincerity in taking these measures for protection of the frontiers; nor can there be any as to his acting in good faith toward Virginia, in negotiating with the Indians the peace that followed."**

* See "The Washington-Crawford Letters," p. 90.

Reuben G. Thwaites says: *"There seems to be no doubt that Dunmore was thoroughly in earnest; that he prosecuted the war with vigor and knew when to stop in order to secure the best terms."**

*Note in Withers' "Chronicles of Border Warfare," p. 178.

The story of the treachery of Lord Dunmore is shown to have been an afterthought—a thought originating after the Revolution— due to his adherence to his Home Government during that struggle.

Did General Lewis Disobey Orders?

The highest virtue of a soldier is his obedience to the orders of his superiors. The overzealous friends of General Andrew Lewis have for a century done to his memory a great injustice, by asserting that when, on his arrival at the Pickaway Plains, he pressed on toward the Indian towns, after having received orders from Lord Dunmore to halt his army, because a treaty of peace was being negotiated with the Indians; also that there was bitter animosity between him and the Governor. Fortunately for the truth of history and the reputation of General Lewis, Captain John Stuart, the historian of the Southern Division of the army— he who had been in the thickest of the fight at Point Pleasant, and also in front of the line in the march through the Ohio Wilderness—was present at the meeting at Camp Charlotte, and here is his account of it:—

"*Having finished our entrenchments (at Point Pleasant) and put everything in order for securing the wounded from danger after the battle, we crossed the Ohio River in our march to the Shawnee towns. Captain Arbuckle was our guide, who was equally esteemed as a soldier and a fine woodman. When we came to the prairie on Killicanic Creek, we saw the smoke of a small Indian town, which was deserted and set on fire upon our approach. Here we met an express from the Governor's Camp, who had arrived near the nation and proposed peace with the Indians. The governor promised them that the war should be no further prosecuted, and that he would stop the march of Lewis' Army before any more hostilities should be committed upon them. The governor, therefore, with the White Fish warrior, set off and met us at Killicanic Creek, and then Colonel Lewis received his orders to return his army as he (the Governor) had proposed terms of peace with the Indians, which he (was) assured should be accomplished. His Lordship requested Colonel Lewis to introduce him to his officers; and we were accordingly ranged in rank, and had the honor of an introduction to the Governor and Commander-in-Chief, who politely thanked us for services rendered on so momentous an occasion, and assured us of his high esteem and respect for our conduct. On the*

*Governor's consulting Colonel Lewis, it was deemed necessary that a garrison should be established at Point Pleasant, to intercept and prevent the Indians from crossing the Ohio to our side; as also to prevent any whites from crossing over to the side of the Indians."**

* See Stuart's "Memoirs of the Indian Wars and Other Occurrences," p. 57.

It cannot be that these statements will continue to be made in the future as in the past. Original sources of information are now abundant, easily available, and research among these will supply proof that Captain Cresap was not the leader of the men who killed Chief Logan's relatives; that General Lewis was not so lost to the dignity and character of a true soldier, as to disobey the orders of his superior officer in the presence of an enemy; that Lord Dunmore was not guilty of double-dealing with the Virginians; that the Indians were not, in 1774, the allies of Great Britain, and that they did not become such, until the spring of 1778. Henceforth let there be accuracy of historic statement, and this will add to, rather than detract from the importance and glory of the victory won at the mouth of the Great Kanawha by the men of 1774—a victory won in a battle in which only Virginians and Indians were engaged.

CHAPTER XI
POETRY OF THE BATTLE OF POINT PLEASANT
THE CAMP SONG AT POINT PLEASANT
THE SHAWNEE BATTLE ON THE BANKS OF THE OHIO
THE BATTLE SONG OF THE GREAT KANAWHA
BATTLE OF POINT PLEASANT: A CENTENNIAL ODE

Battles have been in all ages a favorite theme for the poets lay. That of Point Pleasant has been thus commemorated in verse as well as prose. The first of these productions appears in the Journal of Ensign James Newell, of Captain William Herbert's Company. He was wounded in the battle, but crossed the Ohio with the Army, October 16th—six days thereafter. The following verses appearing in his Journal were written on the battlefield, or possibly on the opposite bank of the Ohio:—

THE CAMP SONG AT POINT PLEASANT

Bold Virginians all, each cheer up your heart.
We will see the Shawnees before that we part,
We will never desert, nor will we retreat,
Until that our Victory be quite complete.

Ye offspring of Britain! Come stain not you name
Nor forfeit your right to your forefathers' fame,
If the Shawnees will fight, we never will fly,
We'll fight & we'll conquer, or else we will die.

Great Dunmore our General valiant & Bold
Excells the great Heroes—the Heroes of old;
When he doth command we will always obey,
When he bids us fight, we will not run away.

Good Lewis our Colonel, courageous and Brave,
We wish too command us—our wish let us have.
In camp he is pleasant, in War he is bold
Appears like great Caesar—great Caesar of old.

Our Colonels & Captains commands we'll obey,
If the Shawnees should run we will bid them to stay,

Our Arms, they are rifles, our men Volunteers
We'll fight & we'll conquer you need have no fears.

Come Gentlemen all, come strive to excel,
Strive not to shoot often, but strive to shoot well.
Each man like a Hero can make the woods ring,
And extend the Dominion of George our Great King.

Then to it, let's go with might & with main,
Tho' some that set forward return not again;
Let us quite lay aside all cowardly fear
In hope of returning before the new year.

The land it is good, it is just to our mind,
Each will have his part if his Lordship be kind.
The Ohio once ours, we'll live at our ease,
With a Bottle & glass to drink when we please.

Here's a health to King George & Charlotte his mate
Wishing our Victory may soon be complete
And a kind female friend along by our Side
In riches & splendor till Death to abide.

Health to great Dunmore our general also,
Wishing he may conquer wherever he go.
Health to his Lady—may they long happy be
And a health, my good friends, to you & to me.

When Henry Howe, the author of "Historical Collections of Virginia," was in Mason County, now West Virginia, in 1844, collecting data for his work, he visited a number of early settlers. Of one of these he writes as follows:—

"There is living on Thirteen-mile Creek, Mr. Jesse Van Bibber, an aged pioneer of this County. His life, like his own mountain stream, was rough and turbulent at its commencement; but as it nears its close, calm and peaceful, beautifully reflects the Christian virtues. From conversation with him we gathered many interesting anecdotes and incidents illustrating the history of this region. I wrote the following down from his lips: It was made on the Battle of Point Pleasant, sometimes called 'The Shawnee Battle.' "

THE SHAWNEE BATTLE ON THE BANKS OF THE OHIO

Let us mind the tenth of October,
Seventy-four which caused woe,
The Indian savages they did cover
The pleasant banks of the Ohio.

The battle beginning in the morning,
Throughout the day lasted sore,
Till the evening shades were turning down
Upon the banks of the Ohio.

Judgment proceeds to execution,
Let fame throughout all dangers go,
Our heroes fought with resolution
Upon the banks of the Ohio.

Seven score lay dead and wounded
Of champions that did face their foe,
By which the heathen were confounded,
Upon the banks of the Ohio.

Col. Lewis and some noble captains,
Did down to death like Uriah go,
Alas! their heads wound up in napkins,
Upon the banks of the Ohio.

Kings lamented their mighty fallen
Upon the mountains of Gilboa,
And now we mourn for brave Hugh Allen,
Far from the banks of the Ohio.

o bless the mighty King of Heaven
For all his wondrous works below.
Who hath to us the victory given,
Upon the banks of the Ohio.

The manuscript of the following poem was sent to Dr. Lyman C. Draper, in 1845, by Charles H. Lewis of Staunton, Virginia, with the statement that he had found it on one of the lids of his grand-mother's Bible. It is published in the "Documentary History of Dunmore's War," pp. 436, 437, it being printed from the manuscript in the Draper Collection in the Library of the State Historical Society of Wisconsin.

THE BATTLE SONG OF THE GREAT KANAWHA

Ye daughters and sons of Virginia incline
Your ears to a story of woe;
I sing of a time when your fathers and mine
Fought for us on the Ohio.

In seventeen hundred and seventy four,
The month of October, we know,
An army of Indians, two thousand or more,
Encamped on the Ohio.

The Shawnees, Wyandots and Delawares, too,
As well as the tribe of Mingo,
Invaded our lands, and our citizens slew,
On the south of the Ohio.

Andrew Lewis the gallant, and Charlie the brave,
With Mathews and Fleming also,
Collected an army, our country to save,
On the banks of the Ohio.

With Christian, and Shelby, and Elliot, and Paul.
And Stuart and Arbuckle and Crow
And soldiers one thousand and ninety in all
They marched to the Ohio.

These sons of the mountains renowned of old
All volunteered freely to go
And conquer their foeman, like patriots bold,
Or fall by the Ohio.

They marched thro' the untrodden wilds of the west,
O'er mountains and rivers also,
And halted, at Point Pleasant, their bodies to rest,
On the banks of the Ohio.

The Army of Indians in battle array,
Under Cornstalk and Ellinipsico,

Was met by the forces of Lewis that day,
On the banks of the Ohio.

They brought on the battle at breaking of day,
Like heroes they slaughtered the foe,
Till two hundred Indians or more, as they say,
Were slain by the Ohio.

The army of Indians were routed, and fled,
Our heroes pursued the foe,
While eighty soldiers and Charley lay dead,
On the banks of the Ohio.

The Brave Colonel Field and the gallant Buford,
Captains Wilson and Murray also,
And Allen, McClennahan, Goldsby and Ward,
Were slain by the Ohio.

Col. Fleming, and Mathews, and Shelby and Moore,
And Elliot, and Dillon, also,
And soldiers one hundred and thirty and four
Were wounded by the Ohio.

Farewell, Colonel Lewis, till pity's sweet fountains
Are dried in the hearts of the fair and the brave,
Virginia shall weep for her Chief of the mountains
And mourn for the heroes who sleep by his grave.

As Israel mourned for Moses of old,
In the valley of Moab by Nebow
We'll mourn for Charles Lewis the hero so bold,
Who fell by the Ohio.

As Israel did mourn and her daughters did weep,
For Saul and his host at Gilboa
We'll mourn Colonel Field and the heroes who sleep
On the banks of the Ohio.

Harry Maxwell Smythe was a native of Virginia who abandoned the profession of law for that of journalism. When about forty years of age he came to Moundsville, West Virginia, about 1872, and with George A. Creel, he established *The New State Gazette,* a publication which had but a brief existence. Later he removed to Kansas City, Missouri, where he died in 1883. In August 1875, there was a great flood in the Ohio River. Mr.

Smythe was then at Point Pleasant where he wrote the following, which appeared in the *Moundsville Reporter* at that time:—

BATTLE OF POINT PLEASANT—A CENTENNIAL ODE

An hundred years have breathed their changeful breath
Upon this field of glory and of death;
A century of change, yet round me still,
The self-same valley, plain, and glen and hill.
Where all day long the sound of battle rolled;
Where all day long the fearful and the bold
Behind their slender bulwarks, stern and pale,
Stood face to face, the white man and the red,
Their cause the same, the same their gory bed.

The same great rivers meet and mingle here,
That on that day of doubt, and dread and fear,
Flowed calmly on, unheedful of the strife,
The sound of battle and the wreck of life.
Now sweet the sunlight falls upon the dell,
Where heroes fought and brave Charles Lewis fell.

Today when rains have swollen the river's tide,
The rich soil crumbles from the water's side;
There white and ghastly, bedded in the clay,
The bones of those who fell that Autumn day;
And ere they sink beneath Ohio's wave,
The sunlight, for a while, gleams in the grave
Of sires of noble sons, and sons of noble sires;
A nation's incense, all her alter fires,
Can scarce repay the labor of that day,
From dewy dawn, till sunlight fled away.

A nation's songs, through all the coming time
Can scarce give language to thy thoughts sublime;
As standing there beside the crimsoned rills
You thought of dear ones far across the hills,
Of West Augusta homes, where warm and bright,
The firelight gleamed on household gods at night,
And dawn awoke each weary, weary day,
When bright eyes waiting, watched the western way,
For forms those eyes might never never greet;
For forms then stark in death, where two great rivers meet.

Erected In memory of *Keigh-tugh-qua,* a chieftain of the Shawnee Nation known to the Virginians as Cornstalk, his Indian name signifying a cornstalk, the chief support of his people; he commanded the Indian army at Point Pleasant. October 10, 1774; and was killed by the Whites at that place, November 10, 1777. It is four feet and three inches square at the base, and twelve feet high. Erected in the courthouse yard on October 13, 1800 by Samuel II Reynolds who was in charge of the construction of Lock No. 11, in the Great Kanawha River; he contributed the stone and the inscription. Other expenses were borne by the citizens of the town. The monument was removed from near Sixth Street, to its present position August 7, 1000. Cornstalk's grave is South 45° East 118 feet from the base of the monument

"Cornstalk died a grand death, by an act of cowardly treachery on the part of his American foes: it is one of the darkest stains on the checkered pages of frontier history."—Roosevelt's *Winning of the West,"* Vol. I., p. 24.

CHAPTER XII

THE MURDER OF CORNSTALK AT POINT PLEASANT, NOVEMBER 10, 1777.

Many persons have an impression that Cornstalk, the famous Shawnee chieftain who led the savage forces at Point Pleasant, was killed in the battle at that place. This is not true. His tragic death occurred there November 10, 1777. We have seen that at the treaty of Camp Charlotte, Captain William Russell with his company was detailed to build a fort at Point Pleasant. This was done and the little stockade received the name of "Fort Blair." It was abandoned by Captain Russell in June 1775, by direction of Lord Dunmore, and a few days later, the deserted stockade was burned by the Indians. In the autumn of that year, Captain Mathew Arbuckle with a body of troops, arrived at Point Pleasant and erected another stockade which received the name of "Fort Randolph." Here Captain Arbuckle continued in command of the garrison for more than two years, and it was while he was here that Cornstalk, his son Ellinipsico, and Red Hawk, a chief of the Delaware nation, suffered death at the hands of enraged Virginians. It is fortunate for the truth of history, that Captain John Stuart, the historian of Lord Dunmore's War, was present and an eye-witness of the tragic scene. He has left to us the following graphic account of it.*

* See Stuart's "Memoirs of the Indian Wars and Other Occurrences," pp. 1620.

"In the year 1777, the Indians, being urged by British agents, became very troublesome to frontier settlements, manifesting much appearance of hostilities, when the Cornstalk warrior, with the Red-hawk, paid a visit to the garrison at Point Pleasant. He made no secret of the disposition of the Indians; declaring that, on his own part, he was opposed to joining in the war on the side of the British, but that all the nation except himself and his own tribe, were determined to engage in it; and that, of course, he and his tribe would have to run with the stream, (as he expressed it.) On this Captain Arbuckle thought proper to detain him, the Red Hawk, and another fellow, as hostages, to prevent the nation from joining the, British."

In the course of that summer our government had ordered an army to be raised, of volunteers, to serve under the command of

General Edward Hand; who was to have collected a number of troops at Fort Pitt, with them to descend the river to Point Pleasant there to meet a re-enforcement of volunteers expected to be raised in Augusta and Botetourt counties, and then proceed to the Shawnee towns and chastise them so as to compel them to a neutrality. Hand did not succeed in the collection of troops at Fort Pitt; and but three or four companies were raised in Augusta and Botetourt, which were under the command of Colonel George Skillern, who ordered me to use my endeavors to raise all the volunteers I could get in Greenbrier, for that service. The people had begun to see the difficulties attendant on a state of war and long campaigns carried through wildernesses, and but few were willing to engage in such service. But as the settlements which we covered, though less exposed to the depredations of the Indians, had showed their willingness to aid in the proposed plan to chastise the Indians, and had raised three companies, I was very much desirous of doing all I could to promote the business and aid the service. I used the utmost endeavors and proposed to the militia officers to volunteer ourselves, which would be an encouragement to others, and by such means to raise all the men who could be got. The chief of the officers in Greenbrier agreed to the proposal, and we cast lots who should command the company. The lot fell on Andrew Hamilton for captain, and William Renick lieutenant. We collected in all, about forty, and joined Colonel Skillern's party (at old Camp Union) on their way to Point Pleasant.

When we arrived, there was no account of General Hand or his army, and little or no provision made to support our troops, other than what we had taken with us down the Kenawha. We found, too, that the garrison was unable to spare us any supplies, having nearly exhausted, when we got there, what had been provided for themselves. But we concluded to wait there as long as we could for the arrival of General Hand, or some account from him. During the time of our stay two young men, of the names of Hamilton and Gilmore, went over the Kenawha one day to hunt for deer; on their return to camp, some Indians had concealed themselves on the bank amongst the weeds, to view our encampment; and as Gilmore came along past them, they fired on him and killed him on the bank.

Captain Arbuckle and myself were standing on the opposite bank when the gun fired; and whilst we were wondering who it could be shooting, contrary to orders, or what they were doing over the river, we saw Hamilton run down the bank, who called out that Gilmore was killed.

Gilmore was one of the company of Captain John Hall, of that part of the country now Rockbridge County. The Captain was a relation of Gilmore's, whose family and friends were chiefly cut off by the Indians, in the year 1763, when Greenbrier was cut off. Hall's men instantly jumped into a canoe and went to the relief of Hamilton, who was standing in momentary expectation of being put to death. They brought the corpse of Gilmore down the bank, covered with blood and scalped, and put him into the canoe. As they were passing the river, I observed to Captain Arbuckle that the people would be for killing the hostages, as soon as the canoe would land. He supposed that they would not offer to commit so great a violence upon the innocent, who were in nowise accessary to the murder of Gilmore. But the canoe had scarcely touched the shore until the cry was raised, let us kill the Indians in the fort; and every man, with his gun in his hand, came up the bank pale with rage. Captain Hall, was at their head, and leader. Captain Arbuckle and I met them and endeavored to dissuade them from so unjustifiable an action; but they cocked their guns, threatened us with instant death if we did not desist, rushed by us into the fort, and put the Indians to death.

On the preceding day, the Cornstalk's son, Ellinipsico,* had come from the nation to see his father, and to know if he was well, or alive. When he came to the river opposite the fort, he halloowed. His father was, at that instant, in the act of delineating a map of the country and the waters between the Shawnee towns and the Mississippi, at our request, with chalk upon the floor. He immediately recognized the voice of his son, got up, went out, and answered him. The young fellow crossed over, and they embraced each other in the most tender and affectionate manner. The interpreter's wife, who had been a prisoner among the Indians, and had recently left them on hearing the uproar the next day, and hearing the men threatening that they would kill the Indians, for whom she retained much affection, ran to their cabin and informed them that the people were just coming to kill them; and that, because the Indians who killed Gilmore, had come with Ellinipsico the day before; He utterly denied it; declared that he knew nothing of them, and trembled exceedingly. His father encouraged him not to be afraid for that the Great Man above had sent him there to be killed and die with him. As the men advanced to the door, the Cornstalk rose up and met them; they fired upon him, and seven or eight bullets went through him. So fell the great

Cornstalk warrior,—whose name was bestowed upon him by the consent of the nation, as their great strength and support. His son was shot dead, as he sat upon a stool. The Red-Hawk made an attempt to go up the chimney, but was shot down. The other Indian was shamefully mangled, and I grieved to see him so long in the agonies of death.

* Doubtless an English corruption of Al-lan-i-wis-i-ca.

The Cornstalk, from personal appearance and many brave acts, was undoubtedly a hero. Had he been spared to live, I believe he would have been friendly to the American cause; for nothing could induce him to make the visit to the garrison at the critical time he did, but to communicate to them the temper and disposition of the Indians, and their design of taking part with the British. On the day he was killed we held a council, at which he was present. His countenance was dejected; and he made a speech, all of which seemed to indicate an honest and manly disposition. He acknowledged that he expected that he and his party would have to run with the stream, for that all the Indians on the lakes and northwardly, were joining the British. He said that when he returned to the Shawnee towns after the Battle at the Point, he called a council of the nation to consult what was to be done, and upbraided them for their folly in not suffering him to make peace on the evening before the battle—"What," said he, "will you do now? The Big Knife is coming on us and we shall all be killed. Now you must fight, or we are undone." But no one made an answer. He said, "Then let us kill all our women and children, and go and fight till we die." But none would answer. At length he rose and struck his tomahawk in the post in the center of the town house; "I'll go," said he, "and make peace!" And then the warriors grunted out "ough, ough, ough," and runners were instantly dispatched to the Governor's army to solicit a peace and the interposition of the Governor on their behalf.

When he made his speech in council, with us, he seemed to be impressed with an awful premonition of his approaching fate; for he repeatedly said, "When I was a young man and went to war, I thought that might be the last time, and I would return no more. Now I am here among you; you may kill me if you please; I can die but once; and it is all one to me, now or another time." This declaration concluded every sentence of his speech. He was killed about one hour after our council.

A few days after this catastrophe General Hand arrived, but had no troops. We were discharged and returned home a short time before Christmas. Not long after we left the garrison a small party of Indians appeared near the fort, and Lieutenant Moore was ordered with a party to pursue them. Their desire was to retaliate the murder of Cornstalk. Moore had not pursued one-quarter of a mile until he fell into an ambuscade and was killed, with several of his men."

Efforts to Punish the Men Who Killed Cornstalk

Captain Stuart states that the company of Captain James Hall was from "that part of the country now Rockbridge County, Virginia. This County was formed by act of the Assembly in 1777, and the first Court held therefore, convened at the house of Samuel Wallace where Lexington now stands April 7, 1778, but five months after Cornstalk was killed. The following is taken from the records of that Court:—

"April 30, 1778.—At a court held this day in the second year of the Commonwealth for the examination of Captain James Hall, who stands bound in recognizance for his appearance, charged with suspicion of felony in being concerned in the murder of the Cornstalk Indian, his son Ellinipsico, Redhawk, and another chief of the Indians on the 10th day of November last, there were present Charles Campbell, Samuel Lyle, Alexander Stewart and John Trimble, gentlemen. The above named James Hall appeared, and upon examination desired the facts with which he was charged, whereupon the sheriff proclaimed who could give evidence against the prisoner in behalf of the Commonwealth to appear and do the same, but none appeared. The Court were of the opinion that the said James Hall be further bound to appear before a court to be held for his examination on the 28th day of this instant, which he agreed to and entered into recognizance accordingly." At the appointed time he again appeared, was placed on trial and acquitted. Similar entries appear showing that Hugh Galbraith, Malcolm McCown and William Rowan were each tried upon the same charge and acquitted.*

* See first Order-Book In Clerk's office of Rockbridge County, Virginia

Captains Arbuckle and Stuart gave respectful burial to Cornstalk and those who perished with him, the graves being located at what was afterward the corner of Viand and Kanawha Streets in the town of Point Pleasant, where they were kept marked. Stephen T. Mitchell, Editor of *The Spirit of the Old Dominion,* published at Richmond, Virginia, was at Point Pleasant in 1827. The inhabitants pointed out the grave of Cornstalk and he wrote the following:

"The remains of the warriors—Cornstalk and his son Ellinipsico—lie alone beneath the sod of the common as if their bodies, even in death disdained to have communication with those of the treacherous foe by whom they were slaughtered, whilst depending on their pledges of faith and hospitality. A slight mound of earth scarcely distinguished from the plain around it marks the tomb of the most relentless, yet the most generous foe that ever menaced the frontiers of America."

In 1840, when the streets mentioned above were opened, the bones of these warriors were removed with military honors, and re-interred all together in one common grave, in the Court-House yard, at a spot where a westward extension of the north wall of the old jail, bisects a southern extension of the east wall of the Court-House, about twenty-five feet from the southeast corner thereof. Prior to the Civil war, Mr. Charles Rawson, a son of the jailor of the County, at his own expense, put a rail fence around the grave, and his sister, Miss Susan, in the kindness of her heart, planted rose-bushes on and about it; but during the occupation of the town by the armies, in the Civil War, the rails were burned, and stock destroyed the shrubbery. Since then, it has been a neglected spot, but now—in 1909—it has been enclosed with concrete columns and connecting chains, and otherwise beautified. This work has been done by the principal—Miss Bertha J. Steinbach—and students of the Point Pleasant High School.

ADDENDA

CORNSTALK was a name that once thrilled the heart of every man on the Virginia frontier and struck terror into every inmate of a mountain home. He had no youth in history; the first known of him being his connection with the Muddy Creek massacre in 1763, in Greenbrier, and that of Carr's Creek now in Rockbridge County, a little later. He was gifted with oratory, statesmanship, heroism, a military strategist, straight in form, and majestic in movement. It was his anxiety to preserve the frontier of Virginia from desolation and death that prompted him to make his visit to Point Pleasant, and the untimely and perfidious manner of his death caused a deep and lasting regret to pervade the bosoms even of those who were enemies of his nation.

Colonel Benjamin Wilson, afterward prominent in the affairs of Monongalia, Harrison and Randolph counties, West Virginia, was with Dunmore at Camp Charlotte and heard the speech of Cornstalk. Of it he said:—

"When he arose, he was in no wise confused or daunted, but spoke in a distinct voice, without stammering or repetition, and with peculiar emphasis. His looks, while addressing Dunmore, were truly grand and majestic; yet graceful and attractive. I have heard the first orators in Virginia—Patrick Henry and Richard Henry Lee—but never have I heard one whose powers of delivery surpassed those of Cornstalk."

* Drake's "Indians of North America," Book V., p. 546

Red-hawk was a chieftain of the Delaware nation and like Ellinipisco, had been in the thickest of the fight at the Battle of Point Pleasant. He was the chief speaker in behalf of the Indians at the treaty with Colonel Bouquet at the Forks of Muskingum, November 12, 1764, where he said:—

"Brother, listen to us your younger brothers. As we see something in your eyes that looks dissatisfaction, we now clear them. You have credited bad stories against us. We clean your ears, that you may hear better hereafter. We wish to remove everything bad from your heart, that you may be as good as your ancestors. (A belt) We saw you coming with an uplifted tomahawk in your hand. We now take it from you, and throw it up to God. Let him do with it as he pleases. We hope never to see it more. Brother, as you are a warrior, take hold of this chain (handing a belt) of friendship, and let us think no more of war, in pity of our old men, women and children. We, too, are warriors."

* Drake's "Indians of North America," Book V., p. 695.

    The remarkable figure made use of in this speech, of throwing the hatchet up to God, is new; and it was remarked by Thomas Hutching, afterward the first Geographer of the United States, who heard it, that by it the speaker wished probably to be understood that, by this disposition of it, it would be out of the reach of bad men, and would be given only to the party in the future, to whom the right of revenge belonged; whereas if it were buried in the ground, any miscreant might dig it up. Red-Hawk promised, on behalf of his nation, that all the prisoners should be delivered up at Fort Pitt the next spring.

    Ellinipsico though having at first appeared, disturbed, met his death with great composure. He was shot upon the seat on which he was sitting. He had been beside his father throughout the battle day at Point Pleasant in 1774. Cornstalk had a son, The Wolf, who was one of the Shawnee hostages taken by Dunmore to Williamsburg, and after escaping, was connected with some of the events on the border in the early years of the Revolution.

APPENDIX A

THE ONLY ROSTERS PRESERVED OF THE COMPANIES WHICH WERE IN THE BATTLE OF POINT PLEASANT OR ARRIVED WITH COLONEL CHRISTIAN IN THE EVENING AFTER IT HAD BEEN FOUGHT AND WON.

But few of the rolls of Companies which participated in the Battle of Point Pleasant, or which arrived on the field that evening with Colonel William Christian, are known to be in existence. Far the greater number have been lost in the shades of oblivion. It is possible that some others, in addition to those we now have, may yet be found, among the musty and dusty documents of public record offices and libraries; but this is not probable. There were eleven companies in the Augusta Regiment, under Colonel Charles Lewis; eight companies in the Botetourt Regiment, under Colonel William Fleming; and seven companies in the Fincastle Battalion, under Colonel William Christian. In addition thereto, there were one company of Minute Men from Culpeper County, under Colonel John Field, (acting Captain); a company of Volunteers from Dunmore (now Shenandoah) County, commanded by Captain Thomas Slaughter; a company of Riflemen from Bedford County, at the head of which was Captain Thomas Buford; and a company of Kentucky Pioneers, led on by Captain James Harrod. Of the rolls of these companies—thirty in number—only the following eleven are known to exist. We print them by permission of the copyright proprietors, from Thwaites and Kellogg's "Documentary History of Dunmore's War;" the originals being in the library of the State Historical Society of Wisconsin.

IN THE AUGUSTA COUNTY REGIMENT

A List of Captain William Nalle's Company of Volunteers in the Augusta County Regiment,

Officers

William Nalle	Captain
Martin Nalle	Lieutenant
Jacob Pence	Ensign

John Bush	Sergeant
William Bush	Sergeant
Bernard Crawford	Sergeant

Privates

Shadrick Butler	John Owler
William Feavill	George Fuls (or Fultz)
Robert Hains	James Miller
Moses Smith	George Harmon
Stephen Washburn	John Chisholm
Israel Meaders	Adam Hansbarger
Henry Owler	Henry Cook
John Griggsby	John Breden
Richard Welch	Thomas Brooke
Zacarias Lee	Henry Miner
John Goodall	Chesley Rogers
Benjamin Petty	Zapaniah Lee
Michael Jordan	Micajah Smith
Bruten Smith	William Smith
James Todd	John Deck
William Spicer	John Fry
James Washburn	John Williams
Charles Brown	Joseph Butler
James Alexander	James Selby
George Rucker	James Reary
Joseph Ray (or Roay)	Abraham Rue
William Scales	Jacob Null
John Bright	John Null
Yenty Jackson	Total 54

IN THE BOTETOURT COUNTY REGIMENT

A List of Captain John Murray's Company of Volunteers in the Botetourt County Regiment,

Officers

John Murray	Captain*
William McKee	Lieutenant**
Samuel Wallace	Lieutenant
Adam Wallace	Ensign
William Taylor	Sergeant

286

Moses Coller	Sergeant
John Larken	Sergeant
John Simpson	Sergeant
Barney Boyls	Sergeant

•Killed at Point Pleasant.
••Assumed command of the company when Captain Murray was killed.

Privates

John Gilmore,	Hugh Logan,
James Hall,	James Arnold,
Stephen Arnold,	William Moore,
John Nelson,	John Sedbury,
William MacCorkle,	Joseph McBride,
George Milwood,	John Lapsly,
Andrew Evans	Ezekiel Kennedy,
Thomas Nail,	John Moore,
James Walker,	Robert Wallace,
John Jones,	John Griggs,
William Simpson,	Daniel Blair,
Thomas McClure,	James Simpkins,
Peter Cassady	Stephen Harris,
Thomas Pearry,	James Gilmore
George Cummings,	Joseph Gibson,
John Eager (or Edgar),	Thomas Hedden,
James Crawley,	John Coiler,
Thomas Burney,	James Neely,
Daniel Simpkins,	Peter Higgins,
William Lyons	William Bradley,
Nicholas Mooney,	William Brown,
Solomon Brundige,	William Johns,
John McClure	James Brambridge,
Daniel Fullin (or Pullin),	Hugh Logan,
David Wallace,	William Neely
Moses Whitby,	John Miligan,
James Cunningham,	William Conner,
John Kelsey,	John McGee,
Hugh Moore,	James McCalister,
William Cochran,	John Barkley,
James Logan,	Andrew Wallace,
John Logan,	Isaac Trimble,

Prisley Gill,	Peter McNeal,
Jonathan Watson,	Andrew Alden,
John Murray,	Total 78

A List of Captain Philip Love's Company of Volunteers, In the Botetourt County Regiment,

Officers

Philip Love	Captain
Daniel McNeill	Lieutenant
John Mills	Ensign
William Ewing	Sergeant Major
Francis McElhaney	Quarter M. S.
Shelton Taylor	Sergeant
James Alexander	Sergeant*
John Crawford	Sergeant

Privates

Robert Owen	James Neeley
Samuel Andrews	Abraham Moon
William Scott	George Craig
Samuel MtGumery (Montgomery)	Richard Wilson
William Teasy	Robert Smith
John Todd	John Buchanan
Thomas Pierce	Charles Davis
Thomas Armstrong	William Franklin
John Dunn	James Franklin
Charles Byrne	William Hanson
Thomas Gilbert	James McDonald
Abraham DeMonts	Richard Collins
William Hooper	James M. Guillin
Samuel Savage	John McGinnis
Thomas Welch	Griffin Harris
Thomas Welch Jr.	John Marks
John Jones	John Robinson
Patrick Conner	John Todd
Joseph Pain	Daniel Ormsbey
William Armstrong	Thomas Brown
Daniel McDonald	James Simpson
	Total 50

*Wounded at Point Pleasant.

A List of Captain John Lewis' Company of Volunteers in the Botetourt County Regiment,

Officers

*John Lewis	Captain
John Henderson	Lieutenant
Robert Alliet (Eliott)	Ensign
Samuel Glass	Sergeant
William Bryans	Sergeant
Peter Huff	Sergeant
William Wilson	Sergeant
Samuel Estill	Sergeant
John Donnally	Fifer
Thomas Alsbury	Drummer

Privates

John Swope	Thomas Edgar
Alexander Kelley	Thomas Canady (or Kanady)
James Carlton	William Jones
Edward Eagin	Richard Packwood
Matthew Polug (or Pogue)	John Arthur
James Ellison	Edward Wilson
John Deniston	Robert Boyd
James Stuart	Solomon White
John Savage	Thomas Carpenter**
Christopher Welch	Solomon Carpenter
William Robinson	David Cook
James Crawley	John Bowman
Samuel Huff	Jacob Bowman
James Dulin	James Burnsides
Isaac Fisher	Matthew Jewitt
Peter Ellenburg	Henry Howard
John Reyburn	Dennis Nail
Andrew Kissinger	Molastine Peregrine
Isaac Nichol	Hugh Caperton
Samuel Barton	Walter Holwell
Philip Hammond	Matthew Creed
William Clifton	James McNutt
James Burtchfield	Samuel Burcks
Joseph Love	Adam Cornwell
Leonard Huff	Nathan Farmer

Thomas Huff**	William Boniface
Jeremiah Carpenter	Gabriel Smithers
Samuel Croley	Robert Davis
William Isum	John Carpenter
Isaac Taylor	Henry Bowyer
Martin Carney	Thomas Burnes
Peter Hendricks	Mathias Kissinger
Robert Bowles	Adam Caperton
John Hundley	William Mann
	Total 78

* This Captain John Lewis was a son of General Andrew Lewis, and a cousin of Captain John Lewis, (son of Thomas) of the Augusta Regiment, his father being a brother of the General.—V. A. L.

**Wounded at Point Pleasant.

A List of Captain John Stewart's Company of Greenbrier Valley Volunteers in the Botetourt County Regiment (Manuscript torn)

Officers

John Stuart	Captain
James Donnally	Sergeant
Charles O'Hara	Sergeant
Skidmore Harriman	Sergeant

Privates

Daniel Workman	William Dyer
Samuel Williams	Edward Smith
William O'Harra	John Harris
Robert O'Harra	Joseph Currence
James Pauley	Joseph Day
William Clendenin	Jacob Lockhart
James Clarke	George Clendennin
Spencer Cooper	John Burke
John Pauley	Charles Kennison*
Daniel Taylor	William Ewing
Archibald McDowell	John Doherty
William Hogan	John McNeal
Andrew Gardiner	Joseph Campbell

Quavy Lockhart	Samuel Sullivan
Thomas Ferguson*	Thomas Gillispie
John McCandless	Henry Lawrence
John Crain	Total 37

* Wounded at the Battle of Point Pleasant

A List of Captain Robert McClennahan's Company of Greenbrier Valley Volunteers in the Botetourt County Regiment.

Officers

Robert McClennahan	Captain
William McCoy	Lieutenant
Mathew Bracken	Ensign*
Thomas Williams	Sergeant
William Craig	Sergeant
Samuel Clarke	Sergeant
William Jones	Drummer

Privates

John Harmon	Richard Williams
Edward Barrett	John Patton
James Kinkaid	Thomas Ellias
John Williams	Charles Howard
George Kinkaid	Thomas Cooper
David Cutlip	William McCaslin
James Burrens	John Cunningham
James Morrow, Sr.	Francis Boggs
James Morrow, Jr.	Edward Thomas
James Gilkeson	Patrick Constantine
Evan Evans	William Custer
James Guffy	Lewis Holmes
William Stewart	John Vaughn
William Hutchinson	Total 34

•Wounded In Battle of Point Pleasant.

A List of Captain Henry Pauling's Company of Volunteers of the Botetourt County Regiment,

Officers

Henry Pauling	Captain
Edward Goldman	Lieutenant*
Samuel Baker	Ensign
Obediah H. Trent	Sergeant
Robert Findley	Sergeant
James Woods	Sergeant

Privates

Robert Watkins	William Canaday
Philip Hanes,	John Frazer
John Clerk	George Davis
James DeHority	Thomas McCrary
William Thompson	John Gibson
William Honey	Charles Ellisson
Joel Doss	James Donahoo
Richard Rollins	Thomas Wilson
William Ray	William Gilliss
Michael Looney	David Condon
Dangerfield Harmon	James King
Stephen Holston	Edward Carther
James Wilson	William Glass
John Agnew	John Fitzhugh
Dudley Callaway	Thomas Reid
David Belew	Joseph Whittaker
Andrew Rogers	Isham Fienquay
Robert Terrell	Richard LeMaster
Andrew Harrison	John Hutson
George Zimmerman	William McCalister
Alexander Caldwell	Jeremiah Jenkins
Edward Ross	Martin Baker
Matthew Ratcliff	James Lynn
	Total 52

•Wounded In Battle of Point Pleasant.

THE FINCASTLE COUNTY BATTALION

A List of Captain Evan Shelby's Company of Volunteers from the Watauga Valley, in the Fincastle County Battalion,

Officers

Evan Shelby	Captain*
Isaac Shelby	Lieutenant**
James Robertson	Sergeant
Valentine Levier	Sergeant

*Assumed chief command on the field of battle after Colonels Lewis, Fleming, and Field had fallen.
**Took command of his father's company, who had assumed command on the field.

Privates

James Shelby	William Casey
Arthur Blackburn	Mark Williams
John Sawyer	John Stewart*
Robert Herrill (Handley)	Conrad Nave
John Findley	Richard Burck
George Armstrong	John Riley
Henry Shaw (Span)	Elijah Robison (Robertson)
Daniel Mungle	Richard Holliway
Frederick Mungle	Jarrett Williams
John Williams	Julias Robison
John Carmack*	Charles Fielder
Andrew Torrence	William Tucker
George Brooks	Benjamin Grayum (Graham)
Isaac Newland	Patrick St. Lawrence
Reece Price*	John Bradley
Abram Newland	Samuel Hensley (Handley)
George Ruddle	Samuel Samples
Emanuel Shoatt	Andrew Goff
Abram Bogard	Hugh O'Gullion
Peter Torney (Forney)	Barnett O'Gullion
John Fain	Joseph Hughey
Samuel Vance	Bazaleel Maxwell
Samuel Fain	Total 49

* Wounded at the Battle of Point Pleasant

A Partial List of Captain William Campbell's Company* in the Fincastle County Battalion,

Officers

| William Campbell | Captain |

Privates

Philemon Hoggins	Benjamin Richardson
Joseph Newberry	John Johnston
Stephen Hopton	Richard Woolsey
John Lewis	Coonrad Sterns
Auldin Williamson	William Champ
William Hopton	Richard Lyhnam
John Neil	John Boles
Wiliam Richardson	Total 15

* There were 39 men in Captain Campbell's Company, but the names of only 15 of them have been preserved.

A List of Captain James Harrod's Company of Kentucky Pioneers

IN THE FINCASTLE COUNTY BATTALION
(From Collin's "History of Kentucky," Vol. II, p. 517)

Officers

| James Harrod | Captain* |

Privates

James Blair	James Harlan
James Brown	Thomas Harrod
Abraham Chapline	Isaac Hite
James Harrod	John Crawford
John Clark	Jared Cowan
Evan Hinton	James Knox

*In the spring of 1774, Captain James Harrod, a Pennsylvanian by birth, collected at the mouth of Grave Creek, now Moundsville,

Marshall County, West Virginia, a party of thirty-one young men, for the purpose of making a settlement in Kentucky. Descending the Ohio to the mouth of the Kentucky River, they thence Journeyed through the wilderness to the Big Spring, now in Mercer County. Here they were engaged in founding Harrodsburg, the oldest town in Kentucky, when they were discovered by Daniel Boone and Michael Stoner who had been sent by Lord Dunmore to warn John Floyd, Deputy Surveyor of Fincastle County, Virginia, which then included all of Kentucky, together with his assistants, then at the Falls of the Ohio, that an Indian War was begun. Harrod and party abandoned their settlement, and proceeded to the Holston Valley, where he and twenty-seven of his men joined the Fincastle Battalion, and with Christian, arrived at Point Pleasant the evening after the battle.

Privates

John Cowan	James Wiley
James McCulloch	David Glenn
John Crow	James Sodousky
Alexander Petrey	Thomas Glenn
Azarlah Davis	Benjamin Tutt
Azariah Reece	James Hamilton
William Fields	Silas Harlan,
Jacob Sandusky	David Williams
Robert Gilbert	John Wilson
Jonn Shelp	Total 32

THE INDEPENDENT COMPANIES

Of the Independent Companies,—the Dunmore County Volunteers, the Culpepper Minute Men, and the Bedford County Riflemen, but one roster, that of the latter, has been preserved. This follows:—

A List of Captain Thomas Buford's Company of Bedford County Rifle Company of Volunteers,

Officers

Thomas Buford	Captain*
Thomas Dooley	Lieutenant
Jonathan Cundiff	Ensign
Nicholas Mead	Sergeant

William Kenedy	Sergeant
John Fields	Sergeant
Thomas Fliping	Sergeant

•Died of wounds the night after the battle.

Privates

Abraham Sharp	Thomas Hall
Absalom McClanahan	William Hamrick
William Bryant	Nathaniel Cooper
William McColister	John Cook
James Scarbara	Mr. Waugh
John McClanahan	John McGlahlen
James McBride	Jonn Campbell
John Carter	Thomas Hamrick
William Campbell	Joseph White
Adam Lynn	Thomas Owen
Robert Boyd	John Read
Thomas Stephens	John Roberts
William Kerr	William Overstreet
James Boyd	Robert Hill
Gerrott Kelley	Joseph Bunch
James Dale	Samuel Davis
James Ard	Jacob Dooley
Robert Ewing	Zachariah Kennot
William Deal	Augustine Hackworth
Francis Seed	William Cook
John Bozel	John Wood
William Hackworth	Uriah Squires
John Welch	Total 52

From the foregoing official rosters it will be seen that they contain five hundred and thirty-one names. If to these we add those of the captains, of the nineteen companies, whose names are known, but of which we have no rosters, we shall have a total of five hundred and fifty names of the men who were with the Southern Division, or left wing of Dunmore's Army, commanded by General Lewis.

Note—The "Documentary History of Dunmore's War" is the chief and by far the most reliable source from which to obtain rosters of the companies engaged in the Battle of Point Pleasant, and we print there -from all of those which participated in that struggle. In addition to these, that work contains rolls or lists of men engaged in defending the frontier in 1774. These included the companies of Captains Daniel Smith, page 396; Robert Doak, p. 399; men in Michael Woods' Muster District, p. 396; Thomas Burk's Muster District, p. 398; and the Garrisons at Elk Garden Fort, p. 401; at Glade Hollow Fort, p. 402; at Maiden Spring Station, and Upper Station, p. 403; and a list of scouts on p. 404. Not one of these organizations was in the Battle of Point Pleasant, as is shown by the regimental and battalion organizations on page 413, 4.14, 415, 416, 417, 418, of the said work.

APPENDIX B

THE AFTER-LIFE OF THE MEN WHO FOUGHT THE BATTLE OF POINT PLEASANT

"It is worth noting that all the alter time leaders of the West were engaged in some way in Lord Dunmore's War."— Roosevelt's *"Winning of the West."* Vol. I, P. 242.

"This battle was the most bloody and the best contested in the annals of forest warfare. The heroes of that day proved themselves worthy to found States."— Bancroft's *"History of the United States."* Vol. IV, p.87.

How true are these statements of eminent historians! They won the Battle of Point Pleasant, which changed the course of history on this continent; and when the War for Independence came, they met the heroes of Lexington, Concord, and Bunker Hill, and together with them, were at Monmouth, Brandywine, King's Mountain, and Yorktown. Seven officers in the Battle of Point Pleasant rose to the rank of general in the Revolutionary Army; six captains in that battle commanded regiments on continental establishment in the war for independence; four officers in that battle led the attack on Gwynn's Island, in Chesapeake Bay, in July 1776, which resulted in the dislodgement of Lord Dunmore, the late governor, who was thus driven from the shores of Virginia never to return; one captain in that battle was the most prominent American officer in the battle of Brandywine where he was severely wounded; another officer in that battle led the advance at the storming of Stony Point, one of the most daring achievements of the Revolution; still another officer in that battle, won lasting fame as the "Hero of King's Mountain." Hundreds of men in that battle were afterward on revolutionary fields and many of them witnessed the surrender of Cornwallis to the united armies of the United States and France, at the close of that struggle, at Yorktown. Indeed, it is a matter of history that these Point Pleasant men were on nearly every battlefield of the Revolution. And one of them, when sixty-three years of age, led the Americans at the battle of the Thames, in 1813, secured a great victory, and thus broke the English power in the Northwest.

But it was not alone on fields of carnage that the men who fought the Battle of Point Pleasant, distinguished themselves. Six of them afterwards occupied seats in the American House of Representatives; three of them were members of the United States Senate; four of them became governors of states; one of them a Lieutenant Governor; one of them a Territorial Governor; one of them military and civil commandant of Upper Louisiana; one of them a surveyor-general of one of the thirteen original states; one the father of a governor of Virginia; one, the father of a supreme judge of Kentucky; one of them the largest manufacturer and wealthiest man in eastern Ohio at the time of his business career; one of them president of the Bank of St. Louis; one of them a framer of a constitution for Ohio; one of them a receiver of public monies in a western State; and a hundred of them state legislators and framers of state constitutions ; while more than a thousand of them went forth to conquer again—not with a rifle, but with the axe— that they might fell the forests from which they had driven barbarism and change the land into fruitful fields.

Was another such battle ever fought, by an army composed of such men? Their fame then resounded, not only in the backwoods, but throughout Virginia. Now, it is known to a nation. Historians have not done them justice. Still, they have not been forgotten. Their names are all around us. Of the men who made national history at Point Pleasant, the name of one is preserved in that of a County in Pennsylvania; the names of three in those of counties in Ohio; of four of them in County names in Indiana; of four of them in the names of counties in Illinois; of four of them in County names in West Virginia; of five of them in the names of counties in Tennessee; and ten of them in the names of counties in Kentucky. Towns named in memory of men who were in the Battle of Point Pleasant are found in many states, prominent among them being Christiansburg, Virginia; Lewisburg, and Clendenin, West Virginia; Flemingsburg and Harrodsburg, Kentucky; Clarksville and Sevierville, Tennessee; and Shelbyville, Indiana.

It was in commemoration of the historic achievement of these men that a Nation and a State—the United States and West Virginia— have united in rearing a towering and enduring monument on the battlefield of Point Pleasant.

APPENDIX C

EXTRACTS FROM THE VIRGINIA GAZETTE, RELATING TO LORD DUNMoRE'S WAR

The Virginia Gazette, the first newspaper published in that Colony, was founded at Williamsburg in 1736; and was the official Journal of the Colony, it was published in 1772 by William Kind; he died the next year and his wife, Clementina, assumed the management of the paper. She died September 24, 1774, after which it was continued for her children by her relative, John Pinkney, a prominent printer of that time. It was then the only newspaper published in the Colony. The following extracts relating to Dunmore's War are copied from it:

"It is reported, and we believe with too much certainty that an Indian War is inevitable, as many outrages have lately happened on the frontiers; but whether the Indians or White people are most to blame, we cannot determine, the accounts being so extremely complicated."—Virginia Gazette, Thursday, May 26, 1774.

"We likewise hear that the Frontier inhabitants are all in motion at the behavior of the Indians, and seem determined to drive from among them so cruel and treacherous an enemy."—Virginia Gazette, Thursday, June 2, 1774.

Cave Cumberland writes the Gazette under date of June 21, 1774, saying:

"I have had no accounts of my brother since he left Fort Pitt, nor is there any news or word of any of the traders at the Shawnee towns. What has become of them, God only knows. But all accounts of that quarter are very bad. We have received accounts this day by express that one Captain McClure, a Virginian, is killed and another man mortally wounded, by a party of Indians which was out near Red Stone. All the poor people who were settled over the Allegheny mountains, are either moved off or gathered in large numbers and making places of defense to secure themselves."—Virginia Gazette, Thursday, July 14, 1774.

"Last Sunday morning his Excellency, our Governor, left this city in order to take a view of the situation of the frontier of this Colony. It seems his Lordship intends to settle matters amicably with the Indians if possible, and proposes to have conferences with the different Nations, to find out the causes of the late Disturbances."—Virginia Gazette, Thursday, July 14, 1774.

"Lord Dunmore before leaving Williamsburg, July 10th, issued a proclamation stating that the House of Burgesses was summoned to meet on Thursday, August 11, ensuing. He, because of absence on the Frontier, prorogued that body until the first Thursday in November next."—Virginia Gazette, Thursday, July 14, 1774.

"Wednesday evening last an express arrived in this city who reports that many families have very lately been barbously murdered on the Frontiers of Pennsylvania and Virginia, and that his Excellency, Lord Dunmore, is endeavoring all in his power to repel those hostile and inhuman savages. Colonel Preston and General Lewis, it seems, have raised a thousand men each, and it is reported also that a like number has enlisted under his Lordship's banner, he, as well as them, being greatly exasperated at the late cruel and intolerable treatment of the Indians towards the white people residing at or near the back parts of his Colony."—Virginia Gazette, Thursday, August 25, 1774.

"The Indians are daily committing some foul murder or other. Their cruel and inhuman treatment towards the people on the Frontiers loudly calls for vengeance."—Virginia Gazette, Thursday, September 8, 1774.

"His Excellency, Lord Dunmore, we hear has amicably settled matters with the Delaware, Wyandot, and Seneca Indians, who have lately brought many tokens of their peaceable disposition and of their determination to maintain peace. His Lordship, set off some time since with a detachment in order to compromise affairs with the other Nations and it is supposed that he will be equally successful."—Virginia Gazette, Thursday, October 6, 1774.

An extract of a letter from Colonel William Preston, dated Fincastle, September 28, 1774, states:—

"That part of the army under the command of General Lewis who is to meet Lord Dunmore at the mouth of the Great Kanawha, or New River, assembled at the 'Great Levels' of Greenbrier, to the amount of about fifteen hundred men, rank and file. Colonel Charles Lewis marched with about six hundred men on the 6th, for the mouth of Elk, a branch of New River which empties in some distance below the Falls, there to build a small fort, and to prepare canoes. General Andrew Lewis marched with another large party on the 12th instant for the same place, and Colonel Christian was to march yesterday (September 27th) with the remainder, being about four hundred, and the last supply of provisions. This body of Militia being mostly armed with Rifle Guns, and a great part of them good woodsmen, are looked upon to be at least equal to any Troops, for the number that have ever been raised in America. It is earnestly hoped that they will, in conjunction with the other party, be able to chastise the Ohio Indians for the many murders and robberies, they have committed on our Frontiers for many years past.

On the 8th instant, one John Harvey, was dangerously wounded and his wife and three children taken prisoners on the head of Clinch River. The man at that time made his escape, but Is since dead of his wounds. The same day a man was taken prisoner by another party of the enemy, on the north Fork of the Holston. On the 13th a soldier was fired upon by the Indians on Clinch River; but as he received no hurt, he returned the fire and it is believed killed an Indian, as much blood was found where he fell and one of the plugs which burst out of his wound was also found. The soldier was supported by some men who were near, and gave the two Indians a chase; who it is supposed threw the wounded one into a deep Pit that was near. These parties of the enemy were pursued several days by Captain Daniel Smith; who could not overtake them, they having stolen horses to carry them off.

On the 23rd, two Negroes were taken prisoners at Blackmore's Fort, on Clinch River, and a great many horses and cattle shot down. On the 24th of September, a family was killed and taken at Reedy Creek, a branch of Holston, near the Cherokee Line; and on Saturday morning, the 25th, Hallooing, and the report of many guns, were heard at several houses, but the damage done was not known when the express came away. These last murders are believed to be perpetrated by the Cherokees, as two men lately returned from that country and made oath that two parties had left the towns, either to join the Shawnees, or to fall upon some of the Settlements; and that the Cherokees, in general, appeared in a very bad temper, which greatly alarmed the traders.

It is impossible to conceive the consternation into which the last stroke has put the inhabitants on Holston and Clinch Rivers, and the latter as many of their choice men are on the expedition, and they have no ammunition. Two of these people were at my house this day, and, after traveling about a hundred miles, offered ten shillings a pound for powder; but there is none to be had for any money. Indeed, it is very alarming; for should the Cherokees engage in a war at this time it would ruin us, as so many men are out and ammunition is so scarce. Add to this the strength of those people, and their towns being so near our settlements on Holston."—Virginia Gazette, Thursday, October 13, 1774.

"This morning an express arrived in this city, from his Excellency, Lord Dunmore, with intelligence relative to his Lordship and the Indians. Far advanced as the week is, we think it our indispensible duty to communicate, at all times, anything that may be important to the public, and have therefore given a supplement to this week's paper."—Virginia Gazette, Thursday, October 14th, 1774.

The First Printed Account of The Battle of Point Pleasant

This appeared in the *Virginia Gazette* of November 10, 1774. Some authorities say that it was written by Captain Mathew Arbuckle; others that it was prepared by Lieutenant Isaac Shelby. The fact is that it was written by Captain Thomas Slaughter, commanding the Dunmore County Volunteers, on the battle-field, on the 17th of October, 1774. This he sent to his brother in Culpeper County, who sent it to the *Gazette* for publication, it being accompanied by the following letter:—

"Culpeper, (Va.), November 3, 1774. Mr. Finkney:—

I received yesterday, from my brother, by an express from the banks of the Ohio, at the mouth of the Great Kanawha an account of a battle between our troops and the Indians, which I have enclosed, to be inserted in your Gazette, with a list of the killed and wounded. My brother, likewise, writes me of our Governor being still on his march to the Indian towns, and as the account is certain, he may not be expected for some time. His Excellency was not in the engagement, being about 75 miles up the Ohio, on the Indian Side. An Express arrived from him the evening after the battle, with orders for their troops to meet him at some distance from the towns so that when the express came off he had no account of the battle.

I am, Sir, your Obedient Servant,

Francis T. Slaughter."

Following this letter is a description of the battle which is substantially the same as that written by Lieutenant Isaac Shelby, and printed elsewhere in this work.*

*See ante pp. 43, 44, 45

"In the afternoon of December 4, 1774, Lord Dunmore arrived at the palace in this city from his expedition against the Indians who have been humbled into a necessity of soliciting peace themselves and have delivered hostages for the due observance of the terms which cannot fail of giving satisfaction as thy confine the Indians to limits which entirely remove the grounds of future quarrel between them and the people of Virginia and lay a foundation for a fair and extensive Indian trade, which if properly followed must produce the most beneficial effects to this country. We hear that four of the principal Shawnee warriors are expected here in a few days, and that twelve head men and warriors of the Delaware and other nations are left at Port Dunmore as hostages. The Indians have delivered up all the white prisoners in their towns, with the horses and other plunder they took from the inhabitants, and offered to give up their own horses. They have agreed to abandon the lands on this side of the Ohio, which river is to be the boundary between them and the white people and never more take up the hatchet against the English. Thus, in little more than the space of five months, an end is put to a war which portened much, trouble and mischief to the inhabitants on the Frontier, owing to the zeal and good conduct of the officers and commanders who went out in their country's defense and the bravery and perservance of all the troops."—"Virginia Gazette, Thursday, December 8, 1774.

APPENDIX D

A PARTIAL LIST OF MEN WOUNDED IN THE BATTLE OF POINT PLEASANT, WHO WERE AFTERWARD GRANTED PENSIONS BY THE COMMONWEALTH OF VIRGINIA

For the reason that the men who fought the Battle of Point Pleasant were never included in any pension legislation of the United States, no pensions were ever paid by the General Government to any of the participants therein. It was a battle between Virginians and Indians, and for that reason, the Commonwealth of Virginia granted numerous pensions to her sons who were wounded in that conflict. Among these were the following:—

John McKinney, a member of Captain George Moffatt's Company; shot through the left thigh and wrist of the left arm, and cut by tomahawk between the shoulders; granted £20:00:0 for immediate use and £10:00:0 per annum during his life. (See "Journal of the House of Burgesses," session beginning June 1, 1775.)

Abram Field, one of the Culpeper County Minute Men in Colonel John Field's Company; wounded in right arm, unable to support wife and three small children; allowed the sum of £20:00:0 for present relief, and £10:00:0 per annum during his life. (See "Journal of the House of Burgesses," session beginning June 1, 1775.)

Colonel William Fleming, commanding the Botetourt County Regiment; wounded in the breast and left arm, thus rendering him unable to practice his profession as a surgeon; granted £500:00:0 instead of a pension as a recompense for his gallant behavior and the wounds he received in this army. (See "Journal of the House of Burgesses," session beginning June 1, 1775.)

William Shepherd, wounded in left shoulder and arm so that he was rendered unable to earn a subsistence; granted pension of £7:10:0 per annum during his life; also the sum of £16:14:2, to pay William Smith, a surgeon, for treating his wounds. (See

"Journal of the House of Burgesses," session beginning June 1, 1775.)

William Lynn, a Lieutenant wounded in action; granted £30:00:0 per annum during his life. (See "Journal of the House of Burgesses," session beginning June 1, 1775.)

Elizabeth Croley, widow of Samuel Croley, killed in battle; granted £25:00:0 and the further sum of £10:00:0 per annum for ten years, to be disbursed by the Church-Wardens in the Parish of Camden, in the County of Pittsylvania, for her use during her widowhood or for her children by Samuel Croley, after the death or marriage of their mother. (See "Journal of the House of Burgesses," session beginning June 1, 1775.)

John Stewart, wounded in the left arm, allowed the sum of £20:00:0 for his present relief. See Journal of the House of Delegates, session beginning October 20, 1777, p. 124.)

Thomas Price, of Randolph County; granted pension of £15:00:0, December 16, 1790, payable annually. (See "Hening's Statutes at Large," Vol. XIII., p. 205.)

Alexander Stuart, in Captain Moffatt's Company; shot through the thighs; granted pension of £8:00:00 payable annually, December 20, 1792. (See "Hening's Statutes at large," Vol. XIII., p. 616.)

Benjamin Blackbourne, Sergeant in Lewis' Augusta Regiment; granted pension of £15:00:0, payable annually, December 2, 1793. (See "Shepherd's Statutes at Large," Vol. I., p. 278. also "Hening's Statutes at Large," Vol. XIII., p. 616.)

James Robinson, of Bath County; shot through the head; granted pension of £10:00:0, payable annually, December 22, 1794. (See "Shepherd's Statutes at Large," Vol. T., p. 332.)

James Curry, in Captain Moffatt's Company; shot through right elbow; granted pension of £5:00:0, payable annually, in 1776; died July 14, 1834. (See "Session Acts, General Assembly of Virginia," 1815-16, p. 256.)

APPENDIX E

KINSHIP OF THE MEN WHO FOUGHT THE BATTLE OF POINT PLEASANT

Nothing connected with General Lewis' army is more remarkable than the kinship existing among the men composing it. General Andrew Lewis and Colonel Charles Lewis, the latter killed in action, were brothers; Captain John Lewis (son of Andrew) commanding a company in the Botetourt Regiment, was of course a nephew of Colonel Charles Lewis; and Captain John Lewis, of the Augusta Regiment, son of Thomas (a brother of Andrew and Charles) was a nephew of both of them, and a cousin of Captain John Lewis of the Botetourt Regiment. Colonel Charles Lewis had wedded Sarah Murray, a half sister of Lieutenant Charles Cameron, of his own regiment, who was killed at Point Pleasant; and a full sister of Captain John Murray likewise killed in action; thus it was that the three were brothers-in-law, all of whom were killed. Major Thomas Posey, the Commissary-General of the Southern Division, had married the daughter of Sampson Mathews, Commissary of the Augusta Regiment, who was a brother of Captain George Mathews, commanding the first company of that Regiment. The former was therefore the father-in-law of Major Posey, and the latter his uncle by marriage. Colonel William Fleming commanding the Botetourt Regiment, had married Nancy, a sister of Colonel William Christian, commanding the Fincastle Battalion; and they were therefore brothers-in-law. Colonel Christian, and Captain William Campbell commanding a company in this battalion, had both married sisters of Patrick Henry, and were of course brothers-in-law. When Captain Campbell died his widow became the wife of Captain, (then General) William Russell, who commanded a company in the Fincastle Battalion, and thus he became a brother-in-law of Colonel Christian.

Captain Alexander McClennahan commanding a company in the Augusta Regiment, was a brother of Captain Robert McClennahan, of the Botetourt Regiment, the latter killed in the battle. He had wedded Margaret Ann, a daughter of Thomas Lewis, a brother of General, and Colonel Charles Lewis, both of whom were therefore his uncles by marriage, while he himself became the uncle of George E. Gilmer, a Governor of Georgia, and a brother-in-law of Captain John Lewis, of the Augusta Regiment. John Frogge, the sutler of the Augusta Regiment, who was killed in the first fire at Point Pleasant, had also married a daughter of Thomas Lewis, and was therefore a brother-in-law of Captain Robert McClennahan. After the death of John Frogge, his widow became the wife of Captain John Stuart, the Historian of Dunmore's War, who commanded a company in the Botetourt Regiment, and thus General Andrew and Colonel Charles Lewis became his uncles by marriage, and Captain John Lewis, of the Augusta Regiment, his brother-in-law. Captain Evan Shelby, who commanded a company in the Fincastle Battalion, had for his Lieutenant, his own son, Isaac Shelby; and Valentine Sevier, a sergeant in Captain Shelby's Company, was a brother of Lieutenant John Sevier, of Captain William Russell's Company of the Fincastle Battalion. Thus we might continue until it would be shown that the army which fought the Battle of Point Pleasant was largely composed of blood-kin men, and those related by marriage.

The End

Some Questions, Facts, Speculations and Assertions
By C. Stephen Badgley

Now that you have read the books of both adversaries in the controversy surrounding the Battle of Point Pleasant as being or not being the first battle of the Revolution, you are probably leaning towards one or the other, but, before you come to a final conclusion, consider the following. Keep in mind that some things stated are speculation. There are no historical documents found (yet) that could verify that any of these events actually occurred (or didn't occur).

Was Lord Dunmore capable of committing such a dastardly deed to sacrifice the southern wing of the Militia as the theory suggested? The answer is yes. Lord Dunmore was not an elected Governor of the Colony of Virginia. The people of Virginia had no voting power. He was appointed to his position by King George III of England. Lord Dunmore's position, his title, his fortune were all because of his allegiance to the British Crown. His main responsibility as Governor of Virginia was to see that the wishes of the British Government were carried out. He was a true, loyal subject to the Crown and if he was told to create a situation on the frontier to divert the Militia and perhaps set them up for annihilation he would have done so... maybe reluctantly, but he would have followed the orders of the Crown.

What could possibly be the reason for doing this? According to Edward E. Curtis PHD, Wellesley College, in 1774 there were 8,580 British Troops in America just prior to the Revolution. The estimated population of the Colonies at that time, according to Evart Boutell Greene and Virginia Draper Harrington of Columbia University was 2,590,000 broken down as follows:

Massachusetts: 360,000, New Hampshire: 80,000, Connecticut: 200,000, Rhode Island: 50,000, New York: 180,000, New Jersey: 130,000, **Pennsylvania: 300,000**, Delaware: 40,000, Maryland: 220,000, North Carolina: 260,000,

South Carolina: 180,000, Georgia: 30,000, **VIRGINIA: 560,000.**

Let's take the colony of Virginia and run some figures. Let's conservatively say that half the population were males. That would be 280,000 males. Let's say half of these males were less than 40 years old and were of fighting age. That would be 140,000. Let's say half of these were unable or unwilling to fight, or were loyal to the Crown. That would be 70,000. Virginia alone could conceivably field a force of 70,000 Militiamen vs. 8,580 total British Soldiers on the American Continent. Keep in mind that during the French & Indian War the brunt of the fighting was done by Colonial Militia so most of these men probably had experience in warfare.

The British Army was the strongest and best army in the world. They had over 45,000 well trained men in arms at the beginning of the American Revolution...the only trouble is that most of them were in other parts of the world. They had over 15,000 in England and over 12,000 in Ireland. The rest were in, Scotland, Minorca, The Isle of Man, Gibraltar and Africa. So there is good reason to believe they would do whatever they could to buy time in America so they could gather their forces and send a sufficient number of them to the Colonies to quell the rebellion they knew was coming. And if a major defeat of the Militia by Indians on the frontier were to occur, weakening the Colonial forces...that would be even better for Britain.

What could the British do to delay the start of the Revolution they knew was coming and could start at any time? Britain knew they needed time to bolster their forces in America. Their leaders probably considered many different ways other than political to achieve this. They needed something to happen that would infuriate the Indians west of the Alleghenies so much that they would go on the warpath and force the Colonies of Pennsylvania and Virginia to send their Militias west to protect the people on their frontiers. The other Colonies would have to delay starting anything because Pennsylvania and Virginia, the Colony with the largest population and Militia, would be tied up fighting Indians. Also, if the British could find a way to cast the blame for this on the Colonists, they could possibly gain the alliance of the Ohio Tribes. Isn't it strange...the way the events played themselves out as if they were planned?

If Dunmore was ordered to do this by the Crown, how could he have accomplished it? Dunmore knew he would have to keep it a secret operation and take in as few confidents as possible, because, if Britain was successful in putting down the coming rebellion, he would still be the Governor and if found out, his life would not be worth a farthing. He probably also knew, by past dealings with the Crown, that if word got out that the British had set the thing up, they would protect the integrity of the Crown and deny it. He, being the Royal Governor, would have the blame placed directly on his shoulders. Secrecy had to be paramount.

Dunmore had a very close friend at Fort Pitt (At that time under Virginia's control.) named Dr. John Connolly and in January of 1774, he appointed his friend as "Captain of the Militia at Pittsburg" and "Head of Indian Affairs." Dr. Connolly was a staunch loyalist just like his good friend Lord Dunmore and would have been the first point of contact on the frontier for Dunmore.

About 40 miles downriver from Pittsburgh was the early settlement of Wheeling. Two brothers, Daniel and Jacob Greathouse, who were part of the local militia under the command of Michael Cresap, roamed the area generally creating havoc with their drinking and cavorting. They had a nasty reputation...in other words; they did not possess the characteristics of your average, heroic, everyday frontiersman.

Cresap would have been ruled out as a possible co-conspirator by Connolly and Dunmore as he was not considered a loyalist. They would have had to go around him to find someone else to perform a dastardly act that would bring the Indian nations to war. What better choice than the Greathouse boys?

Connolly knew that Logan was probably the best loved Indian in the country. He was well respected and revered by both the Indians and the whites. He always remained neutral in time of war and every man, red or white, was always welcome to come to his village and they were treated like V.I.P.'s regardless of their station in life. To have him murdered by frontiersmen would surly incite the Indians to war. Once the war was started,

Dunmore would make plans to order the Militia to the frontier to quell the uprising.

Dunmore's plan was to order his Militia split into two wings to proceed to the Ohio Country and confront the Indians. Dunmore was probably counting on the Indians to defeat the southern wing. Connolly would make sure the Indians knew of the advance so the Indians could gather sufficient force to annihilate the southern wing. Dunmore would then engage the Indians and calling for more militia, he could keep the war going for as long as Britain needed to get her forces over here. Once the Crown felt they had sufficient forces or were ready to fend off any Patriot attacks, Dunmore would then treat with the Indians, in the name of Great Britain, and make them allies for the British cause.

Could the Indians actually have defeated Lewis's wing of the Militia? The answer is yes, if Cornstalk hadn't made a decision to attack them at the Point. The most successful ploy used by Indians against large bodies of enemy was to ambush them but not totally surround them. By giving the enemy an avenue of escape, most generally the enemy would panic and flee rather than fight to the death. The Indians could then follow them and pick them off as they ran. This happened with Braddock, St. Clair and Crawford. All had large numbers of soldiers, but were defeated with terrible losses.

In this instance, Cornstalk waited too long. Had he set up an ambush further up the Kanawha, the Militia probably would have retreated and the same outcome as stated above would have occurred. By attacking the Militia after they had reached the Point with their backs to the Kanawha and Ohio Rivers, he left them no escape route. They had to fight or die. They chose to fight. When Cornstalk's warriors pushed the lines back towards the rivers, they actually became stronger as they fell back... the lines of Militia closing in together.

What was the northern wing of the Militia doing at this time? The original plan of battle was for General Lewis to take his southern wing of the army as far as Point Pleasant where the Great Kanawha River runs into the Ohio River and wait there. Dunmore was to take the Northern Wing of the army and ford the Ohio River near the mouth of the Little Kanawha River, near present day Parkersburg, West Virginia. Once on the Ohio side of the river, Dunmore's wing would travel downriver, burning crops and destroying the small villages along the way. He would join General Lewis at Point Pleasant and the united army was to proceed on downriver to the Scioto River which they would follow northward and attack the Indian towns in the Scioto Valley.

Dunmore reached the Ohio Country and crossing the river into it he set up camp at the mouth of the Hocking River and began to build a fort. He named it Fort Gower and had a few detachments burn some small villages nearby. He never made a move to join Lewis at Point Pleasant.

It has been said that on the day before the fight at Point Pleasant, Dunmore was visited at his camp by Blue Jacket, a warrior chief of the Shawnee. Isn't it strange that Blue Jacket appeared there? I'm sure he didn't just drop in to say "hello". And stranger still, if Dunmore was at war with the Shawnee, why didn't he hold Blue Jacket hostage? The next day, the day of the battle, it is said that Dunmore was overheard saying, *"Lewis is probably having hot work about this time."* If he knew this, why hadn't he sent his forces downriver to assist Lewis?

Upon finding out that the southern wing of the army was not wiped out and receiving messengers from the Indians wanting peace out of fear that those Virginians at Point Pleasant would advance and destroy their villages, Dunmore was probably in quite a quandary. What was he to do now? He had about 800 bloodied Virginians, angry and spoiling for a fight, wanting to cross the river and attack the Indians, Britain's potential allies. It was obvious now that there would be no prolonged Indian war to tie up the militia as he had initially planned so he had to come up with something that would appease both the Virginians and his King and at least keep the Indians in a favorable position to become allies of the British.

He sent dispatches to Lewis ordering him not to advance and to old the army at the point. He, instead of going to the point to team up with Lewis, headed straight towards the main Shawnee town of Chillicothe near present day Circleville, Ohio. (Not the present town of that name.) There he met with Cornstalk and other leaders of the tribes and negotiated a peace treaty.

Probably, with his Virginia Governor's hat on, he advised the Indians that they could no longer cross the Ohio River into Virginia territory. To the peace treaty he also added that Kentucky, the Indian's sacred hunting grounds, was now part of this agreement and would be open for settlement. This raised the ire of the Indians, but they could not do anything about it...they were the ones suing for peace. Dunmore probably added this to keep the sentiments of the Indians towards settlers on edge so when he would need them as allies, they would not hesitate to act. Putting on his British Tory hat, he probably told the Indians that their alliance with Britain was expected in case the Colonists revolted. If they did not agree to these terms he would turn loose those angry Virginians at the Point and join them with his army to wipe them out.

When Dunmore returned to Williamsburg, his true "Tory" nature was exposed in the actions he took there.

In the 1883 Hardesty's Historical and Geographical encyclopedia, Virgil Lewis stated, *"To the student of history no truth is more patent than this, that the Battle of Point Pleasant was the first in the series of the Revolution,"* (see page 38.)

Why did Virgil change his views and become an adversary of Mrs. Poffenbarger and her theory? Please don't misinterpret this as an attack on Mr. Lewis character. I never knew the man, but I have the utmost respect for him and the work he did. But, he was just that...a man, not a demigod. Could it be that he felt he was being upstaged by a woman...an amateur historian? Remember, it was through her efforts that the Battlefield and the Monuments became a reality. At that time, coming out of the Victorian Age, many people felt that women were intellectually inferior to men. Was he trying to bring her down from her lofty perch? Could he have been seeking revenge in a way? And isn't it strange that he doesn't even mention Mrs. Poffenbarger's name in his book? Even when tells of the monument and the park? It was Livia Poffenbarger that started the ball rolling and kept it rolling until the battlefield was purchased, cleaned up and the dead respectfully buried. It was through her efforts that West Virginia received help in purchasing the monument from congress.

Mrs. Poffenbarger, in her book, refuted a claim made by Mr. Lewis that the Benjamin Lewis was a descendant of John Lewis, the founder of Staunton, Virginia. (See page 86.)

In regards to the letters written after the battle to Lord Dunmore and praising him for stopping the depredations on the frontier, they were indeed warranted. He did stop the Indians and opened up the Kentucky country for settlement...but was that his intentions in the first place...or did it just happen because Cornstalk and his warriors failed to defeat the southern wing? Had there been a secret conspiracy as suggested, the entities who wrote those letters would not have known about it and Dunmore would have been the last person to bring the matter up.

Lewis presents a Resolution of the Officers Who Served Under Dunmore. (See Pages 258) There was another resolution at that meeting at Fort Gower that he doesn't present. Here it is:

"Resolved, That we will bear the most faithful allegiance to his Majesty King George the Third, *whilst his Majesty delights to reign over a brave and free people;* **that we will, at the expense of life and everything dear and valuable, exert ourselves in support of the honor of his Crown and the dignity of the British Empire".**

In this same resolution it says:

But as the love of liberty, and attachment to the real interests and just rights of America, outweigh every other consideration, we resolve that we will exert every power within us for the defense of American liberty, and for the support of her just rights and privileges; not in any precipitate, riotous, or tumultuous manner, but when regularly called forth by the unanimous voice of our countrymen."

This resolution seems to say, that these officers will be loyal to the Crown as long as the British Government recognized their rights to be treated like other Englishmen but if the British failed to recognize this, they, along with the other Colonies, would fight for them. Dunmore and the Crown had to be aware of their sentiments before this Indian war was created. These sentiments were common in all the Colonies. The British needed this Indian war to occupy the Pennsylvania and Virginia militia while they reinforced their troops in America.

Here are the rest of the minutes of that meeting:

"At a meeting of the officers under the command of his Excellency, the Right Honorable the Earl of Dunmore, convened at Fort Gower, situated at the junction of the Ohio and Hockhocking rivers, November 5, 1774, for the purpose of considering the grievances of British America, an officer present addressed the meeting in the following:

"Gentlemen:

Having now concluded the campaign, by the assistance of Providence, with honor and advantage to the colony and ourselves, it only remains that we should give our country the strongest assurance that we are ready, at all times, to the utmost of our power, to maintain and defend her just rights and privileges. We have lived about three months in the woods, without any intelligence from Boston or from the delegates at Philadelphia. It is possible, from the groundless reports of designing men, that our countrymen may be jealous of the use such a body would make of the arms in their hands at this critical juncture. That we are a respectable body is certain, when it is considered that we can live weeks without bread or salt; that we can sleep in the open air without any covering but the canopy of heaven, and that our men can march and shoot with any in the known world. Blessed with these talents, let us solemnly engage with one another, and our country in particular, that we will use them to no purpose but the honor and advantage of America in general, and of Virginia in particular. It behooves us then, for the satisfaction of our country, that we should give them our real sentiments, by way of resolves, at this very alarming crisis."

"Whereupon the meeting made choice of a committee to draw up and prepare resolves for their consideration, who immediately withdrew; and after some time spent therein, reported that they had agreed to and prepared the following *resolves, which were read, maturely considered, and unanimously adopted by the meeting:* Followed by the resolve listed above and the one on page 258.

Excerpt from "The History of Virginia" 1852

The following is taken verbatim from the book "The History of Virginia" by T. S. Arthur and William Henry Carpenter published over a hundred and fifty years ago. Here, Dunmore's true nature and character are shown and you can get a pretty good picture of what was happening when Dunmore was appointed Governor of Virginia and why he and Connolly are considered by many to be the perpetrators of the murder of Logan and the subsequent Indian uprising in an effort to tie up the militia of Virginia and Pennsylvania in face of the upcoming Revolution. This theory has been around for a long, long time as evidenced by the entry in this book which was published ten years before Livia Poffenbarger was even born and Virgil Lewis was only three or four years old.

Preface from the book

As the first Anglo-Saxon colony in America, Virginia has always occupied an important historical position. But while detached portions of her early annals, full of romantic interest, have become familiar to all classes of persons, the connected narrative of the dangers and privations which attended her early settlement, and subsequent progress, has remained, for the most part, imperfectly known to the general reader.

To give this history in a compact form, neither colored by prejudice nor distorted by party feeling, the present volume has been written.

The materials for the work have been drawn from the most reliable sources and it has been rendered as accurate as possible by patient investigation and by a careful comparison of conflicting authorities.

The History of Virginia
Chapter 23, Page 280

By the death of the lamented Botetourt, the duties of governor devolved upon William Nelson, president of the council, until the arrival of Lord Dunmore in 1772. The quartering of troops in Boston, the riots in that city during the spring of 1770, and the obstinate persistence of the British ministry in retaining the duty on tea, all tended to increase the agitation of the public mind. Slight events became causes of grave suspicion; and while everyone felt that a crisis was rapidly approaching, none knew upon which province the blow was first to fall. The delay of Dunmore, in New York, for several months after his appointment, was by no means favourable to his reputation in Virginia. The resignation by Captain Foy of his office as Governor of New Hampshire, for the purpose of accepting the inferior post of private secretary to Dunmore, was regarded by many as originating in some latent purpose. Foy had obtained a brilliant military reputation by his conduct at the battle of Minden; and it was supposed, not without plausibility, that the British ministry intended to employ his talents in carrying out those measures of coercion which had already been devised. To provide an adequate salary for his distinguished secretary, Dunmore had directed that he should receive a fixed sum of five hundred pounds a year, besides the lucrative emoluments arising from a list of fees established expressly for his benefit. This assumption of an authority vested in the assembly alone, received, at the first-meeting of that body, a prompt rebuke; and Dunmore, conscious of the impolicy of creating an open rupture with the indignant Burgesses upon a question of so little moment when compared with the one at issue between the provinces and the mother country, consented to annul the new list of fees, and sought by his courtesy and condescension to efface the unfavorable impression his conduct had created. For a brief period harmony was apparently restored, but before the assembly again met, in 1773, a forgery of colonial paper money to an alarming extent, while stimulating the governor to bring the supposed offenders to justice, had led him to overstep the strict limits of the law. Conscious that one uncensored illegal act might afford a pretext for others, the assembly resolved upon an address to Dunmore, in which they stated, that as a doubtful construction, and various execution of the criminal code, would greatly endanger the safety of the innocent, they trusted that the proceedings in the case under notice might not be adduced in future as a precedent. Stung by the rebuke, Dunmore answered tartly, "In apprehending and bringing to justice the forgers of your paper currency, I little imagined when I was endeavoring to punish the guilty, that my conduct could by any means be thought to endanger the safety of the innocent." This display of acerbity had no effect upon men who were sustained by the consciousness of having performed a duty which they owed to their constituents.

After having thus zealously defended the privileges of the subject, the burgesses proceeded to organize a committee of correspondence, for the purpose of keeping up a frequent communication with the other colonies, and of obtaining the earliest intelligence from abroad. The subsequent movements of Dunmore were also subjected to the closest scrutiny.

During the summer he proceeded on a pleasure excursion to the back settlements. He remained sometime at Pittsburg, examining the nature of the country, conciliating the inhabitants and holding frequent interviews of a private nature with one **Connolly** whom he had appointed Indian Agent. **This man, able and unscrupulous, was known to possess considerable influence, not only over the surrounding tribes of savages, but also with the hardy and unsuspicious borderers. The object of Dunmore's journey soon became apparent. It was to create a territorial dispute between Virginia and Pennsylvania and thus weaken the existing bond between the two provinces; or failing in that, to divert the attention of Virginia from the designs of the British Government by <u>provoking an Indian war</u>.** He had scarcely set out on his return before Connolly commenced the formation of settlements in Pennsylvania under Patents granted by Dunmore. These encroachments were immediately resisted, Connolly was seized and imprisoned by the officers of Pennsylvania and the settlers secured and punished as outlaws. Dunmore instantly issued a proclamation, which was well calculated by its violent and haughty tone, to increase the excitement already existing. Fortunately his scheme was foiled by the sagacity and moderation of his council, who firmly rejecting all violent measures, agreed to settle the controversy by arbitration.

In the meanwhile, the general adoption of the non-importation agreement having had the effect of virtually annulling the tax upon tea, the British government endeavored to force its introduction into the colonies by offering the East India Company a drawback equal to the amount of duty. As the tax was by this means rendered merely nominal, the hope was indulged that resistance would cease, and the proposition was accepted by the company, but as the principle involved remained the same as ever, the people would not yield.

At Charleston, the tea was allowed to be stored, but its sale was expressly prohibited. The cargoes intended for Philadelphia and New York, were sent back at once to England. At Boston, the popular indignation displayed itself far more violently. On the evening of the 16th of December, 1773, three ships, containing tea, were boarded by an organized party, disguised as Indians, who forcibly broke open the chests containing the obnoxious commodity, and emptied their contents into the water. This bold act was no sooner known in England, than a bill was passed by Parliament, closing the port of Boston, and removing the seat of government to Salem.

The assembly of Virginia was in session when a rough draft of the bill reached Williamsburg. All other business was at once thrown aside. An order was passed forthwith, protesting against the conduct of the ministry as subversive to American freedom, and setting apart that day week—the 1st of June, 1774—for the purpose of fasting, humiliation, and prayer. To put a stop to proceedings so alarming, **Dunmore summoned the members to the council chamber, and dissolved the assembly.**

On the following day, the whole of the delegates repaired, by agreement, to the Raleigh Tavern, where, after drawing up an address to the American people, they authorized a correspondence to be opened with the several colonial committees, suggesting the expediency of appointing delegates to meet in a general Congress. The proposal everywhere met with a favourable response. On the 1st of August, 1774, a convention was held at Williamsburg, which, after adopting, in a more stringent form, the old non-importation agreement, appointed seven delegates to the proposed Congress. Prominent among those chosen, were Randolph, Washington, Henry, and Jefferson.

The Continental Congress met at Philadelphia on the 4th of September following. It consisted of fifty-three delegates, the leading men of twelve provinces. Of this select assembly, Peyton Randolph was chosen president.

But while the patriotism of Virginia was being thus honored by her sister provinces, she was suffering all the horrors of an Indian war upon her frontiers. Preluded by a series of atrocious murders, it suddenly burst in full fury upon the defenseless inhabitants. The parties of border militia which had assembled to check the progress of the enemy were swept away and such settlers as did not seek safety in flight, were either barbarously massacred, or hurried into captivity. No longer dreading the effects of French skill, superadded to Indian ferocity, large numbers of volunteers immediately took the field. An army of twenty-seven hundred men was speedily raised. **Dunmore, to whom, by means of his agent Connolly, the war has been attributed**, placed himself at the head of a division of fifteen hundred men, and marched against the Shawanese towns on the Scioto. The remaining division under Colonel Andrew Lewis proceeded to Point Pleasant, at the mouth of the great Kanawha.

As a junction was to have been made at this place with the troops under Dunmore, Lewis halted his men and encamped until the first division should arrive. On the 9th of October, orders were received from the governor for the troops to cross the Ohio and join him at, or near, the Shawanese towns. Early the next morning, while the men were actively engaged in preparing for their march, several wounded scouts came into camp with intelligence that the Indians had been discovered in great force at a distance of less than a mile from the point. The main body of the army was immediately ordered out under Colonels Charles Lewis, and Fleming. The advance, under Lewis, had not proceeded more than four hundred yards before it was assaulted by the Indians, and the action commenced. At the first fire Colonel Lewis fell mortally wounded. Fleming being disabled soon after, the men fell back in some confusion toward the camp, but were speedily rallied under cover of a reinforcement commanded by Colonel Field. The engagement then became general, and was continued, with unabated fury, from sunrise until near the close of evening. A skilful manoeuvre, executed under the orders of Colonel Andrew Lewis, at length decided the victory in favour of the Americans. Three companies, commanded by Shelby, Matthews, and Stuart, were directed to proceed secretly up the Kanawha, turn the position of the enemy, and suddenly fall upon their rear. This movement was successfully accomplished. Alarmed at being placed unexpectedly between two fires, the Indians were thrown into disorder, and about sunset commenced a precipitate retreat across the Ohio to their towns on the Scioto. In this hard fought battle the Virginians sustained a loss in killed and wounded of two hundred and fifteen.

As soon as the dead were buried, and arrangements made for the comfort of the wounded, Lewis pressed forward to form a junction with Dunmore. While he was on his march, he was met by an express bearing orders for the troops to return at once to Point Pleasant. Suspicious of the motives by which the governor was actuated, Lewis continued to advance, until he came in sight of one of the Indian towns, where he encountered Dunmore in person, who informed him that he had already consented to enter upon negotiations for a peace.

At the treaty, which was concluded soon after, Logan, one of the principal Chiefs was not present. To avoid, however, any misconstruction of his motives, he sent, by General Gibson, the following speech to Lord Dunmore: "I appeal to any white man to say, if ever he entered Logan's cabin hungry, and he gave him not meat; if ever he came cold and naked, and he clothed him not. During the course of the last long and bloody war, Logan remained idle in his cabin, an advocate for peace. Such was my love for the whites that my countrymen pointed, as they passed, and said, Logan is the friend of the white man. I had even thought to have lived with you, but for the injuries of one man. Colonel Cresap, the last spring, in cold blood, and unprovoked, murdered all the relations of Logan, not even sparing my women and children. There runs not a drop of my blood in the veins of any living creature. This called on me for revenge. I have sought it: I have killed many: I have fully glutted my vengeance. For my country I rejoice at the beams of peace. But do not harbor a thought that mine is the joy of fear. Logan never felt fear. He will not turn on his heel to save his life. Who is there to mourn for Logan! Not one."

The war was closed upon the frontier; but a sterner, grander, and more prolonged contest was speedily approaching. Resolutions, addresses, and resistance, both passive and forcible, had fully aroused the spirit of the American colonies, and prepared them for the bloodier struggle which was to follow. The common cause, at first imperfectly embraced, because imperfectly understood, was now sustained by unanimity of action, as forcible as it was imposing.

In the early part of 1775, the various provincial governors received instructions from England, to check the disposition to rebellion in the colonies, by seizing upon all depots of arms and ammunition. Gage, of Massachusetts, was the first to undertake the fulfillment of this order, by an attempt to capture some cannon and military stores collected at Concord, a small town some twenty miles from Boston. Eight hundred troops were detached on this service, and on the nineteenth of April, at sunrise, reached Lexington, where, for the first time, they came into collision with a body of continental militia. The regulars were at first successful, but were subsequently compelled to retreat to Boston, with a loss in killed and wounded of three hundred men.

On the 22d of April, two days only after the battle of Lexington, **Dunmore secretly removed the gunpowder from the magazine at Williamsburg, to an armed vessel lying off York Town**. This act was no sooner discovered than the volunteers of Williamsburg assembled in arms, with the avowed purpose of seizing the person of the governor.

Restrained with difficulty from the immediate execution of their threat, they dispatched a deputation to the governor, demanding a restitution of the powder. His reply was courteous, but evasive. In the midst of the excitement, news arrived of the fight at Lexington. The tidings spread like wild-fire throughout the province. Fifteen hundred men collected at Fredericksburg from the upper country, prepared to march at a moment's warning to the defense of the capital, which **Dunmore had threatened to lay in ashes at the first signal of insurrection.** By the influence of Randolph, and other patriotic gentlemen, this large force was prevailed upon to abstain from active hostilities until the continental congress should decide upon the proper course to be pursued. Firm in his belief that the time for action had arrived, Patrick Henry alone refused to consent to any proposition involving delay. Placing himself at the head of his own company of volunteers from Hanover County, he marched at once upon Williamsburg. By the time he had reached Doncastle's ordinary, sixteen miles from the seat of government, his force had swelled to five hundred men. As he approached the city he was met by deputies from Williamsburg, accompanied by Corbin, the king's receiver, who consented to give bills for the value of the powder taken away. The particular cause of quarrel being thus removed, Henry returned to Hanover County, and on the 4th of May disbanded his followers.

While the deputies were treating with Henry, Dunmore sent his family on board the Fowey man-of-war, and after fortifying his palace, garrisoned it, in addition to his own armed servants, and the Shawanese hostages, with a party of marines which he had ordered to his assistance from one of the ships in the river.

These preparations for resistance, joined to the threat made by Captain Montague, that if his detachment met with any interruption, he would open a fire upon the town of York, brought on a renewal of the excitement. A proclamation by Dunmore declaring Henry and his followers guilty of rebellion, added fuel to the flame.

Stimulated to increased activity, meetings were held in every county, and volunteers pledged themselves to be in readiness to march wherever their services might be required. In this threatening aspect of affairs, Dunmore, fearing to trust himself beyond the walls of his palace, called his council together and asked their advice. They suggested that the marines should be dismissed, and an assembly convened. The governor reluctantly consented. A brief period of quiet succeeded, but confidence was not restored. It was rumored abroad that a scheme was being arranged for the seizure of the newly elected deputies, who were openly warned to come prepared. Undeterred by the mysterious danger with which they were menaced, the delegates fearlessly set out for the capital. Those from distant counties entered Williamsburg dressed in their hunting shirts, and bearing their rifles. Nearly all who attended were armed. They had scarcely reached the city before an attempt was made to break open the magazine. In the act of entering it, a spring gun exploded, wounding one of the persons engaged in the affair. An alarming riot followed, and Dunmore, fearful for his personal safety, fled secretly by night, and took refuge on board the Towey.

The flight of the governor was no sooner discovered, than the council and assembly agreed upon a joint address, entreating him to return to the palace, and offering to concur in any measure that might be considered necessary for his personal security. On his refusal to do so, the assembly declared his office vacant, and appointed the president of the council in his place. They adjourned themselves soon after, having first agreed to meet in convention at Richmond, for the purpose of organizing a provisional government, and arranging a plan of defense. While the Virginia Assembly were thus endeavoring to induce Dunmore to return to Williamsburg and resume the duties of his office, the continental congress, then in session at Philadelphia, after declaring that hostilities with Great Britain had commenced, had appointed George Washington commander-in-chief of the Continental Army. This appointment was made on the 15th of June, 1775.and strongly garrisoned, effectually protected the approach to the city. Woodford threw up a breastwork at the end of the causeway, and waited for the arrival of reinforcements. Deceived by a stratagem as to the number of the provincials, Captain Fordyce, at the head of three hundred and fifty Regulars, Tories, and Negroes, sallied out from the fort on the morning of the ninth of December, 1775, to attack Woodford in his entrenchments. While advancing along the causeway, Fordyce fell mortally wounded, and his troops, after having sustained a loss of nearly one-third of their whole number, in an action which lasted only thirty minutes, gave way and retreated precipitately to the fort. Alarmed at this unexpected defeat, **Dunmore hastily spiked his artillery, abandoned his works, and embarked with the remainder of his army on board the vessels in the harbor.** Five days after the skirmish at Great Bridge, the Virginians, reinforced by the North Carolina militia under Colonel Robert Howe, took possession of Norfolk, and opened a fire upon the British ships. In retaliation for this rash provocation, and for the rough treatment which certain royalists had experienced from the conquerors, **Dunmore, strengthened by the arrival of the frigate Liverpool, bombarded the town on the first of January, 1776, and, landing a party of marines and seamen under cover of the cannonade, set fire to it in several places.**

On the 17th, was fought the battle of Bunker's Hill. Four days afterward, Washington left Philadelphia to assume command of the troops, then stationed at Cambridge.

On the 17th of July, according to previous agreement, the Virginia convention met, entrusted the executive authority to a committee of safety, and ordered the immediate enlistment of two regiments of Minute Men. The royal government of Virginia was at an end.

Dunmore, having with him several armed vessels and two companies of regulars, still hovered about Old Point Comfort, and threatened the lower counties. **Hoping to create a diversion in his favour west of the mountains, he had sent to his former agent Connolly, the commission of a lieutenant-colonel; but his project failed of success by the arrest of Connolly in Maryland, while returning from a visit to General Gage at Boston.**

Landing at Norfolk, then just rising into a town of some commercial importance, Dunmore seized a printing press, and on the 17th November, issued a proclamation, declaring martial law, and offering freedom to all slaves belonging to rebels who would join the royal standard. A large number of Negroes and Tories responded to the call. With this mixed force he commenced offensive operations. Marching to Kempsville, in Princess Anne County, he destroyed some arms collected there, and took several prisoners, among whom was Captain Mathews, of the Minute Men. Having threatened the inhabitants of Hampton with an attack, the committee of safety sent Colonel Woodford with a hundred riflemen to assist in defending the place. Before he could arrive, six tenders, filled with men, entered Hampton Creek, and endeavored to effect a landing, for the purpose of burning and plundering the town; but as the enemy approached the shore in boats, they were driven back by a party of concealed riflemen. Night set in and, in the meantime, the reinforcement under Woodford arrived. In the morning a second attempt to land was resisted with even greater success than the former; the enemy then withdrew to Norfolk.

Desirous of striking a decisive blow, the committee of safety determined to force Dunmore to evacuate Norfolk. Woodford's second Virginia regiment and the Culpepper battalion were ordered upon this service. At Great Bridge, a few miles from Norfolk, the enemy occupied a stockade fort, which, being furnished with artillery. Of a thousand houses, nearly nine hundred were consumed. The remainder were destroyed soon after by order of the committee of safety.

During the whole of the summer following, Dunmore, sailing up the various rivers of eastern Virginia, carried on a series of petty predatory incursions, by which the loyalists sustained great losses. Plantations were ravaged, houses were burned, and nearly a thousand slaves abducted from their masters. At length, although moving with celerity from point to point, and retreating to his boats whenever menaced with a serious attack, he found himself so continually harassed by armed parties of volunteers and militia, that he was constrained to withdraw his motley force, and retire to St. Augustine with the plunder he had accumulated.

The general assembly of Virginia met at Williamsburg on the 6th of May, and after appointing Edmund Pendleton president, and John Tazewell clerk, proceeded to the business before them. On the 15th of the month it was unanimously agreed upon to instruct the Virginia delegation to the continental congress, then in session at Philadelphia, to propose in that body a formal declaration of independence, and the absolution of the United Colonies from all allegiance to Great Britain. A committee was also appointed to prepare a declaration of rights, and a plan of government suitable to the new condition of the province. On the 29th the constitution, framed by George Mason, with a preamble sent by Jefferson from Philadelphia, was unanimously adopted. Patrick Henry received the appointment of Governor. On the 5th of July the assembly adjourned. At Philadelphia, the day previous, the Declaration of Independence as drawn up by Jefferson was passed by Congress. It was proclaimed at Williamsburg on the 25th of the same month amid the firing of cannon, and the exulting shouts of the assembled people. The assembly again met on the 7th of October, 1776, and appointed a committee to revise the state laws. By the strenuous efforts of Jefferson and Mason, an act was passed at this session, by which dissenters were relieved from the disabilities under which they had labored previously, and all forms of religion placed upon an equal footing.

What are your thoughts?

Was there a conspiracy of some kind? Was the Battle at Point Pleasant indeed the first Battle of the American Revolution? Mrs. Poffenbarger believed it was, from the bottom of her heart, and managed to convince Congress that it was. If you haven't reached a final conclusion yet, I'm sure you have developed personal opinions and we would love to know what they are. Please go to our website and click on the book cover. You will then find a link to a page where you can give your comments on this controversial issue. Or, if you would rather, just send an email to BadgleyPubCo@AOL.com and we'll post it for you.

WWW.BadgleyPublishingCompany.com

Printed in Great Britain
by Amazon